FAITH, RIGHTS, AND CHOICE

The Politics of Religious Schools in Canada

The Canadian provinces have evolved quite different ways of responding to the policy problems posed by religious schools. Seeking to understand this peculiar reality, *Faith, Rights, and Choice* articulates the ways in which the provincial governance regimes developed for religious schools have changed over time.

Covering nearly three centuries, the book begins with the founding of schooling systems in New France and continues into a variety of present-day conflicts that emerged over the question of religion in schools. James Farney and Clark Banack employ a method of process-tracing, drawing on 88 semi-structured interviews with key policy insiders. They also reference archival material documenting meetings, political speeches, and legislative debates related to government decisions around issues of religious education. Relying on the theoretical foundations of both historical institutionalism and Canadian political development, *Faith, Rights, and Choice* presents a new analytic framework to help make sense of the policy divergence witnessed across Canada.

(Political Development: Comparative Perspectives)

JAMES FARNEY is the Regina academic director and an associate professor in the Johnson Shoyama Graduate School of Public Policy at the University of Regina.

CLARK BANACK is the director of the Alberta Centre for Sustainable Rural Communities and an adjunct professor of political studies at the Augustana campus of the University of Alberta.

Political Development: Comparative Perspectives

Editors: Jack Lucas (University of Calgary) and
Robert C. Vipond (University of Toronto)

Political Development: Comparative Perspectives publishes books that explore political development with a comparative lens, with a particular focus on studies of Canadian, American, or British political development. Books in this series use historical data and narratives to explain long-term patterns of institutional change, public policy, social movement politics, elections and party systems, and other key aspects of political authority and state power. They employ cross-country comparison, within-country comparison, or single-case analysis to illuminate important debates in comparative political science and history.

Faith, Rights, and Choice

The Politics of Religious Schools in Canada

JAMES FARNEY AND CLARK BANACK

UNIVERSITY OF TORONTO PRESS
Toronto Buffalo London

© University of Toronto Press 2023
Toronto Buffalo London
utorontopress.com

ISBN 978-1-4875-4580-2 (cloth)   ISBN 978-1-4875-5198-8 (EPUB)
ISBN 978-1-4875-4828-5 (paper)   ISBN 978-1-4875-4911-4 (PDF)

Library and Archives Canada Cataloguing in Publication

Title: Faith, rights, and choice : the politics of religious schools in Canada /
    James Farney and Clark Banack.
Names: Farney, James Harold, author. | Banack, Clark, 1981– author.
Series: Political development: comparative perspectives.
Description: Series statement: Political development: comparative
    perspectives | Includes bibliographical references and index.
Identifiers: Canadiana (print) 20220484619 | Canadiana (ebook)
    20220484635 | ISBN 9781487545802 (cloth) | ISBN 9781487548285
    (paper) | ISBN 9781487551988 (EPUB) | ISBN 9781487549114 (PDF)
Subjects: LCSH: Religious education – Government policy – Canada –
    Provinces. | LCSH: Education and state – Canada – Provinces. |
    LCSH: Church schools – Government policy – Canada – Provinces.
Classification: LCC LC114 .F37 2023 | DDC 379.2/80971 – dc23

We wish to acknowledge the land on which the University of Toronto
Press operates. This land is the traditional territory of the Wendat, the
Anishnaabeg, the Haudenosaunee, the Métis, and the Mississaugas of the
Credit First Nation.

This book has been published with the help of a grant from the Federation
for the Humanities and Social Sciences, through the Awards to Scholarly
Publications Program, using funds provided by the Social Sciences and
Humanities Research Council of Canada.

University of Toronto Press acknowledges the financial support of the
Government of Canada, the Canada Council for the Arts, and the Ontario
Arts Council, an agency of the Government of Ontario, for its publishing
activities.

Canada Council   Conseil des Arts
for the Arts   du Canada

ONTARIO ARTS COUNCIL
CONSEIL DES ARTS DE L'ONTARIO
an Ontario government agency
un organisme du gouvernement de l'Ontario

Funded by the   Financé par le
Government   gouvernement
of Canada   du Canada

Canadä

For Bridget, Gus, Brynn, and Everett

Contents

Acknowledgments

Beginning with a pair of rough, solo-authored conference papers in 2014, the lengthy process of writing this book was interwoven with far more professional and personal challenges than we ever would have anticipated at the outset. That we managed to complete it is largely a testament to how many supportive people we encountered along the way to whom we are significantly indebted. First, we must acknowledge David Rayside, who nudged us to work together on this project after listening to us individually present those aforementioned conference papers at the American Political Science Association Meetings in 2014. Next, we are especially grateful for the time and insight shared with us by all those "education-insiders" from across Canada who agreed to be interviewed for this project. Quite simply, this book would not have been possible without the vast amounts of knowledge they shared with us. Thank you as well to the two anonymous reviewers who raised very thoughtful critiques that ultimately made this manuscript much better than it initially was. And to Daniel Quinlan of University of Toronto Press, thank you for your enduring patience and positive support as we dragged this project on over the years.

This research was supported by institutional funds generously provided by the University of Regina, York University, and the Augustana Campus of the University of Alberta, as well as a SSHRC Insight Grant #435-2016-0629. This SSHRC grant supported the Comparative Education Policy Group, led by Linda A. White at the University of Toronto. This group provided us with wonderfully supportive peers who helped us work through the arguments in this book. It also allowed for our attendance at a number of academic conferences wherein we shared aspects of this project with very diverse and engaged audiences who helpfully challenged us on many fronts. The grant also allowed us to work with an excellent group of research assistants: Michael

Chmielewski, Katelynn Kowalchuk, Bethany Kulaway, and Ann Loz-
kina at the University of Regina; Sean Lewis, Umar Khan, and Nicole
Kiselyov at York University; and Beaudon Rogers at the Augustana
Campus of the University of Alberta.

  We are also so grateful to our supportive colleagues: Jim would especially like to thank Tom McIntosh and Rick Kleer at the University of
Regina, and Clark acknowledges Ian Wilson and Lars Hallstrom at the
Augustana Campus of the University of Alberta. Finally, and most of
all, we are grateful to our families – this project has been a presence in
the lives of our children from the time that they began school themselves. It's been coloured by, and its writing enlivened with, the joys
provided by Gus, Bridget, Brynn, and Everett. And, of course, we are
both so grateful for the patience and encouragement of Christina and
Kendell in its research and writing.

James Farney and Clark Banack,
Regina and Camrose,
31 May 2022

FAITH, RIGHTS, AND CHOICE

Introduction: The Puzzle of Religious Schools in Canadian Politics

In 2007, then Ontario Progressive Conservative (PC) leader John Tory was in the midst of a close election campaign. Because he saw it as the right thing to do, and after relatively little consultation inside his party, he pledged public subsidies to independent religious schools like those which already existed in Quebec and the four Western provinces. This promise proved hugely unpopular in Ontario and was widely credited with derailing his campaign and costing the PCs the election. This reaction, in a province that has funded Roman Catholic separate schools since 1867, embodies a contradiction in Ontario's educational landscape. In 1985, an influential government-commissioned report recommended the introduction of subsidies to independent and religious schools outside the separate system. This recommendation was reinforced when the United Nations Human Rights Committee rebuked the province in 1999 for the discriminatory practice of funding *only* Catholic religious education. However, something about the mixture of religion and education profoundly troubled Ontario voters. As a result, extending government support to religious schools beyond Catholic separate schools has never been politically possible in Canada's largest province.

In 2003, in response to the government's decision to close their rural public school due to declining enrolment, families from the town of Theodore, Saskatchewan, banded together to create a Catholic School Division. They purchased the school building and renamed it "St. Theodore Roman Catholic School," though most students who would attend were not Catholic. Nevertheless, the province's constitutional obligations to Catholic schools meant that the reopened facility had to receive full public funding. In 2017, Saskatchewan's Court of Queen's Bench ruled that such government funding of non-Catholic students in Catholic schools was unconstitutional, because it created an indirect avenue for non-Catholic Christians to receive a form of fully funded religious education that is unavailable to non-Christian faith communities. Overturned on appeal in 2020 by the Saskatchewan Court of Appeal and then denied leave to appeal to the Supreme Court in 2021, the legal aspect of this case has been resolved. But that the provincial government's immediate response was to both appeal the initial ruling and to pass legislation invoking the Constitution's Section 33 notwithstanding clause shows that separate schools still have the capacity to provoke significant political and legal controversy. It also highlights the rather awkward fact that in Saskatchewan, as well as in Alberta and Ontario, large pockets of non-Catholic students currently attend fully funded and constitutionally protected Catholic schools.

In 2018, the Alberta government introduced legislation that required all schools to create Gay-Straight Alliance student clubs and prohibited schools from disclosing to parents whether their children were participants in these clubs. With their public funding threatened should they fail to comply, a group of independent religious schools took the Alberta government to court, arguing their right to religious freedom was being violated. Although the United Conservative government, elected in 2019, subsequently altered aspects of Alberta's Education Act to appease religious schools on these matters, battles over the duty of schools to affirm and protect LGBTQ students and the rights of publicly subsidized, independent, and "separate" religious schools to opt out of such activities continue to be a source of discord in many provinces across Canada.

As these brief pan-Canadian vignettes demonstrate, the issue of religion in school governance, which significantly challenged Canadian policymakers well before Confederation, continues to present unique challenges today. Indeed, religious diversity is the oldest of the forms of diversity which Canada has consciously tried to incorporate, and multiple methods of accommodation continue today. This book examines the history of this accommodation, seeks to understand the peculiar reality that Canada's provinces have evolved quite different ways of responding to the policy problems posed by religious schools, and articulates the way in which the provincial governance regimes developed for religious schools have changed over time. Today, the Atlantic Canadian provinces provide support only to a single secular public system. Ontario funds both public schools and constitutionally protected separate schools (almost all Roman Catholic) but does not support independent religious schools. In Quebec, British Columbia, and Manitoba there are no fully funded religious separate schools, but there are substantial networks of partially subsidized independent schools (most

Table I.1. Contemporary Funding of Religious and Independent Schools

Province	Fully Funded Separate Catholic Schools	Fully Funded Separate Protestant Schools	Partially Funded Independent Schools	Fully Funded "Alternative" Religious Schools
Nova Scotia	No	No	No	No
PEI	No	No	No	No
New Brunswick	No	No	No	No
NFLD	No	No	No	No
Quebec	No	No	Yes	No
Ontario	Yes	Yes	No	No
Manitoba	No	No	Yes	No
Saskatchewan	Yes	Yes	Yes	No
Alberta	Yes	Yes	Yes	Yes
British Columbia	No	No	Yes	No

of which are religious). Saskatchewan and Alberta combine a partially funded independent school sector with constitutionally entrenched and fully funded Roman Catholic separate schools and fully funded alternative and independent schools (both religious and secular) within their public systems (see table I.1 above). With each of these different models of financial support come different means of government oversight of issues such as teacher accreditation, curricula, and religious instruction. Taken together, we can say that the provinces have constructed markedly different regimes (Manzer 2003) of managing religious schools.

This contrast becomes especially interesting in light of the fact that, despite substantial jurisdictional room for policy divergence, in most areas of educational governance and policy there have been powerful patterns of convergence across the provinces (Wallner 2014). For more than a century, primary and secondary education have been universal programs, with curricula, teacher accreditation, and educational administration generally converging on similar models and following similar trends across the country. Since at least the Second World War, the idea that the public system be fully government funded through to the end of secondary school has been commonplace. The ideational space and political economic structures within which debates about education are broadly similar across Canadian provinces and, as one would expect, deeply influenced by trends in the rest of the anglophone world (Manzer 2003). So why is it that Canadian provinces have evolved such different ways of regulating and supporting religious schools?

By tracing the long-term patterns of political development (Lucas and Vipond 2017) in comparative perspective, we highlight the unique

ways by which provinces have responded to demands to accommodate religion within their education system. In doing so, we offer an
important and largely untold aspect of Canada's broader story of
accommodating diversity while also illustrating the important role
that provincial governments and religious institutions have had in constructing Canada's approach to secularism. We establish that there is
no one single and simple answer that explains all of this divergence.
Rather, the policy diversity that exists in Canada is the result of provincial polities wrestling with a myriad of complex issues related to
religious schooling through unique processes of political development
over significant stretches of time. The origins of today's distinctive patterns of school governance lie deep in the origins of the Canadian state
yet have also been impacted by a series of particular choices made in
particular provincial political contexts and cultures in recent decades.
In basically every case, the way the issues at the heart of the debate
were conceptualized by provincial policymakers evolved over time in
different ways. This is a story that contains both seemingly immediate
and significant policy shifts in some provinces, much more incremental
change in others, and in Canada's most populous province, Ontario,
almost no significant change at all since Confederation. Overall, each
of the chapters that follows will demonstrate how the contexts and cultures of each province, especially the unique educational policy regimes
that evolved in each, conditioned the responses of policymakers to
both large-scale exogenous shocks to the education policy system and
to more gradual endogenous pressures. These differential dynamics,
played out over time, generated the policy divergence we find today.

Underlying our approach to the evolution of provincial policy with
respect to religious schooling is the position that politics takes place
in time and understanding it requires paying attention to feedback
effects, timing, and sequence (Pierson 2004; Boychuk 2016). Specifically,
we draw on two intellectual traditions: Canadian political development (Lucas and Vipond 2017) and the theories of institutional change
developed in historical institutionalism (Mahoney and Rueschemeyer
2003). By drawing on both, we can use history not simply as a source
of raw data but also treat it as an important space within which politics
unfolds. Combined with the leverage that comparison across provinces
makes possible, this book demonstrates how religious identities and
institutions – in some cases in forms politically mobilized two hundred
years ago – are deeply embedded within the Canadian state and continue to structure political debates about schools today.

To organize this history, as well as to highlight the different ways
in which religious schooling has been understood across Canadian

provinces by policymakers over time, we identify three basic regimes governing religious schools: *faith*, *rights*, and *choice*. These serve both to illustrate the broad historical periods in which each of these regimes dominated the politics of religious schooling in Canada and to categorize the very different ways in which the policy problems of religious schools were understood by policymakers. The *Faith* regime – a view on religious schools that sees communal religious identity and institutional autonomy as the primary political challenge – dominated debate during the nineteenth century, was entrenched in the 1867 Constitution, and continues to define the debate in some provinces into the contemporary period. Visible almost as soon as legally actionable rights to religious schools were entrenched in the Constitution, but becoming increasingly important after the Second World War, a *Rights* regime allowed both groups seeking change and groups seeking to preserve the status quo access to the courts and to a potent set of political arguments to argue both for and against public funding for private religious schools. It was a crucial part of Catholic mobilizing in support of separate schools (Mulligan 2006), but other minority groups (perhaps most notably Canada's francophone minorities) also found rights arguments to be powerful (Buckingham 2014). Finally, since the 1970s, arguments rooted in market-derived visions of *Choice* in education have become increasingly common and influential in structuring the governance of religious schools (Bosetti and Gereluk 2016). Visible both inside and outside public systems, mechanisms to facilitate school choice have been widely taken up and, in some provinces, have provided a framework for religious schools to successfully argue in favour of receiving state support. We utilize this faith, rights, and choice framework throughout the empirical chapters that follow as a way to demonstrate the evolution of the debate over religious education in each province and also to highlight the manner in which certain regimes continue to be important in certain provinces, thereby helping to explain the divergence we find in contemporary provincial responses to the issue.

In the sections that follow in this introductory chapter, we lay out how our approach to these regimes is informed by Canadian political development and our understanding of institutional change by historical institutionalism. We then briefly describe our methodological approach, broaden the discussion with a consideration of the normative complexity of the issue of religious schooling, and offer a more detailed exploration of the faith, rights, and choice framework we apply in our study. This introductory chapter closes with a comparative overview of the evolution of approaches to religious education we find in each of the provinces studied.

It is worth noting, however, that there are two sizeable omissions in our analysis: the development of policy related to religious education in the Territories of Canada, as well as the creation and operation of religion-based Indian Residential Schools throughout Canada. In both cases, the most obvious reason that these issues have been set aside in this book is that they are/were areas of federal rather than provincial jurisdiction and thus evolved according to very different logics than the development of provincial policies around religious education. Similarly, references to the residential school system or the evolution of education in the Territories were simply not part of the calculations made by policymakers grappling with the issue of religious schooling in their respective provinces. In the case of residential schools more specifically, the explicitly racist and colonial motivations behind the establishment of the system on the part of the federal government stands in marked contrast to the very different and far less harmful sets of reasons that underlie the evolution of various provincial policies related to religious education. Those readers wishing to learn more about this history, especially as it pertains to the involvement of religions institutions and efforts to de-establish Indigenous religions, are urged to consult the final reports of Canada's Truth and Reconciliation Commission as well as additional scholarly literature on the topic (for instance: MacDonald 2019; Miller 2001; Reid 2015). As for Territorial education policy, it too, in many cases, exists within a much more complicated context related historically to a similar colonial mission with respect to Indigenous Peoples, and more recently, within individually negotiated self-government arrangements between the federal government and First Nations residing in the Territories (see Jamieson 1994; King 1998; McGregor 2013; Rasmussen 2011).

Theory

Sitting at the difficult intersection between citizenship, state structure, and the provision of education, religious schools pose big and complicated questions for policymakers. Our approach to the complex reality represented by two hundred years of political contestation over the relationship between religious schools and provincial governments is grounded in the reality that politics takes place in time (Pierson 2004; Boychuk 2016). From the Canadian political development tradition (and its American counterpart), we derive our focus on the historical origins of contemporary political structures and our interest in the question of "how did we get here?" Historical institutionalism is in broad theoretical alignment with this sensibility (Smith 2009), and from it we draw especially on recent work that has developed frameworks for understanding the ways in which institutions change.

American political development is a well-established tradition in American political science (Sheingate 2014; Mettler and Valelly 2016). Grounded in the recognition of the power of path dependency and of policy layering, it is a tradition that has developed a rich set of theoretical insights into how historical decisions have shaped contemporary American public policy and politics. Running through this literature is a recognition that political outcomes are often contingent and sometimes internally inconsistent, but they are embodied in regimes or political orders that define the rules of the game for the practice of politics (Orren and Skowronek 2004). A foundational recognition is that processes of incremental reform and change lead to the formation of regimes that embody these rules (Skowronek 1982). Internal regime inconsistency, referred to as intercurrence in political development literature (Lucas 2017), can be papered over for a long time but can also act as a catalyst for significant change as internal pressures grow. This understanding of political development has significant overlaps with historical institutionalism through shared concepts such as path dependence, feedback effects, exogenous and endogenous triggers of change, and policy entrepreneurs.

In drawing on the American political development tradition to understand Canadian politics, we are following the lead of important articles by Smith (2009) and Lucas and Vipond (2017). Reviewing the existing scholarship in Canadian political science that takes a historical approach, Lucas and Vipond (2017, 220) identify four ways of using history in political science: the use of history to expand datasets, a focus on key events and turning points, themes of change and stability, and examinations of the "legacy of the past" on contemporary political decision-making. This book engages in the latter three enterprises, as we seek to understand the key political turning points that have led to our contemporary situation with regards to religious schooling, to examine the long periods of institutional stability and incremental change between major turning points, and to explain why decisions taken in the mid-nineteenth century are still so influential today. In doing so, we embrace the core claim that "history provides a solid platform from which to advance the basic mission of political science, namely, to describe, explain, and explore the use (and abuse) of (state) power" (Lucas and Vipond 2017, 229).

Though not cited by either Smith or Lucas and Vipond, a landmark study of Canadian education policy, Ronald Manzer's comparative *Educational Regimes and Anglo-American Democracy* (2003) clearly

embodies a developmental approach. Manzer identifies five successive, but interdependent, political regimes at play in the governance of
public education in anglophone democracies that resulted from political contestation over the answers to five key political problems: how
to provide public instruction, how to educate for industrial efficiency,
how to provide mass education in the era of the welfare state, how to
educate for a pluralist society, and how to educate for global capitalism.
Each regime builds on preceding patterns of political contestation, and
different polities could create different (albeit constrained) answers to
the policy problems that defined each period. Earlier work by Manzer
(1985, 1994) makes it clear that this typology for the evolution of public
education in Canada is grounded in a political development perspective on the evolution of Anglo-American democracies. This approach is
extended by Miriam Smith in her 2009 Canadian Political Science Association Presidential address: "Diversity and Canadian Political Development." Here, Smith argues that there is a natural overlap between a
Canadian political development approach and historical institutionalism. Both approaches "are distinguished by their attention to the structures ... that limit political actors and by their attention to the unfolding
of large-scale processes of political, economic, and social change over
time" (Smith 2009, 844). They use similar tools and are similarly focused
on the state and the programs that the state delivers. She argues that
this historical and structural approach is useful in approaching questions of diversity and human rights and crucial to understanding the
"role of the state, law and public policy in producing and reproduc-
ing racialized and gendered power relations" (Smith 2009, 849). It is
an approach particularly useful in placing Canada within its North
American context and in understanding the colonial past of Canadian
government and society.

In emphasizing provincial variation and differentiation in the policy
regimes around religious schools, we recognize that we are situating
religious schools in Canada in contrast to the remarkable record of
inter-provincial convergence in education policy established by Jennifer Wallner in *Learning to School: Federalism and Public Schooling in Canada*
(2014). Wallner attributes this convergence, in the absence of formalized
coordination mechanisms such as a federal Ministry of Education, to
four factors: education being properly understood as developmental
(rather than social) policy, strong policy networks that facilitate policy
diffusion, unconditional fiscal arrangements, and equality among the
provinces creating strong opportunities for cooperation and shared
learning (Wallner 2014, 237–50). Recognizing that these factors are
present for religious schools, too, in the accounts that follow we pay

attention to what differentiates religious schools from other elements of education governance and what leads to such markedly unique patterns of differentiation across provinces.

Like this book, Manzer (2003), Wallner (2014), and the examples in Smith (2009) focus on the politics of education as a macro question that plays out on the level of national and provincial governments. But it is important to recognize that the political development approach can also draw on micro-histories to document important political dynamics. This is the approach taken by Vipond in his *Making a Global City: How One Toronto School Embraced Diversity* (2017). This detailed study of the Clinton Street Public School in Toronto describes how public education in Canada changed both in its understanding of religious and ethnic identity during the twentieth century and how different groups of new Canadians interacted with the resulting practices that sought to create citizens and to define citizenship. Focused on the outcomes of policy, rather than its political origins, Vipond's book makes a strong argument for examining the development of the Canadian school as an important site in understanding our country's approach to diversity, democratic engagement, and citizenship formation. Vipond's approach is shared by Lucas in *Fields of Authority: Special Purpose Governance in Ontario* (2016). While we do not engage with the internal governance of religious schools, we would argue that whether provincial governments permit or financially support religious schools does throw additional light on how much authority and autonomy are delegated to schools operating outside the public system.

The political development tradition offers a guide to understanding the importance of previous political debates and decisions that influence contemporary structures and policies. There is something of a bias towards path dependence built into the framework. Though intercurrence offers a starting point for understanding whether potential exists for political change, it is less fully developed as a theory of change than historical institutionalism, which has better models to deal with it. Having a model capable of identifying both change and continuity is critical to our project: the differentiation across Canadian provinces in the policy regime within which religious schools operate is the result of multiple moments of contention and institutional change. To address this gap, we draw on theories of institutional change developed in the historical institutionalist tradition in comparative politics.

Like Canadian and American political development, historical institutionalism as a conscious intellectual tradition emerged in the 1970s as a part of the "new institutionalism." This return to institutionalist analysis is usually divided into three types: rational choice institutionalism, sociological institutionalism, and historical institutionalism (Hall and Taylor 1996). Rational choice institutionalism drew heavily from economics and sought to understand the role that political institutions play in creating stability in situations where individual rationality alone could not. Sociological institutionalism (as the name suggests) grew out of sociological studies of organizational life and sought to understand the interaction of institutions and culture in creating organizations. Historical institutionalism tends to have a relatively broad notion of institutions, recognizes the asymmetries of power that exist in institutions, emphasizes path dependence, and seeks to integrate the study of institutions with other factors (Hall and Taylor 1996, 938). In historical institutionalism we find a rich body of theory that elaborates on the core point that "it is more enlightening to study human interactions: (a) in the context of rule structures that are themselves human creations; and (b) sequentially, as life is lived, rather than to take a snapshot of those interactions at only one point in time" (Sanders 2008). Overlapping intellectually with the political development tradition discussed above, early applications of historical institutionalism leaned heavily on path dependence as an analytic tool. While analytically powerful, this naturally led to the charge that historical institutionalism overemphasized political stability and, as a result, failed to develop reasonable tools to address change. Though perhaps a fair charge in the 1990s, the concern that change has not been appropriately addressed in historical institutionalism has generated an impressive response.

Fundamental to historical institutionalist examinations of institutional change is a distinction between the type of change and the sources of change. Change can be caused by dynamics exogenous to institutions and by endogenous factors within them (Koning 2016). Examining big changes in institutions, driven by exogenous changes in institutions, ideas, or interests, has been the stock and trade of historical institutionalism from its beginnings. Here, dramatic shocks – a completely new set of economic ideas, the Great Depression, or the American Civil War being three classic examples – sufficiently destabilize existing institutions or create irresistible pressures for the formation of new ones that create moments of dramatic change. Over long periods, attention to exogenously driven changes points scholars both to the founding moments of a polity or an institution (Wiseman 2007; Sanders 2008) and to patterns of punctuated equilibrium, where long stretches of stability are interrupted by periods of dramatic change driven by forces outside the institution (Baumgartner and Jones 1993). Understanding such patterns of change requires paying careful attention both to the forces that define critical junctures and the forces of path dependence that exist in periods of institutional stability.

But significant change need not happen simply as the result of external shocks to institutions. Instead, it can be the result of more gradual processes of endogenously driven development within institutions. One particularly important model of endogenous change has been developed by Kathleen Thelen and her co-authors James Mahoney (2010, 2015) and Wolfgang Streeck (2005). As described in Mahoney and Thelen there are four patterns of incremental institutional change:

1 Displacement: the removal of old rules and the introduction of new ones
2 Layering: the introduction of new rules on top of or alongside old ones
3 Drift: the changed impact of existing rules due to shifts in the environment
4 Conversion: the changed enactment of existing rules due to their strategic redeployment

(2010, 15–16)

Each of these types of incremental change can add up to significant changes in the operation and nature of an institution over time. In our historical chapters, we find moments of change being motivated by both exogenous factors and all four endogenous patterns. Though we identify a diverse range of factors at play in each of these circumstances, it is worth highlighting the frequent appearance of policy entrepreneurs, generally understood to be individuals or groups willing to devote considerable resources in pursuit of a future policy outcome (Kingdon 2003, 122–32; Mintrom and Norman 2009; Zahariadis and Exadaktylos 2016). In our concluding chapter, we consider the implications of this multiplicity of ways in which regimes have changed. But for now, it is important to emphasize that there is diversity not just in the policy regimes by which provinces now regulate religious schools but that the paths by which they have arrived at those outcomes are substantively different.

Historical institutionalism, for our purposes, usefully builds a flexible understanding of institutions and their capacity for change. It suggests that institutions can be remarkably stable, can change in significant ways as the result of endogenous internal dynamics, and can change as the result of exogenous shocks. In the case studies which follow, we find and track examples of each type of change as different provinces wrestle with the challenges posed by religious schools. Combining a political development approach with the models of institutional change developed within historical institutionalism gives us a robust theoretical toolkit to examine the variations in provincial regimes concerning religious schools. From Canadian political development we take the importance of regimes, long historical time periods, and (theoretically informed) explanations of specific events. From historical institutionalism, we draw on a rich literature on how institutions can create path dependence, the mechanisms of exogenous change, and a typology for tracking and describing endogenous change. Both intellectual traditions stress the need for balancing the role played by institutional structures and policy entrepreneurs in creating these dynamics, as well as carefully tracking insights generated both through comparison between cases and historical work within them.

A Note on Method

Reconstructing the long history of policy development related to the intersection of religion and education in ten distinct provinces proved challenging in several ways. The existing literature on the development of education systems in Canadian provinces from the nineteenth century forward is vast. The reader will quickly notice that we leaned heavily upon much of this literature as a foundation for our analysis. Yet very few of these works were comparative in nature and, of course, none were unable to take account of the many ways in which those key initial policy decisions on the accommodation of religious differences in education systems would shape provincial approaches to religious education going forward. It is at this point that we hope to make our most straightforward contribution: to demonstrate and compare how policy related to religious education evolved across ten provinces over time.

In order to accomplish a fully comparative treatment, we turned both to recent secondary literature that documents a variety of key points in provincial evolution and politics (even if it did not focus particularly on education) and to our own analysis of a large assortment of primary data from each province. Primary material included archival material documenting meetings; political speeches and legislative debates on government decisions about religious education; the position papers produced by religious, secular, and parent groups active within the education policy communities of each province; media reports; and broader statistics on provincial demographics, provincial election results, school enrolment numbers, and various funding models utilized at different points. In addition, our analysis was grounded in data generated from the completion of eighty-eight semi-structured interviews with key policy insiders (past and present) from across the provinces (see the appendix for a full list of those interviewed). Interviewees included current and former members of provincial education ministries, provincial cabinet ministers, premiers, political party leaders, academics, and members of interest groups active in education policy discussion and development. This last group included leaders of faith-based organizations active on educational issues as well as representatives of various secular public education interest groups.

Following Tansey (2007), we acknowledge the vital role such elite interviews with those active in the relevant policy community can play when seeking to reconstruct the processes that led to a particular policy decision being made in recent memory. As such, we employed a non-probability approach in seeking such informants, specifically utilizing a combination of purposive and snowball sampling, while simultaneously working to ensure the quality of the data generated through multiple processes of triangulation. We tended to first reach out to relevant ministers (and deputy ministers) of education (past and present) and, from that contact, were often directed to others within government who participated in the debates/decisions in question. We also relied upon media reports and internet searches to identify and contact relevant interest groups, from which we were very often put in contact with non-governmental officials who were active in the educational debates that interested us. The completion of these interviews with policy insiders provided us a significant window into the debates that took place around the intersection of religion and education in each of the provinces over the past three to four decades.

Overall, our method closely approximates what Beach and Pedersen (2013) have described as "explaining-outcome process tracing," an approach that seeks to provide a thick accounting of policy development by highlighting the causal processes that lead from X to Y. In its simplest formation, such a dedication amounts to the belief that "proper explanations should detail the cogs and wheels of the causal process through which the outcome to be explained was brought about" (Hedstrom and Ylikoski 2010, 50). In particular, we seek to explain a particular policy outcome by crafting "a minimally sufficient explanation ... with sufficiency defined as an explanation that accounts for all of the important aspects of an outcome with no redundant parts being present" (18). However, this approach differs from theory-centric process tracing in that the explanatory story that we tell in each of the ten provinces is often too specific to generalize to a broader theory. Indeed, "nonsystematic" or case-specific factors are a very important aspect of each of our provincial analyses. As such, each of our seven empirical chapters tells an explanatory story that, in general, is too specific to be portable to other cases. This, however, allows us to be more pragmatic and "eclectic" in terms of drawing from differing theoretical traditions in order to

provide greater insight into the outcome in question (Beach and Peder-
son 2013, 34–5, 63–4).

The Politics of Religious Schooling in Canada

Schooling in general is of great political importance and poses significant
political questions related to both citizenship and the roles and respon-
sibilities of the state versus those of parents. Religion and schooling –
our focus in this book – poses its own particular political challenges. In
his summary of debates over religious schools and colleges, the Canadian philosopher Elmer Thiessen (2001) identified a number of charges
against religious schools that weave through debates over their public
funding in Canada: that religious schools promote divisiveness, foster
intolerance, overemphasize parental rights with regards to children, violate the academic freedom of instructors, are elitist, take funds that might
have otherwise supported the public system, violate the separation of
church and state, engage in indoctrination and censorship, and breed
dangerous forms of fundamentalism. Coming to conclusive answers to
any of these questions is made difficult not just by the deeply held values
at play but also because religious believers within even a single tradition
will disagree which religious schools pose these threats and which do
not (McDonough, Memon, and Mintz 2013; Zine 2008).

More specific to the politics of religious schools in Canada, we find two
bundles of issues have been particularly tricky for policymakers. First,
there is the question as to whether being (or being formed into) a rights-
bearing citizen means belonging to a single community. By creating an
institutional space that opens up multiple venues for the practice of
citizenship and the formation of future citizens through schooling, religious schools can challenge the idea of a single, undifferentiated, political community. Religious schools vary widely in how countercultural
they are, but all offer students and parents an alternative community to
belong to. Some schools – Catholic schools in the nineteenth century or
Hutterite and Muslim schools today – seem to some to offer a vision of
alternative community that is robust enough to challenge the Canadian
state for the primary allegiance of those who belong to it (a perception
that linguistically or culturally defined schools have also suffered from
at different times).

Second, even if they do not offer an alternative community, religious
schools may offer an alternative vision of the scope of citizenship. This
can be apparent both on questions of the duties of citizens (can a school
teach pacifism in time of war, for example?) and on questions about
how far state guarantees of the rights enjoyed by the citizens extend

into semi-autonomous spaces like religious schools (are religious schools required to support LGBTQ clubs or hire teachers whose lifestyles run counter to the values promoted by the school?). In both these cases, those who oversee schools are forced to choose between different rights claims and different notions of citizenship. Debates over how school governance affects questions of citizenship have been present throughout the history we examine here.

Of course, there are some distinctive contextual features surrounding these debates in Canada that distinguish it from other developed countries. Canada has no constitutional separation between church and state and, until 1982, had constitutional documents that were largely silent on the questions of individual rights even though they did include entrenched protection for rights of groups. Since 1982, an extensive jurisprudence has grown up around issues of religious freedom and religious equality (Buckingham 2014). This jurisprudence is evolving, but it is worth noting that it has not moved in the direction of creating a bright line between church and state. Instead, it has tended to emphasize the imperative of equal treatment between different faith traditions (as well as the secular "none of the above" option). Canadians have generally been at least somewhat comfortable with claims grounded in group rights and identity, in addition to those grounded in individual rights. This is clearly the case with religious schools, but it is also evident in the recognition of heritage languages in the school system and a model of integration that, in general, emphasizes a mosaic rather than a melting pot model of diversity. The final contextual element worth highlighting is the significant secularization that Canada has undergone since the Second World War. After peaking in the 1950s, levels of religious belief, practice, and affiliation have fallen off across the country, most dramatically in Quebec. At the same time, large scale immigration has seen the number of religious traditions practiced by Canadians grow markedly. This combination of secularization and diversification has created challenges both in the systems of governance that we examine here and within public secular schools (on the latter, see Vipond 2017).

Our task, however, is not to develop philosophical answers to the broad normative questions raised by these debates in Canada or elsewhere. Instead, it is to track how the ideas that Canadian policymakers held as appropriate solutions to such questions interacted with the interests of communities engaged in the process – at particular times and places – to shape the institutions of provincial school governance that we have today. In doing so, we track the evolution in Canada's political accommodation of religious identity across time and identify the variations in how policymakers in different provinces understood the choices they were presented with. The empirical analysis at the heart of this book is largely organized around the notion that the unique ways in which provincial approaches to religious schooling policy have evolved are strongly related to the distinct ways in which provincial politicians and policymakers understood the central policy challenges that the issue of religious schooling has raised at different historical points. Religious schooling has proven to be an incredibly complex, multifaceted issue across Canada, and the specific challenges the issue poses have been understood in many different ways across the country over time. These distinct interpretations of the policy problem have been shaped by, and interacted with, unique provincial contexts and cultures, specific exogenous shocks, and the work of distinct policy entrepreneurs to produce the divergence we find today.

Following the practice of other scholars of education governance in Canada (Manzer 2003; Wallner 2014), we identify clear periodization effects in the development of policy and the nature of the policy environment with respect to religious schooling. In an effort to make analytical sense of this historical evolution across ten provinces over almost two hundred years, we adopt from the Canadian political development tradition the notion of three distinct regimes that map onto this pattern of periodization. At the heart of each of these regimes is a central idea that dominates how the politics of religious schooling has been interpreted in each province. We label these three regimes *faith*, *rights*, and *choice*. Importantly, not every provincial regime changed in every period or in response to a newly emerging dominant idea. Indeed, Ontario – Canada's largest province – has maintained the fundamentals of a focus on faith since 1867. But we argue that the ideas of faith, rights, and choice help identify a crucial element of the different contexts for decision-making as experienced by policymakers. What follows is an introduction to the central ideas at the heart of each of these regimes as well as a brief discussion on the historical period in which these ideas generally dominated debates over religious schooling in Canadian provinces.

Faith

The most obvious and intractable political problem posed by religious schools concerns the question of the religious character of the state itself and the relationship between the state and religious communities. Both normative arguments and political activity have been the most heated around the question of government support for religious schools. The faith regime dominated the period from before Confederation to the Second World War when the divide between Roman Catholics and Protestants was the country's major social cleavage and issues revolving around religious schooling were understood as key "national questions" that overlapped with the linguistic divide. Placing education under provincial jurisdiction was part of the Confederation bargain designed to protect religious minorities. As Quebec (1867), Ontario (1867), Manitoba (1870), Alberta (1905), Saskatchewan (1905), and Newfoundland (1949) entered Confederation, the rights of religious minorities (usually Catholic, but in Quebec and occasionally in other provinces, Protestants) to denominationally defined but state-supported separate schools were constitutionally entrenched. Section 93 did not mean equal protection or equal funding was extended to separate schools, but it did represent a guarantee of public resources for them. In Nova Scotia, New Brunswick, Prince Edward Island, and British Columbia, Section 93 did not apply because there was no formal pre-existing support for separate schools when these provinces entered Confederation. That said, nineteenth century school politics in these provinces did revolve around religion and was often incredibly heated.

Until just prior to the Second World War, religion, overlapping with language and ethnic diversity in many cases, was the deepest divide in educational politics and, in some provinces, the defining social differentiation that underlay the political party system. Since the end of the Second World War, this ability of religion to define school politics has decayed as Canada has grown increasingly diverse and secularized. As we will elaborate on below, in many provinces the issue of faith is far from the centre of contemporary debates over the funding of religious schools. Nevertheless, intense debates over Ontario's decision to extend funding to Catholic high schools in 1984 or John Tory's infamous campaign pledge to extend partial funding to private religious schools in 2007, the constitutional amendments to secularize school systems in Quebec and Newfoundland in the 1990s, ongoing conflicts related to the recognition of LGBTQ identities in schools, and the constitutionality of funding non-Catholic students to attend fully funded Catholic schools illustrate the enduring challenge that the relationship between church and state presents. Indeed, as we will argue in more detail below, faith continues to be the dominant way the problem of religious schools is understood in Ontario and Quebec in particular, thereby helping us understand the unique policy outcomes one finds in each of those provinces.

Rights

The post-Second World War period was more complex and saw the rapid growth of public schooling in Canada, immigration from a much wider range of source countries, the official adoption of "multiculturalism" as a policy principle, a relatively stable constitutional setting, and pre-existing funding for separate schools in several provinces. In some places – especially Ontario – the divide between Protestants and Catholics continued to be politically important but was weakening. In all jurisdictions there were policy entrepreneurs lobbying for funding to be extended to independent schools and/or schools of non-Catholic faith communities. Central to this period, extending into the 1980s, was the way religion came to be understood as one of a number of minority identities seeking accommodation among groups of rights-bearing citizens. Critical to this transition was the example set by francophones who, in a number of provinces in the 1960s, began utilizing rights-based language in their quest for fully funded French-language education. This strategy became especially important in Manitoba, where Catholic Manitobans followed francophones in arguing that a right to public funding existed based on interpretations of legislation stretching back to the late nineteenth century. Of course, it was not until the Charter of Rights and Freedoms was entrenched in 1982 that francophones were able to claim total legal victory in gaining access to fully funded schools, an outcome not ultimately available to faith-based communities. However, the use of a rights-based argument became an important strategy for the faith-based independent school lobby in Manitoba and throughout the country.

In British Columbia and Alberta, for instance, the arguments used by independent school lobbies evolved throughout the 1950s and 1960s from being based on faith (essentially, that governments ought to support religious schools because society benefits from the presence of religion) to ones based explicitly on individual and group rights claims. Employing argumentation drawn from Article 26 of the United Nations Declaration of Human Rights, which identifies both a child's right to an education *and* the parent's right to choose the kind of education given to their children, groups in both provinces successfully swayed reluctant governments to extend partial funding to independent schools. In doing so, these groups were able to convince both governments and large swaths of citizens that, in a truly democratic society, parents' rights to send their children to schools of their choice must be protected, and true protection requires state support. Even in Quebec, wherein the formalization of state support for private schools in the 1960s was due largely to the grand bargain struck between church and state that allowed for the creation of a Ministry of Education and the secularization of the public school system, the right of parents to choose the form of education their children received was enshrined in the preamble of the historical legislation in 1964.

Today, it is common to refer to such an argument as rooted in "parental rights," and this notion still holds much sway, especially in provinces wherein the partial funding of independent religious schools is largely uncontroversial. Indeed, we suggest that a key reason why funding for religious schools is largely uncontroversial in Western Canada is due to the fact that the issue has largely come to be understood by both governments and citizens as one of "parental rights," a much more palatable conception compared to the more potentially explosive issue of state-supported faith in a secular society. Of course, inherent in the notion of "parental rights" is the notion of choice in education, a seemingly innocuous principle in the 1960s and 1970s that has nevertheless become very controversial in contemporary debates over education in Canada and elsewhere. In this way, the argument from parental rights served as an important transition into the dominant current regime of school choice.

Choice

Separation of church and state, group rights, and the place of religious schools relative to these themes are perennial topics for political debate. But – especially in more recent years – a good part of the debate over religious schools in Canada has had less to do with religion or rights in the constitutional sense than with school choice, and, especially, whether the state ought to support schools of choice in one way or another. As Manzer (2003) has pointed out, debates over whether education ought to be publicly or privately provided go back to the 1840s in Canada and are closely linked to broader ideological contexts about the role of the state (as opposed to the market, the family, or the third sector) in delivering social services. The contemporary "school choice" movement traces its intellectual heritage back to the writings of classical liberals Friedrich Hayek (1960) and Milton Friedman (1955, 1962). In essence, proponents of school choice argue that increased state support of a variety of schooling options increases competition between service providers thereby stimulating innovation, responsiveness, and overall performance while simultaneously reducing costs (Chubb and Moe 1990, 1998; Daniels and Trebilcock 2005; Levin 1998).

In their recent overview of debates over school choice in Canada, Bosetti and Gereluk (2016) identify a wide range of considerations specific to education that play into the debates between school choice and the common school model on the level of ideas.[1] These debates raise important questions: Should schools embody a single notion of community or help minority communities preserve their identity? How do

---

1   Other important treatments of school choice in Canada include Holmes (1992, 1998), Daniels and Trebilcock (2005), Allison and Van Pelt (2012), and Campbell (2004).

we weigh equality of opportunity against equality of treatment against reasonable pluralism against individual rights? Does bringing the market and competition into educational provision create incentives for innovation and improvement or commodify and degrade a public good that ought to be equally accessible to all? These are powerful and important questions about how school governance ought to be structured. But, just as with questions of religion and rights, questions of choice are bound up with issues of material interests and worked out within institutions defined at some point in the past.

The *choice* regime corresponds to the contemporary, post-Charter era wherein certain provinces attempted to stretch regimes of accommodation developed previously to accommodate a much more diverse range of faiths and a generally more secular society under circumstances of financial pressure on governments, the emerging acceptance of neoliberal theory, and a centralization of school governance. At the heart of this policy period is the framing of the issue of religious schooling as one centrally of enhancing school choice for parents within the context of the supposed benefits to the schooling system by introducing principles of marketization as key guidelines. Today, the framing of the issue of religious schooling around the notion of school choice is the dominant interpretation in Alberta and British Columbia and determines some aspects of the politics and policy of religious schools in Saskatchewan, Manitoba, and Quebec.

Conclusion: Exploring the Evolution of Religious Schooling in Canada through the Regimes of Faith, Rights, and Choice

This book is built around case study chapters examining how the politics of religious schools have changed in each province, presented in the order in which the provinces entered Confederation. Each chapter shares the faith, rights, choice framework – insofar as it matches the realities of that province's politics. By way of introduction to those chapters, and as a way of highlighting the variation across provinces, we close this introduction with a short overview of the history of the politics around religious schools in each province.

Ontario stands alone among Canadian provinces in possessing an approach to religious schools that has remained essentially unchanged since 1867. The province supports a secular system as well as a separate Catholic one, but offers no government support for independent schools, faith based or otherwise. A central reason for the persistence of this structure has been the fact that the faith regime has remained the dominant lens through which many of the issues related to school governance have been politically debated. Like other provinces, debates in Ontario over education in the pre-Confederation period and up until about the Second World War were largely considered in relation to the divide between Protestants and Catholics. Although claims framed more so in terms of rights rather than religion emerged in post–Second World War Ontario, especially from the Franco-Ontarian community, which applied it in a successful attempt to gain self-governing status for their schools, the rights or choice regimes never emerged as dominant. This is not to say the *choice* regime was non-existent in the province. As in other provinces, certain policy entrepreneurs in Ontario did make arguments in favour of government support for religious independent schools rooted in choice. Indeed, the Shapiro Report of 1985 put forward a set of ideas in favour of government support with a very heavy element of "choice" in its framing and in its recommendation that government financial support be extended to religious and independent schools. But this report was submitted in the midst of a much larger and more bitter fight over the extension of funding to Catholic high schools and neither the Peterson government nor the broader public were in any mood to consider additional funding to independent faith-based schools. That the "faith" component of these private schools remained front and centre in such debates goes a long way to explaining the unique refusal of Ontario to provide support to private religious schools. In fact, the long-running and oft-mentioned fear of societal fragmentation in the face of growing cultural and religious diversity that has been paramount in Ontario policy debates related to the question of government support for religious schools, a fear not nearly as pronounced in the rest of Canada, makes sense only when one comes to see that debates in most other Canadian provinces on this question are not understood through the volatile context of *faith*, but rather as an issue of *rights* and increasingly related to the benefits of school *choice*. This transition away from the *faith* frame and towards that of rights or choice has simply not taken place in Ontario. Since the challenges policymakers are trying to solve have not changed, it is perhaps not surprising that the resulting institutional structures have not changed either.

Although Quebec's current approach to the funding of religious and independent schools is nearly identical to that of both Manitoba and BC (a fully funded secular public system alongside partial state support for independent schools), the way its system of school governance has evolved is unique within Canada. This is largely due to the near total control over education that Churches, especially the Catholic Church, held in Quebec from the early days of the New France settlement and well into the second half of the twentieth century. The second cause for

Quebec's unique system is the monumental policy changes enacted in the wake of the Quiet Revolution, highlighted by the establishment of a Ministry of Education in 1964, long after the state had claimed authority over education in all other provinces. Throughout the long period of Catholic Church control over education, and even into the first decades after the Quiet Revolution, the *faith* regime remained the dominant lens through which education debates of all kinds were understood. That said, prior to the 1950s, very few if any in the province openly questioned the total control possessed by the Church – rather, it was simply assumed that the Church ought to operate all aspects of the education system. With the Quiet Revolution, and the simultaneous rapid secularization and liberalization that took place in the province, the *faith* regime remained dominant although the fundamental way the question of *faith* was interpreted changed drastically. Rather than continuing to defend the Church's central role in education, the focus of the majority of Quebecois, and especially the governing elite, became how quickly the state could take control from the Church and fully secularize the province's public education system.

The Quiet Revolution, then, can be understood as a dramatic exogenous shock to the education policy system, eventually resulting in the strict curtailment of the Church's influence over education – a radical shift in policy direction if there ever was one. Yet the public education system in Quebec did not become fully secular until 2008, some forty-four years after the creation of an Education Ministry. The process of secularization moved in a far more incremental fashion than many likely assumed would be the case in the mid-1960s. The Catholic Church still possessed essential pockets of support throughout the province, and it took sensitive and long-running negotiations between church and state to move the issue forward. In addition, the new nationalism that was emerging in the province would place linguistic concerns front and centre, knocking concerns over religion in schools off the political agenda for a time in the 1970s and '80s. Finally, the constitutional impediment inherent in Section 93 of the British North America (BNA) Act seemed to prevent definitive movement on this front until finally, in the late 1990s, the political will emerged to pursue a series of significant educational reforms between 1998 and 2005 that, for all intents and purposes, finally delivered the secular education system that seemed inevitable in the 1960s.

Even though the *faith* regime remained the central lens through which policy debate around the evolution of Quebec's public education system evolved, debates over state support for independent religious schools took a slightly different path. In short, while the state commitment for funding such schools (established officially in 1968) was the product of the larger compromise struck between the Catholic clergy and the state in the early 1960s that led to Bill 60 and the creation of a Ministry of Education in 1964, the issue of public support for religious independent schools has come to be understood, at least in part, through the lens of parental *rights* and school *choice*. Indeed, the preamble of Bill 60 in 1964 did not defend religious education directly but rather spoke to the right of parents to choose the type of instruction best suited for their children and the role the state ought to play to protect such a right. Such support for independent schools was certainly not unanimously supported in Quebec and the issue remains quite polarizing today. Yet, in complete opposition to the situation in Ontario, *faith* is simply not the sole focal point of these debates around independent schools. Rather, nearly all opposition to funding such schools hinges on notions of "elitism" in the private sector and the importance of directing scarce state resources to the public sector. Similarly, defenders of public funding for independent schools most often refer to the importance of maintaining the tradition of private schools in Quebec (which is of course related to a traditional, Catholic, Quebecois identity), defending the principle of school *choice* enshrined in Bill 60, and the broader benefits of competition between the private and public sector.

In Atlantic Canada, two different arrangements received recognition when those provinces (separately) entered Confederation. In New Brunswick, Prince Edward Island, and Nova Scotia there were localized political compromises leading to informal separate schools that received government support in the nineteenth and early twentieth centuries, based simply on whether there was a Protestant or a Catholic majority in any given area. These accommodations for (usually Catholic) minorities were not formalized systems; thus, they did not count as pre-existing separate schools under the terms of Section 93 of the Constitution. Though there were occasional political and legal controversies over this arrangement, the informal system of separate schools seems to have been satisfactory enough to have prevented significant mobilization to either formalize a separate system in any of the Maritime provinces or to see government support extended to other independent or religious schools. When, in the 1960s, school amalgamations created larger and religiously mixed schools, it occurred with very little political controversy either at the time or since. Rights-based controversy did arise around francophone school boards but, unlike in other provinces, the extension of a rights regime to other groups seems not to have been of significant import. Similarly, the relative poverty, small size, and lack of immigration to these provinces seem to have prevented any pressure to create more choice in the system even though each Maritime province does have a long history of elite independent schools in its education landscape.

Newfoundland and Labrador's history, also addressed in chapter 3, is quite different. When it entered Confederation in 1949, seven denominational educational systems received government support and constitutional protection. There was, in fact, no public school system because the colonial and then provincial government had long lacked the resources for such a system and, instead, had chosen to subsidize church schools as a way to extend educational access. This arrangement began to be questioned in the 1960s, when the post-war baby boom, increasing demand for secondary education, and an ecumenical religious mood saw the amalgamation of three Protestant systems and a Royal Commission examining educational governance. Though there was discussion in the 1960s about radical change, the constitutional protection for the existing church school system and ongoing strong public support for it prevented such change from being seriously considered. Thus, the Confederation era system continued until the 1990s, when economic hardship, demographic decline, and rapid secularization created a crisis in Newfoundland schools resolved with a Constitutional amendment and the creation of a single public system in 1997. Importantly, these systemic pressures were reinforced by provincial government leadership that had a strong commitment to driving change.

Canada's Atlantic provinces have evolved regimes where there is a more or less binary choice: secular public schools or Christian separate schools (usually Catholic). In Western Canada, both of these options are available, but there is also – like with Quebec – a notable presence of partially publicly supported independent schools. The extension of public support to these schools beginning in the 1970s brings an important aspect of policy layering into the Western Canadian chapters, as these were changes produced not by crisis nor (often) introduced suddenly.

In Manitoba, independent-school funding was introduced in the 1980s as a solution to religious and rights claims left unresolved from that province's establishment and entry into Confederation in 1870. Though the Catholic minority did have legal protection for its schools upon Manitoba's formation, these protections were set aside by the provincial government from the 1880s forward. These actions triggered the Manitoba Schools Crisis – the national unity crisis of its day. However, despite significant political mobilization, the Manitoba government's move to a single public system operating in English was maintained for most of the twentieth century. This was first challenged by francophone mobilization in the 1960s. When the Catholic minority threatened to launch a constitutional challenge seeking the protection of its rights in the 1980s, a choice-based compromise was reached: the Manitoba government would partially support all independent schools. This compromise has been politically stable.

Since the early 1990s, the funding and regulatory model for independent schools in Manitoba has been similar to that of British Columbia and to post-1997 Quebec: a secular public system alongside partial government support for independent schools. For the most part, this has been a politically stable compromise for about three decades. However, the path by which Manitoba arrived at this structure was anything but smooth. Indeed, debates over religious and independent schools in Manitoba have been complicated, politically explosive, and nationally important in a way those of no other province have been. As is well known, Manitoba's education system has long been at the centre of much larger debates about how to manage three critical (and mutually reinforcing) divides in Canadian life: between settler and Indigenous communities, English and French speakers, and Catholics and Protestants. From its earliest days until the 1960s, the faith regime was dominant in such debates, although it is without doubt that the English-speaking Protestant majority was the clear victor in the many policy battles that took place. Yet the structure of Manitoba's educational system began to shift in response to the mobilization of the province's francophone community, who would find success in their quest to access and eventually control their own schools via arguments based in constitutional rights which culminated in the famous *Mahe v. Alberta* (1990 CanLII 133 (SCC), [1990] 1 SCR 342). Even before this court victory, francophone successes, in turn, opened a broader policy window in the province wherein arguments rooted in school choice made on the part of an alliance of religious and secular independent schools would find sympathetic ears with all three major parties in the post-war era, culminating with the Lyon Progressive Conservative government introducing direct grants to private schools in 1980. Thus, we find clear evidence of the *faith, rights,* and *choice* evolution at play in Manitoba though the transitions between the periods are quite muddy.

Initially, British Columbia stood alone among Canadian provinces, intent from its pre-Confederation days on ensuring a strict divide between religion and education, at least in terms of overt church involvement in publicly funded schools or the flow of public money to religious schools. In other words, BC would deal with the problem of *faith* in exactly the opposite way of all other provinces. For over a century, despite the frequent pleas of the province's Catholic community, the education system of BC included a single network of non-denominational public schools and a smattering of wholly unfunded independent schools. This changed dramatically in the 1970s, however, as a result of both exogenous social and political change as well as the strategic actions of a persistent education policy entrepreneur. Similar to Alberta, the independent school lobby in BC, made up of mostly but not wholly of religious citizens, made the explicit decision to frame their arguments in favour of state support not around the principle of religious liberty, as frequently found in Ontario, but rather upon the *right* of parents to choose the type of education their children receive. By shifting the frame from that of *faith* to that of both *rights* and *choice*, these actors successfully defused much of what made the similar debate in Ontario so explosive. In a democratic, pluralistic, and individualistic society like BC, it has proven far more difficult for opponents of state support to independent schools to defeat arguments based on *rights* and *choice* as opposed to those based on *faith*. This shift in framing helped usher in a clear policy window in the late 1970s wherein the BC government capitulated to the demands of the independent school lobby, authorizing the allocation of public funds for qualifying independent schools in 1977 and subsequently raising levels of support to contemporary levels in 1989, a period of change that can be categorized primarily as layering, as the regime established in 1977 was gradually made more generous. Since 1989, a second period of policy inertia has largely descended upon the issue of funding independent schools, best understood again as the product of path dependency. And again, similar to Alberta, the province's embrace of neoliberalism in the 1990s and early 2000s has further entrenched support for such funding given the belief in the tangible benefits of competition, driven by school *choice*, within the education marketplace, creating a regime wherein any type of significant reversal of the existing support for independent schools is unlikely.

Saskatchewan and Alberta, which were formed out of the Northwest Territories in 1905, had school systems designed to avoid the political controversy of Manitoba. This entailed the constitutional protection of Catholic separate schools on the Ontario model in both the *Saskatchewan* and *Alberta Acts* of 1905. There are some small differences between the two provinces when it comes to the politics of Catholic education (it was more controversial in Saskatchewan than in Alberta and Saskatchewan only began to fund Catholic high schools in 1964 while Alberta has done so since 1905), but the general evolution is the same. Again, with some differences in matters of detail, both Saskatchewan and Alberta have layered quite complicated regimes of support for multiple categories of independent school over top of the public-separate system. This is surprising, for the two provinces are usually seen to be quite distinctive in their political cultures and policy orientations.

Of the two, Saskatchewan began with the most contested politics over education. Immediately after 1905 contention over both the funding of separate schools and a strong government bent to enforce English-language only instruction gave debates over schooling in Saskatchewan distinct parallels to Manitoba or Ontario. That is, questions of religious schools were important and deeply divisive. After about 1930, however, Saskatchewan switched course. The politics of education became notably less contentious and incremental changes saw first funding for Catholic high schools in 1964, then funding for francophones and ad hoc arrangements with some private high schools in the 1970s. The modern regime of support for independent schools emerged in the late 1980s. Catholic separate schools and francophone schools represent the incremental establishment of a rights regime, but by the 1980s independent schools (both religious and non-religious) were successful in layering claims rooted in choice over top of these faith and rights regimes. The *Good Spirit* court case (sometimes known as the Theodore case) centred on the ability of the separate school system to receive funding for non-Catholic students was being fought while this book was being written. The initial decision, which found it unconstitutional for non-Catholic students to receive government funding when attending Catholic schools, would have overturned the basis of this regime. Overturned on appeal and strongly opposed by the government, this decision might have triggered substantial contention over the public support of religious schools in Saskatchewan on a faith basis.

Alberta has been the province most supportive of a wide variety of religion-based education in Canada, an outcome that seems to fit well with the perception that it has, essentially since its founding, been an especially religious region. Yet, although the overall evolution of this system of educational governance is attributable to a variety of systematic and case-specific factors, the degree of religiosity in the province is not central to this story. Much of the policy debate in the pre-Confederation days of the Northwest Territories, as well as that occurring in the first few decades after Alberta was created in 1905, was structured around the question of *faith*. Indeed, legislation passed in the 1870s and 1880s laid the foundation for a "concurrent" public system, providing the Protestant and Catholic Churches significant influence over education. Although key officials sought to constrain the autonomy of religious organizations – most especially Catholics – in those early days, the Alberta Act of 1905 solidified the rights of Catholics to form separate, publicly funded schools throughout Alberta, a situation that remains largely unchanged today. The development of the state-supported independent school sector in Alberta, on the other hand, is a story best understood as gradual and incremental change driven by arguments grounded in both the *rights* of parents in general and, more recently, the embrace of *choice*-based arguments that coincide with the province's long-running populist's leanings towards individual autonomy, as well the turn towards neoliberalism in the 1990s and beyond. Indeed, central to the Alberta story are the strategies employed by the faith-based independent school lobby that, beginning in the 1960s, was able to convince a hesitant Social Credit government that the *right* of parents to educate their children according to their convictions was paramount, and the role of a democratic government in a pluralistic age was to protect this right by ensuring independent schools were financially viable. This opened a policy window wherein the first public subsidies for independent schools were introduced in 1967, an outcome layered on top of the constitutionally entrenched support for Catholic separate schools in the province. Over the next several decades, additional layering took place as incremental changes related to the autonomy of, and public funding for, independent schools were introduced. Broader exogenous factors related to both self-interested electoral calculations on the part of Alberta governments and, more importantly, a strong commitment to school *choice* – rooted, in turn, in a wide embrace of the ideology of neoliberalism in the 1990s – are of immense importance when seeking to understand why a variety of these incremental changes were introduced over the past three decades, gradually shaping Alberta's intricate network of schooling options.

1 Ontario's Puzzling Continuity

Introduction

Educational debates in Ontario have often been seen to define the "Canadian" situation (Sweet 1997; White 2003; Zinga 2008), and the province's educational system has been influential across English Canada in almost every area (Wallner 2014). Yet, despite its convergence with the other English-speaking provinces in other areas of educational policy and governance, Ontario's public support for religious and independent schools is different than that of all other provinces in both its configuration and in its stability. The provincial government supports a single public system (today best understood as secular although originally non-denominationally Protestant) and a single separate system (with the exception of a single Protestant board, this is a Roman Catholic system). Both public and separate systems operate parallel French and English subsystems and are funded equally through a mix of provincial grants and property taxes. Particularly in the public system in larger cities, there is a substantial degree of choice between schools of different curricular, linguistic, or ethnic focuses (Thompson and Wallner 2011). Ontario's school system has responded to calls for the rights of linguistic minorities to be recognized with self-governing school boards and for increased parental choice between schools within the public system in fairly significant ways. In 2014–15, 29.7 per cent of Ontario students attended a separate school (Fraser Institute 2017) and, in 2019–20, 6.9 per cent attended (non-government funded) independent schools (Fraser Institute 2022).

Yet religious (and independent) schools fit into a broader educational regime in a way that has been unchanged since 1867: there is government support for a secular system and a separate Catholic system but no support for schools of any other religious groups or for independent schools. The situation of religious (and of independent) schools continues to be defined by faith, operating in a faith regime largely unchanged since the nineteenth century. This situation has come about through a hundred and fifty years of incremental change through processes of drift, conversion, and layering. From the 1960s forward arguments framed in terms of rights have been an important component of other aspects of educational politics, but they served to entrench the status quo regarding independent and religious schools rather than change it. Though policy entrepreneurs have sometimes argued for a regime of choice in Ontario, it has never gained significant support within the province's political system (Davidson, Lucas, and McGregor 2020).

This chapter focuses on three critical episodes in the evolution of Ontario's school system that highlight the constraints on institutional change in the governance of religious schools in the province. First, it examines the creation and constitutional entrenchment of the public-separate structure in the mid-nineteenth century, when policy elites were attempting to resolve the problem of Protestant-Catholic accommodation in the colonial legislature of the United Province of Canada within a faith regime. In the second, we explore the background of religious lobbying and linguistic politics in the extension of full funding to Catholic high schools in 1984–7 and discussions related to government support for independent schools in the context of the Shapiro Report of 1985 – the most significant modern examination of Ontario's school system. Finally, the chapter investigates more recent debates for government support of independent (both religious and secular) schools in Ontario. In each of these episodes – and in contrast to most other provinces – faith continues to define the regime even as the religious groups affected have changed and the scope of public education has expanded. Though both rights and choice arguments have been made, neither has been successful enough to change the regime in Ontario.

Table 1.1. Key Dates in the Evolution of Ontario's Education System

Date	Event
1841	Schools Act
1867	Confederation and Section 93
1912	Regulation 17 debates over French-language education
1969	MacKay Report on Religion in Public Schools
1984	Davis funding extension to Catholic high schools
1997	*Adler* case

The Constitutional Entrenchment of Faith:
Ontario Schools and 1867

The simple answer to the stability of the Ontario system is that the constitutional entrenchment of a division between public and separate schools embedded in the Constitution Act, 1867 has not been changed since Confederation. Then, Section 93 provided that

> In and for each Province the Legislature may exclusively make Laws in relation to Education ...
>
> 1 Nothing in any such Law shall prejudicially affect any Right or Privilege with respect to Denominational Schools which any Class of Persons have by Law in the Province at the Union;
> 2 All the Powers, Privileges, and Duties at the Union by Law conferred and imposed in Upper Canada on the Separate Schools and School Trustees of the Queen's Roman Catholic Subjects shall be and the same are hereby extended to the Dissentient Schools of the Queen's Protestant and Roman Catholic Subjects in Quebec;
> 3 Where in any Province a System of Separate or Dissentient Schools exists by Law at the Union or is thereafter established by the Legislature of the Province, an Appeal shall lie to the Governor General in Council from any Act or Decision of any Provincial Authority affecting any Right or Privilege of the Protestant or Roman Catholic Minority of the Queen's Subjects in relation to Education.

Incorporated into the 1867 Constitution in a way that protected Catholic separate schools in both Quebec and Ontario (but not in the Maritime provinces) the Section 93 compromise provided the template for dealing with religious (and overlapping linguistic) diversity in Manitoba, Saskatchewan, and Alberta when those provinces were created through Confederation. In both Ontario and Quebec, it is important to recognize that Section 93 was not the result of the Confederation deliberations alone. Instead, Section 93 entrenched the result of debates between the 1810s and 1867 about what the nature of schooling in the United Province of Canada ought to be. These debates, begun before the province had even achieved responsible government as a British colony, continued through a period when Upper and Lower Canada were united as one colony and their results were cemented into legislation just before Confederation in a form that was then constitutionally entrenched. But it is only in Ontario that subsequent political events saw this constitutional compromise remain intact. Some, but not all, of the roots of this resilience can be found in the origins of the compromise and the resulting regime of educational governance.

The first phase of this debate, which lasted from roughly the 1790s until the 1830s, centred on whether the scarce educational resources of a frontier society ought to focus on elementary common schools open to all or elite grammar schools. Ultimately, both grammar and common schools would receive state support but would be governed in different ways. Grammar schools were governed by trustees appointed by the government while common school trustees were elected by parents (Di Mascio 2012; Lucas 2016). Beginning in the 1820s, a second set of debates opened up around what the religious character of public schools would be. Initially, the question was whether government support for schools ought to be provided to the Anglican Church, which would then run the schools for the colony, or whether schools should be operated as a single Protestant, but non-denominational, system governed by locally elected trustees and (sometimes) subsidized by churches (Di Mascio 2012; Walker 1955). Adherents of both provisions believed that Christian instruction was an important part of the curriculum and assumed that instruction would be in English. The resolution of this debate by the 1840s was that the religious nature of the public common schools would be non-denominational but clearly Protestant. This compromise might have proved persistent had the province's settler population remained a mixture of anglophone Presbyterians, Anglicans, and Methodists from the United Kingdom and United States. But with significant Irish Catholic immigration throughout the 1840s, the union of the two provinces of Upper and Lower Canada in 1841, and the migration of francophone Quebecois into Northern Ontario, the nascent education system needed to adjust to the presence of a significant number of Catholics and to begin to deal with linguistic diversity (Manzer 2003).

This shifted the problem that political elites were trying to resolve. While there were doctrinal differences between Methodists, Anglicans, and Presbyterians, it was difficult – even in the 1840s – to argue that these differences were a threat to the colonial political order. Catholics were another matter. Only allowed to hold office in the United Kingdom after the 1829 Reform Act, Catholics were discontented – the 1837 Rebellions had made political stability a pressing issue in both Upper and Lower Canada and suggested that the overlapping French/English and Catholic/Protestant divides were real threats to that stability. On the other hand, Catholics were a cohesive community with their own traditions of education, capacity to provide that education even in frontier conditions through various religious orders, and powerful allies among politicians in (majority Catholic) Lower Canada. There were also strong similarities between the position of minority Protestants in Lower Canada and minority Catholics in Upper Canada that played out in the legislature of the united province. Finally, given the strong preference of Protestants that the Bible be taught in schools, it seemed clear even to many Protestant leaders that Protestants and Catholics would have to be educated separately (Walker 1955).

Political struggles over this new form of diversity would define educational politics in Ontario between the late 1830s and 1867. The debate began in the aftermath of the 1837 Rebellions, coinciding with the granting of responsible government to the colony in 1841. Resolving these debates took the better part of twenty years and almost as many revisions to the province's Education Acts. Fundamentally, the question was how to provide both universal elementary education while providing autonomy for the Protestant minority in Lower Canada and the Catholic minority in Upper Canada. The 1841 Act for the Establishment and Maintenance of Common Schools in Upper Canada embodied a compromise that would come to define Ontario's educational regime: "secular central governance, non-denominational common schools, and separate schools for denominational minorities" (understood as Catholics in Protestant townships and Protestants in Catholic ones) (Manzer 1994, 54). Initially, most of the schools that received government funding (from both the colonial and municipal governments) also had to charge tuition or receive financial support from churches to survive. This formula was tweaked in changes to the Education Act throughout the 1840s. From the 1843 Act forward, the legislature treated Canada West (Ontario) and Canada East (Quebec) separately when legislating about education. In 1846, school trustees were given taxing power to support Egerton Ryerson's goal of free elementary education (a goal that would not be completely realized until 1870). These changes were the subject of some political controversy in which religious leaders were as prominent as politicians (Walker 1955; Sissons 1959). Proponents and opponents of the general framework or specific applications could be found both in the Reform group and in the Tory group in the legislature.

These divisions between what would become parties were significant and contributed to the collapse of the Reform movement around 1850. Clear Grits, as the group around George Brown became known and which would eventually evolve into today's Liberal Party, were defined by their opposition to government support for Catholic separate schools. In the unified legislature, they formed an alliance with the strongly anti-clerical French Canadian Parti rouge. Their Tory opponents – evolving into the Liberal-Conservative party of John A. MacDonald at the time – included anti-Catholic members of the Orange

Order and many Catholics (Walker 1955). Making things even more politically combustible – and more focused on faith – was that both the Protestant (Westfall 1989) and Catholic (Fay 2002) communities were in unusually militant theological moods in the 1850s. Catholics were coming under the influence of ultramontanism, which sought the authority of the Pope over both governments and bishops and often rejected both liberalism and democracy. Canadian Protestants, on the other hand, were under the influence of more revivalist forms of their faith that were emerging in the United States and Great Britain. Combined with a growing consensus that schooling ought to be free, publicly supported, and teach some form of Christianity, the stage was set for heated and confused debate over what form faith in schools ought to take.

The policy issue central to these debates was whether or not separate schools in Upper Canada were receiving their fair share of tax revenue and whether they enjoyed the sort of autonomy and equality accorded to separate (Protestant) schools in Lower Canada. At stake were questions both of tax administration and how to account for equality: by the attendance of pupils? By denominational share of the total population? By a transfer of the proportion of taxes paid by members of a denomination to school trustees? Or simply by exempting supporters of separate schools from property taxes? It was with the Taché Bill of 1855, which the Liberal-Conservative government introduced in an effort to resolve these problems, that separate school status was firmly restricted to Catholics for the first time, rather than being open to Protestant denominations in principle (Walker 1955, 169). What became the final Upper Canadian effort to establish a stable school system was the 1863 Scott Act. This followed the broad outlines of the Taché Bill of 1855 and was passed by a Liberal-Conservative government lead by the Catholic J. Sanford Macdonald. As both Catholics and Orangemen from both Canada East and Canada West supported the bill, its passage through the legislature was relatively straightforward (Walker 1955).

Much of the commentary immediately after the passage of the 1863 Act treated it as finally bringing closure to the question of public support for separate schools. However, the political permanency of the bargain depended on decisions being made in a unified legislature where the Catholic majority of Canada East could help to defend the position of the Catholic minority of Canada West and the Protestant majority of Canada West could defend the position of the Protestant minority of Canada East. This political reality would shift if, as seemed likely from the moment that discussions around Confederation began, education became a provincial responsibility, and Upper and Lower Canada became separate provinces. Under such pressure, the possibility that a Protestant majority in the legislature might move to roll back support for Catholic schools seemed a distinct possibility. One response to this question, from both the Protestant minority in Canada East and the Catholic minority in Canada West, was to seek more generous protections in the colonial Educational Bills in 1864. Neither of these bills passed (Walker 1955).

A much more significant protection was the entrenchment of support for separate schools in both provinces in Section 93 of the Constitution Act, 1867 with which this section began. It was the result of a deliberate effort on the part of pro-Confederation leaders in Canada West – both the pro-separate school side of prior debates (such as John A. Macdonald and John Sandfield Macdonald) and opponents of separate schools (most notably George Brown) – to remove the problem from the already complicated public debates around Confederation. In this, they seem to have been successful, for education was not a notable part of the Confederation debates of 1867. The BNA Act's entrenchment of the Scott Act's compromise has been the single dominant feature of Ontario's regime of publicly supported religious schools since 1867, and it has stabilized the core division between public and separate schools. It also constitutionally entrenched in Ontario (and in Alberta and Saskatchewan, which followed the Ontario model in 1905) some important institutional features. Most importantly, separate schools were not church schools in the way that religious schools in Newfoundland and Quebec were. Separate schools in Ontario (and Saskatchewan and Alberta), it was always clear, were responsible to the Ministry or Department of Education and to their boards of elected (Catholic) trustees in ways parallel to schools in the public system. This was the case even for those schools staffed by members of religious orders. Clerics had visiting rights, and there were significant amounts of religious education, but school governance always ran through to the provincial government or to elected trustees and not to Church bodies (Walker 1955; Sissons 1959).

What this constitutional settlement left open for debate was whether government support ought to be more generous, what the place of church leaders in school governance would be, and whether or not the Section 93 guarantees were special ones particular to Catholics or whether they represented a model that might legitimately be extended to other faith groups. Political activity around these questions was very often heated, but the resulting policy changes were almost always relatively minor. In the 1870s, the question was whether bishops or lay boards held the upper hand in separate school governance. In the 1880s, it was whether all Ontario schools ought to use the same Bible translation or whether separate and public schools could use different ones.

Out of these debates emerged the tendency for provincial Conservatives to ally themselves more and more closely to the Orange Order and anti-Catholicism, and Liberals to ally themselves more and more closely to the cause of separate schools and the Roman Catholic Church (Walker 1955, Sissons 1959). There were important exceptions to this rule in both parties, but one's stance on the separate school question came to be an important element of a person's partisan allegiance in Ontario until the 1980s (Interview with Sean Conway, 26 June 2014). Nineteenth and early twentieth century debates in Ontario over the appropriate administration of religious schools were tied in with French Canadian opposition to the hanging of Louis Riel in 1885 and to the Manitoba Schools Crisis that followed. These were central national questions that fused linguistic and religious identity together in explosive ways. In 1912, as part of these debates, the Ontario government passed Regulation 17, which restricted French to only the first two years of school. Those who wanted only English used in any public or separate school in the province were an unlikely alliance of English-speaking Catholics concerned about dividing scarce resources in the Catholic system and triumphalist Ontario Protestants predominantly allied with the Conservative Party. Those who, while wanting English to be the dominant language of instruction, saw the point of allowing and supporting French-language instruction in predominantly francophone communities were closely tied to the Liberal Party, predominantly Catholic, and supported by the Quebec government. As most francophones were Catholic, this debate had an important religious element but was clearly understood to be about language by most concerned. While Regulation 17 was repealed in 1927, bilingual and francophone schools were not publicly supported in Ontario until 1968 (Behiels 2004).

The resolution of these debates did not settle the central issue of unequal funding between separate and public schools. In part, this was produced by industrial property taxes being designated only for public system support (a matter worked out in the 1941 *Ford* case). Increasingly important through the twentieth century was the lack of public support for separate high schools. The last question had seemingly been resolved by the Judicial Committee of the Privy Council's decision in 1928's *Tiny* case. The Council observed that, while more extensive funding could not be required legally, it was a perfectly reasonable political or policy decision for the province to extend funding to separate high schools or to the schools of other faiths (Allison and Van Pelt 2012). *Tiny* led to the province funding separate grades nine and ten at the elementary school rate but leaving grades eleven through thirteen dependent on tuition and church support. This compromise became difficult to maintain after the Second World War, as more and more students attended high school, and a desire for better facilities made those schools more expensive to operate. Similarly, differences in tax assessments still meant that the separate elementary schools received fewer resources than their public counterparts. These fiscal pressures increased dramatically after the Second World War as the children of the baby boom entered schools in record numbers and staying enrolled until the end of high school became normal. These changes, combined with significant Catholic immigration from southern European countries such as Italy and Portugal, put the Catholic system into an impossible situation (Gidney 1999).

Faith or Rights? Post–Second World War Separate Schools

In the 1950s, 1960s, and 1970s the enrolment surge caused by the post-war baby boom and the universalization of high school made questions of capacity critical in both the separate and public parts of Ontario's school system (Gidney 1999). These thirty years also saw the unionization of teachers, the amalgamation of small school boards into larger units, the province's urbanization, and a dramatic increase in the diversity of the population (Gidney 1999; Vipond 2017). It was also a period when the policy question of schools outside the public system was framed in a new way by some groups. In Catholic communities, and even more so in francophone communities, groups began to make claims framed in terms of rights separate from religion. In other provinces, rights would become an important way of arguing for the extension of public support to religious and independent schools. While rights claims were made in education policy and were critical to the creation of self-governing francophone school boards in Ontario, rights never came to define the debates around school choice and religious schools in Ontario. Indeed, after 1985 the provincial policy debate seems to have returned to viewing the issue primarily in terms of religious versus secular public schools in keeping with the faith view foundational to Ontario's regime.

On questions of language, the provincial government had slowly retreated from its Regulation 17 position from the 1920s forward. On an incremental basis, the government extended French-language education at the elementary grades where there was demand for it in the separate system. In 1967, premier John Robarts announced full support for French-language high school education. In order not to offer support to separate high schools (which did not receive public support at the time), this high school French-language education would be in the public system. Further creating a jurisdictional tangle, these programs were to be offered only where numbers warranted as decided by the public school board. While advocates for francophone rights were happy to receive public support, the key question of whether or not stand-alone, self-governing French schools were guaranteed continued to be a sticking point that played out in very heated ways in a number of communities through the 1970s (Behiels 2003).

The constitutional entrenchment of the Charter of Rights and Freedoms in 1982 fundamentally changed this debate. In a 1984 reference case, the Ontario Court of Appeal found that Section 23 of the Charter-required minority-language education (French, in Ontario) could not be limited by a "where numbers warrant" clause but needed to be understood as an individual right. The court also found that these schools needed to be self-governing. The government's response to the ruling was politically obscured by the concurrent controversy over the provision of full funding to Catholic high schools, but it resulted in the creation of French-language sections on local school boards where there were only a few francophones, public French-language boards, and separate French-language boards (Gidney 1999, 142–9) Gidney argues that a similar focus on rights can be seen in the government's response to the teaching of heritage languages, the inclusion of children with disabilities into the school system, and issues of gender equality (149–64). These needs did not require the creation of stand-alone schools, but they were clearly understood as questions of individual rights.

A similar deployment of rights language can be seen emerging in the 1960s around the question of religious observance in Ontario's public schools. Until the 1960s, these schools embedded a non-denominational Protestant form of Christianity throughout their curriculum. The MacKay Report of 1969, commissioned by then education minister Bill Davis with examining the place of religion in Ontario's public schools, found this to be deeply problematic. In a diverse society, the report argued, schools needed to educate students so that they could work out their own morality rather than indoctrinating them with the specifics of a single faith. This change would mean replacing Bible classes with a World Religions course, ending the practice of clergy having visiting rights in public schools, and rooting out the Christian imagery and messaging that ran through the elementary school curriculum. While supported by the educational establishment and reflective of the increasing diversity of the province, these recommendations were politically contentious enough that it took twenty years for them to be (more or less) fully implemented across the province. The complete implementation of these changes, especially in rural Ontario, was not the result of politics or policy decision-making but of court rulings in *Zylberg* (1988) and

Elgin County (1990) that applied the Charter of Rights and Freedoms to the question (Buckingham 2014, 54–63; Gidney and Millar 2001).

Treating diversity and religion as a problem understood in terms of rights was thus an option in Ontario's education policy space in the post-war period. The Franco-Ontarian community used it with success to gain self-governing status for their schools. Inside both the separate and public systems, proponents of heritage language education, disabled students, and secular public schools also found rights arguments to be persuasive to policymakers (Gidney 1999). But this way of framing the question does not seem to have caught on for religious and independent schools. Understanding the policy problem as one of faith rather than rights had much to do with the continuing political dominance of the separate schools funding issue in Ontario through the 1970s and 1980s.

The enrolment pressure on the separate system in the 1950s and 1960s had led its leaders and Ontario bishops to mount a lobbying campaign for the government to fund grade nine and ten in separate schools at high school (rather than elementary) rates and for grades eleven, twelve, and thirteen to receive public support. Initially, this was a relatively quiet, almost administrative, campaign. It became much more public in 1964 when the education minister, Bill Davis, refused to change the laws on corporate taxation to equalize funding between Catholic schools and the public system and rejected the idea of funding grades eleven through thirteen in Catholic schools. Between 1968 and 1971, in response, a very significant mobilization effort was made by Catholics to lobby for full funding to be provided to Catholic high schools (Gidney 1999; Walker 1986). This campaign involved coordinated lobbying by Catholic bishops and the Separate School trustees association. It was directed at the Ministry of Education and the three political parties (all of which opposed the extension of funding in the early 1960s). In the Jesuit priest Carl Matthews, this coalition had an almost classic example of a policy entrepreneur (Power 2005). In response to this campaign, both the New Democratic Party (NDP) and the Liberal Party of Ontario shifted to support funding for Catholic separate schools. In part, this was the result of changing normative commitments by party leadership, but it was also a strategic response to the entrance of large numbers of Catholic Portuguese and Italian immigrants into the electorate. By 1971, both parties supported the extension of full funding to separate high schools (Interviews with Sean Conway, 26 June 2014, Bob Rae, 7 July 2014).

This Catholic campaign failed to convince the Progressive Conservative government, however. Davis's 1971 "This Far and No Further

Speech," given in the midst of his first successful election campaign as PC party leader, seemed to have definitively closed the door on any extension of public support to Catholic high schools. Davis justified his refusal to extend funding to separate high schools using language that continues to define the policy problem in Ontario:

> In the question as to whether or not the government of Ontario should extend tax support to secondary separate schools beyond Grade 10, we do not believe the refusal to do so rescinds any constitutional right, nor does it offer any future limitation or condition to the voluntary decision of any parent or child to choose between a secondary education in the public school system or in the private school of their choice.
>
> If, on the other hand, the Government of Ontario were arbitrarily to decide to establish and maintain, out of public funds, a complete educational system determined by denominational and religious considerations, such a decision would fragment the present system beyond recognition and repair and do so to the disadvantage of all those who have come to want for their children a public school system free of a denominational or sectarian character.
>
> (Davis, as quoted in Paikin 2016, 523)

One of the significant mysteries of Ontario politics is how and why Davis's thinking changed between this speech and his decision in June of 1984 to equalize funding between separate and public high schools. What makes tracing the decision particularly difficult is that it is closely tied up with Davis's personal views, rather than having been brought about through public mobilization and political pressure. One account for the change in Davis's approach emphasizes the political implications of Ontario's changing demographics and the need for the Conservatives to find a way to make inroads into new Canadian communities which, at the time, were heavily Catholic. To some commentators, these demographic realities underpinned a secret promise between Davis and Cardinal Carter during the 1981 election that Davis would extend funding to separate schools sometime during the next mandate (Hoy 1985). Both the premier and the cardinal, though, deny such a promise was ever made (Interview with Bill Davis, 20 October 2014; Paikin 2016, 341).

What is clear is that by 1981 there was no question of Davis's dominance of the PC Party and of Ontario provincial politics. As a former and very successful education minister, Davis paid close attention to educational issues during his time as premier. And, with regards to separate school funding, he clearly felt that he had the ability to make his own independent decisions in the policy area. Indeed, when Davis decided to extend funding to separate high schools, he did not consult with the minister of education at the time, Bette Stephenson, or with Cabinet any further in advance than the day of making the announcement in the legislature (Interview with Bill Davis, 20 October 2014; Paikin 2016). There were meetings in advance of the announcement between Davis and Cardinal Carter, the most senior Catholic bishop in Ontario, and between Davis and Harry Fisher, the deputy minister of education, where some of the details of the funding announcement were worked out (Paikin 2016, 326–43). These meetings drew on positive personal relationships between Davis, Cardinal Carter, and Carter's predecessor as archbishop of Toronto, Philip Pocock (who had retired to Davis's Brampton riding and lived near Davis), each of whom could be seen as policy entrepreneurs seeking full funding for Catholic high schools (Interviews with Bill Davis, 20 October 2014, Sean Conway, 26 June 2014). In Davis's own account, the tipping point in deciding his position on the issue was realizing that he did not have a satisfactory answer to a group of Catholic high school students from Brampton who asked him – while he was mowing his lawn – why their parents had to pay tuition for them to attend high school. He also argued that he might have reconsidered the issue earlier had he not been trying to govern with repeated minority governments through the 1970s (Interview with Bill Davis, 20 October 2014). In announcing the change in the legislature, Davis stated that he was guided by

> three fundamental principles ... First, we must not only respond to the claims of the moment, but we must also work to honour those contracts and obligations that were struck to create a united Canada in 1867. Second, we must not undertake a course of action that by its nature or in its execution would cripple or limit the viability of our non-denominational public secondary school system, which is accessible to all and universally supported and which will always remain the cornerstone of our education system ... The new direction is not compelled by or founded upon a reinterpretation of old statutes or jurisprudence. The letter of the old law cannot substitute for common sense. Further, we must all appreciate that historic benefits must keep pace with changing conditions.
>
> (Davis 1984, as quoted in Paikin 2016, 536)

In the legislature, the announcement was relatively uncontroversial since both the NDP and the Liberals had long committed themselves to support the extension of full funding to Catholic high schools, and few Tories were inclined to criticize their very popular and soon-to-retire leader (Interviews with Sean Conway, 26 June 2014, Bob Rae, 7 July

2014). Additionally, as part of his announcement of government funding for separate high schools, Davis announced that there would be a commission on the implementation of the changes, a second commission on educational finance, and a third – lead by Bernard Shapiro – examining the funding of independent schools and schools of other minority groups (Gidney 1999, 128).

While it did not trigger controversy in the legislature, Davis's change did face strong opposition from the public education establishment, the Protestant community, and grassroots groups concerned about its impact on their local high schools. Just as this political battle was really beginning, Davis retired as premier. The Progressive Conservatives lost the election that followed – perhaps partly because much of their base felt betrayed by Davis's reversal of a long-standing party commitment not to fund Catholic high schools – and a Liberal/NDP coalition led by David Peterson formed the first non-Conservative government in the province in forty-five years (Interview with Sean Conway, 26 June 2014). It was this government that implemented Davis's dramatic change. It introduced Bill 30 in July 1985 but delayed third reading until the Social Development Committee had conducted public hearings. These hearings ended up being the most extensive of their kind in Ontario's history, with 879 submissions and presentations lasting into November 1985 (Gidney 1999). Many local groups were concerned about the closure of their local schools, but the measure also faced very strong opposition from public school trustees groups, the various public Teachers' Federations, and Protestant churches. This public opposition created problems within the coalition government, as parts of the NDP became unwilling to support a measure which seemed to undercut their allies in the labour movement. In order to hold its coalition together, the government modified Bill 30 in four ways: (1) teachers in the public system with a conscientious objection to working for a Catholic school would receive retaining and financial support should their position be transferred to the Catholic system; (2) students would be able to access either system they chose at the high school level; (3) non-Catholic students would not be required to take religious education; and (4) – after 1995 – Catholic boards would no longer be able to make being Catholic a condition of employment in a separate high school nor impose a denominational test for attending those schools (Gidney 1999, 137). In this form, Bill 30 passed in June 1986.

Since 1986, the equal public support of the Catholic separate system has remained a political issue in Ontario. Both the Ontario Secondary School Teachers Federation and the Elementary Teachers Federation of Ontario (Interview with Vivian McCaffrey, 27 June 2014) have called for the creation of a single public system, as has the provincial Green

Party. Those who oppose continued public funding argue that there are considerable costs to maintaining both systems and that the support of a specifically Catholic separate system is problematic as it treats different religions differently. The three major parties continue to be internally divided on the issue and so maintain their support for the status quo (Rayside, Sabine, and Thomas 2017) even though a fairly consistent majority of Ontario residents would prefer having a single, publicly supported, school system (Forum Research 2015). But these general disagreements about the existence of separate schools have not generated sustained and focused political mobilization about their overall situation.

The (official) Catholic position on many issues of sexual identity and orientation have become a new set of flashpoints for Catholic schools, beginning with *Hall v. Durham Catholic School Board* in 2002, continuing with contention over Gay-Straight Alliance groups and the Accepting Schools Act in 2012, and then expanding to include questions of trans-rights (Martino et al. 2019; Callaghan 2018). It has repeatedly brought the province's Liberal government and the Church into conflict over what, precisely, the "Catholic" nature of the separate system is over the last decade and who gets to decide what is and is not "Catholic." However, the long-term political impact of these controversies is difficult to judge, in part because significant groups of parents in the public system have also mobilized against the recognition of LGBTQ students in that province. Further, significant parts of the Catholic educational establishment – especially the Ontario English Catholic Teachers' Association and significant parts of separate school administration – take a strongly inclusive position on sexuality (Interview with Victoria Hunt, 17 April 2014).

Since 1867, the Roman Catholic separate schools have consistently been significant political problems in Ontario's politics. Although rights emerged as a way to frame the problem in other parts of the educational system in the 1960s and 1970s, the political importance of the separate school issue kept the problem firmly framed in faith terms insofar as it applied to schools outside the public system. This continued focus on religion, rather than choice, and the lack of success of advocates either of independent schools or of other faith communities at getting public support for their schools, sets Ontario apart from provinces in Western Canada and Quebec, where choice became an important way of understanding the question. At the same time, support for separate schools has been sufficiently strong that the creation of a single public system has never seriously been on the table. The constitutional entrenchment of the separate system was extended through a process of exogenous change as it took a premier's rather idiosyncratic intervention to extend funding to Catholic high schools after efforts at endogenous change had failed.

The Failure of Choice: The Continuing Dominance of Religion in Ontario

The way that government support for independent schools continues to be defined as a religious problem in Ontario is different from most other provinces. Until the Second World War, this was likely an accurate reflection of the population's deep-seated divide between Protestants and Catholics and of the thinking of the political class. Since then, though, the nature of political and policy discussions that centre the separate school question and the failure of political entrepreneurs to adopt a rights or choice understanding of the issue combine to reinforce the faith regime. As we saw above, the theme of rights could be an effective argument in Ontario school politics, but it was an argument that only those seeking self-governing public schools for francophones or the maintenance of Catholic separate schools successfully made. Rights were not pursued by those seeking public support for either independent or non-Catholic religious schools. Explaining a negative is always difficult, but it is possible to see some of the reasons why choice – so effective in other provinces – did not come to define the policy problem of independent schools in the eyes of Ontario policymakers or the Ontario public.

One aspect of the situation more present in Ontario than in other provinces is that it has long had a sizeable group of independent schools that are not religious. These range from schools modelled on British public schools with roots dating back to the early nineteenth century to "alternative" Waldorf or Montessori schools that blossomed in the second half of the twentieth century. Aside from the discussion triggered by *The Report of the Commission on Private Schools in Ontario* in 1985, there seems to have been little policy conversation and little lobbying around getting government support for non-religious independent schools. Some of this is because the most organized part of the non-religious sector – the elite independent schools grouped as the Conference of Independent Schools of Ontario – have been lukewarm about government support (Interview with Deani Van Pelt, 13 April 2014). In general, these schools do not see a pressing need for that financial support and are worried that gaining government funding would mean giving up autonomy.

Instead, voices arguing for government support for independent schools in Ontario have tended to come from faith communities, which has reinforced the political perception that the issue of funding schools outside the public system is a religious matter. While an issue for some Protestant groups before Confederation, it really emerged as a significant issue in the 1970s as the Evangelical Christian, Christian Reformed, and Jewish communities built extensive networks of private schools. These communities were internally divided over the desirability of public funding. Some members of all three saw public support as a valuable resource that would make their systems more accessible and of better quality. Others believed that public support would so limit the autonomy of their schools that they would no longer be able to fulfil their primary religious purpose. In Evangelical Christian and Christian Reformed communities (which overlap from a political point of view while having important differences in other respects), the initial overall position was that public support was not desirable. In the 1960s, 1970s, and 1980s these schools were dominated by groups that sought a fairly high degree of separation from government and/or from broader society: conservative Anabaptists and Dutch immigrants being two prominent examples (Schryer 1998). Evangelical Christians did start schools during this period, but it also seems that many of them were satisfied – especially in rural Ontario – by the still substantial Christian elements in public schools (Schryer 1998). As a result, it was not until the 1980s that any serious effort was made to pursue public support for non-Catholic Christian schools.

The Jewish community was more interested in state support. Until court cases in the 1980s and 1990s secularized Ontario's public schools, the bulk of Jewish activism was focused on insuring that public schools had room for Judaism as well as Christianity (Sable 1999). That said, by 1971 "lobbying for government funding was taken up by various organizations, including the Ontario Committee for Government Aid to Jewish Day Schools" (Sable 1999, 208). This included negotiations from 1975 to 1977 between the provincial government and Associated Hebrew Schools that resulted in a tentative deal being reached that would have created a separate Jewish school board in North Toronto (Interview with Hugh Segal, 10 July 2014). Under the terms of the agreement, Jewish schools would receive the same per capita funding as other separate schools and be allowed to offer religious instruction during the school day. Additionally, they were to use provincially certified teachers and to be "neighbourhood schools" open to students of any faith within their catchment area. Ultimately, the deal fell apart because a significant part of the Jewish school community board felt uncomfortable with the idea of allowing a religiously mixed student body (Sable 1999).

Though this possibility did not come through, there does seem to have been a willingness to engage more broadly with the possibility that schools of other faiths might have claims to government support as well. As part of his extension of support to Catholic high schools, Davis commissioned a report by noted educational researcher and administrator Bernard Shapiro to investigate public support for both religious and non-religious private schools. The *Report of the Commission on Private Schools in Ontario*, released in October 1985, still stands as an impressive piece of research on schooling in Ontario and independent schooling in Canada that was influential outside of Ontario. The Commission began its work with significant public opinion polling and public consultation. It found that only small minorities of Ontario citizens were in favour of government financial support being provided to independent schools and that only half of families whose children attended independent schools would be in favour of such state support (Ontario 1985, 19). Many people dramatically overestimated the size of the independent school sector and thought that its character tilted far more towards elite schools (which at the time made up about one-third of independent schools in Ontario) than was in fact the case. Everyone consulted as part of the process, including proponents of independent schools, were committed to having a very strong public system. In these consultations, the Commission also found that a majority of people making submissions opposed government money going to support independent schools. Among those submissions that supported government funding, a number of arguments were put forward:

1   The general value of increased diversity, choice, and competition
2   The inappropriateness of limiting public support to the schools of a particular religious group (i.e., the Roman Catholic community)
3   The perceived inequity of parents having to pay both private school tuition fees and the local education taxes
4   The importance of enabling students to choose (without regard to financial constraints) a school that reflects their particular value system
5   The real or imagined shortcomings of particular public school systems and programs

(20–1)

In submissions from organizations, the commission found that public school boards, some Protestant denominational schools, and the Conference of Independent Schools (which represented the elite private schools) opposed the extension of public funding. Separate boards, Jewish schools (for the secular part of their program), and some Protestant schools (usually seeking operational funding) were the organizations that supported the extension of funding (22–36).

On the basis of this consultation, the Shapiro Commission made a sweeping set of recommendations. Most importantly, it suggested extending some funding to independent schools but recommended introducing reporting and teacher accreditation requirements. It advised creating a category of "associated" schools that would receive equal funding to public schools, be open to all students, employ certified teachers, charge no tuition, and report to the school board with which it was in association. Subject to the agreement of local boards, these schools could have a religious character. Taken as a whole, the Shapiro Report is an example of a policy entrepreneur (Shapiro) putting forward a set of ideas with a very heavy element of "choice" in its framing. While it differed in detail and offered less autonomy to independent schools than the frameworks being developed at the same time in the Western provinces, the report offered a broadly analogous set of recommendations.

What differed was the political context. By the time Shapiro submitted his report the Peterson government was in the midst of the bitter fight over extension of funding to Catholic high schools. It was not in the mood to consider the extension of public funding to other faith groups. As Sean Conway, the minister of education at the time, saw the situation, there was "a sense that the fragmentation of the system" had already gone too far, especially since government was creating separate francophone public and separate systems at the same time as it was fully funding separate high schools (Interview with Sean Conway, 26 June 2014). As the minister responsible, Conway made it clear publicly that the government would be extending funding only to the Catholic system even before the report was delivered. With a political option off the table, a group of parents decided to turn to the courts for relief in what became known as the *Adler* case (1997). In this case, a group of parents challenged the province's funding of only Catholic separate schools on the grounds that it infringed on the equality provisions in the Charter of Rights and Freedoms. The Supreme Court dismissed the appeal on the grounds that the Section 93 guarantee could not, by definition, contravene another part of the Constitution. Were the province to decide to extend funding to faith-based schools other than Roman Catholic ones, the Charter equality provisions would apply to that extension. Since it had not, however, Charter equality guarantees could not force the government to act. The parent group later took the case to the United Nations Human Rights Committee, which did find Ontario's regime discriminatory but lacked jurisdiction to force the Ontario government to do anything (Allison and Van Pelt 2012, 116).

While the *Adler* decision might have opened a door to the extension of public funding to schools of other faiths, by the 1990s, Ontario's education sector was dominated by a series of bitter fights between teachers' unions and the government. Both the NDP government of Bob Rae and the Conservative government of Mike Harris focused on cost-cutting and responding to the perceived low academic quality of education in Ontario. For the Harris government, there was the additional goal of reducing the overall size of government and a general commitment to free market principles. Importantly, the application of these principles to education was focused primarily on the reduction of costs, streamlining of governance, and constraining of unions throughout the Harris years. For the most part, the bitter disputes inside the education community had little to do with independent schools or school choice (Ibbitson 1997; Gidney 1999) except for the introduction of a substantial tax credit for private school tuition in 1999. This scheme would have allowed for tax credits of 50 per cent of independent (not only religious) school tuition up to a maximum of $3,500 per year. Opposed by both the Liberals and the New Democrats, and by important elements within the PC party, the initiative was introduced as part of a provincial budget without any consultation with the Education Ministry (Interview with Janet Ecker, 8 July 2014). This credit was scrapped a year after it was introduced by the new Liberal government of Dalton McGuinty.

The most recent controversy concerning non-Catholic religious schools and funding in Ontario occurred during the 2007 provincial election campaign. John Tory, the Progressive Conservative leader, made central to the party's election campaign a promise he had first made in his 2004 leadership bid: full funding for schools of all faiths. In Tory's plan, funding would be conditional on schools teaching the Ontario curriculum, participating in standardized testing, and employing provincially accredited teachers ("Tory Would Expand Religious School Funding," *Toronto Star*, 23 July 2007). Further, Tory promised to establish a commission, led by former premier Bill Davis, to carry out extensive consultations prior to any implementation of the plan. Well-informed sources have suggested that this plan came from a principled commitment to religious equality in light of Tory's role in Davis's extension of full funding to Catholic separate schools (Interview with Janet Ecker, 8 July 2014; Interview with Hugh Segal, 10 July 2014). That commitment was carried out in the face of opposition from the very communities that Tory believed would benefit from it (Van Pelt 2007). Tory's plan probably cost the PCs the election (Sears 2007), for it opened up the party to allegations of simultaneously pandering to religious extremists and threatening to privatize public education. The Tory defeat seems to have definitively moved the extension of funding to non-Catholic religious schools off the political agenda for the time being (Davidson,

Lucas, and McGregor 2020). At the same time, it shows that religion, rather than choice or rights, continues to define the problem for many policy entrepreneurs in Ontario.

Conclusion

Ontario demonstrates a fundamental continuity in the political place of religious schooling and a remarkable resiliency of the faith regime around it. Since before Confederation, a combination of successive political dynamics has created a situation where essentially only Catholic separate schools have received government support. Only the extension of funding to Catholic high schools in 1984 can be described as a classic exogenously driven institutional change with regards to religious schools. But, even at this moment when radical change seemed possible, policymakers drew back from the idea of fundamental revisions to the system that might have extended support to non-Catholic religious groups. As for endogenous change, there are examples of incremental change through displacement (the gradual secularization of the public system) and of layering (the gradual equalization of funding between public and separate elementary schools). However, these processes did not add up to a significant revision of the regime developed at Confederation. In part, this may well be because Catholics in Ontario were successful in using claims based on rights to preserve and extend their status quo while francophones were using a litigation strategy to extend their ability to self-govern their schools.

Just as there have been only minor changes in the education regime of Ontario, the framing of the central question has also been stable. This is a way of understanding the problem that cuts across most of the salient social and political divides: urban/rural, north/south, Liberal/Conservative/NDP, religious/secular, and working/middle/upper class. Certainly, there have been policy entrepreneurs who have sought to change this framing in Ontario, but they have not been successful. Indeed, although the Shapiro Report in 1985 brought choice-based arguments to the table in Ontario in a significant way, no group mobilized behind them, and the Peterson government – otherwise active in reforming educational governance – saw adding elements of choice to the system as further fragmenting an already dangerously divided system. And, though the Conservatives under John Tory did experiment with choice, it was a short-lived experiment under the former and an electorally disastrous experiment under the latter.

2 The Incremental Secularization of Quebec's Education System

Introduction

The story of Quebec's education system, much like the story of Quebec's broader evolution, is one best told in two parts. There is pre-Quiet Revolution Quebec, whose politics and society, including its education system, were dominated by the Catholic Church. Then there is post-Quiet Revolution Quebec, a province that radically shed its attachments to the Catholic Church and is now the most secular society in Canada, complete with a fully secularized public education system. On one level, this story is essentially true. At a deeper level, however, there is far more nuance involved in Quebec's broader political and social development, as well as the evolution of its education system, than this simple depiction allows. It is undeniable that the province's education system was basically controlled in full by religious organizations well into the twentieth century. Indeed, Quebec was the last province in Canada to establish a modern Ministry of Education, finally creating one in 1964. Prior to this, the state exhibited next to no interest in regulating education in the province in any meaningful way – education was simply assumed to be the sole domain of churches. Then came the Quiet Revolution, the famed Parent Commission, and the swift transfer of educational authority from the church to the state. This period represented a dramatic exogenous shock to the education policy system resulting in the strict curtailment of the church's influence over education. For the first time in Quebec's history, a policy window had appeared that allowed for a radical shift in policy direction. However, most observers agree that the public education system in Quebec did not become fully secular until 2008 (or perhaps even 2020!), over four decades after the creation of an Education Ministry and a long process of endogenous change.

Table 2.1. Key Dates in the Evolution of Quebec's Education System

Date	Event
1760	The British Conquest of New France
1793	An Act for the Establishment of Free Schools and the Advancement of Learning
1875	The abolishment of the Ministry of Public Instruction and the creation of separate Catholic and Protestant Committees to govern education
1961	Establishment of the Royal Commission of Inquiry on Education in the Province of Quebec (Parent Commission)
1964	Bill 60 Establishes the Ministry of Education
1968	Bill 56: An Act Respecting Private Education
1996	Commission for the Estates General on Education recommends "unlocking educational confessionality"
1997 (Apr.)	Quebec formally requests an Amendment to Section 93 of the Constitution Act, 1867
1997 (Dec.)	Section 93 Amended, allowing for the dissolution of Religion-Based School Boards
1998	Roman Catholic and Protestant School Boards replaced with French and English Boards
1999	*Religion in Secular Schools* (The Proulx Report) recommends full secularization of Public School System
2008	Mandatory *Ethics and Religious Culture* (ERC) Program introduced, replacing all religious instruction in public schools
2019	Bill 21 bans the wearing of any religious symbols by teachers in public schools
2020	Province announces the cancellation of the ERC program

Why, in a province that became so overtly secular in such a short time after the Quiet Revolution, did it take so long to fully secularize the public education system of Quebec? This chapter attempts to answer this question. After a brief foray into the early development of the education systems in New France, the colony following the conquest of 1760, and the province of Quebec prior to 1960, this chapter delves into the impact of the Quiet Revolution and the varied developments that shaped its education system to this day. The Catholic Church, of course, was not ready to simply turn over full control of education in the early 1960s, nor did the bulk of Quebec's citizens immediately demand a full withdrawal of the Church. Rather, a sensitive set of negotiations took place between church and state, aided immensely by liberalizing reforms that were taking place in the Catholic Church in the wake of the Second Vatican Council. This set the stage for a much more incremental march toward the full secularization of Quebec's schools than one might have predicted given the wave of anti-clericalism that swept across Quebec following the Quiet Revolution. Of course, the constitutional impediment inherent in Section 93 of the BNA Act also seemed to prevent definitive movement on this front until finally, in the late 1990s, the political will emerged to pursue a series of significant educational reforms between 1998 and 2005 that, for all intents and purposes, finally delivered the secular education system that seemed inevitable in the 1960s.

Throughout this incremental evolution, the debate over religious schooling in Quebec remained firmly ensconced within what we are calling a faith regime. That is, the central question at the heart of the debates over religious schooling that took place in Quebec was, and would remain, the appropriateness of mixing religion and state-funded education. The monumental shift that did occur in Quebec related to this issue was not, therefore, the shift from a regime of faith to one of either rights or choice that we see in so many other provinces. Rather, the shift that occurred was related directly to the manner by which most Quebecois, and eventually the state, came to answer the fundamental question at the heart of the faith regime. In essence, after a centuries-long endorsement of the foundational role of religious institutions in public education in the province, post-Quiet Revolution Quebec came to see the issue in exactly the opposite way, strongly opposing any church involvement in public education. In other words, the key change in Quebec happened *within* a single regime, rather than in embracing a new regime.

This pattern was largely replicated in the establishment and evolution of the province's commitment to publicly subsidize private religious schools, an exploration of which closes out the chapter. The initial formalization of public funding for such schools in 1968 took place within the same faith regime discussed above and was a product of the broader negotiations that took place between church and state for control over education in Quebec. The installation of a system of public subsidies was part of a grand bargain wherein the Catholic Church agreed to relinquish its long-held control over most public education in Quebec to the newly created Ministry of Education. Since 1968, a typical path-dependent situation has developed with battle lines drawn on both sides of the policy debate over the funding of private schools, but little reason to expect significant change in policy direction any time soon. Although arguments rooted in choice have emerged in Quebec in defence of this funding, and the notion of "a parent's right to choose," is even mentioned in the 1964 bill that established the Education Ministry, the more common argument in defence of public funding in contemporary Quebec is grounded in the idea that private schools represent an important connection to the traditional Catholic Quebecois identity. In other words, Quebec has not experienced the nearly unanimous shift into a rights or choice regime with respect to the funding of private schooling that has occurred in much of Western Canada. Rather, the debates continue to focus on the question of the appropriateness of formal religious involvement in education in general as well as the connection between Catholicism and the Quebecois identity in particular.

Historical Foundations of the Faith Regime: The Catholic Church and Education in Quebec before 1960

Formal education in New France, like elsewhere in what we now call Canada, was initially directed by various religious orders and had as its purpose the Christianization of the Indigenous Peoples of the region. Such efforts by the Jesuits, Recollects, Sulpicians, and Ursulines can be traced back to the early seventeenth century in New France, with the Jesuits breaking ground for the colony's first elementary school in 1635 (Magnuson 1980, 3–4). Guided at this time by the principle of Gallicanism, various agents of the Catholic Church were heavily involved in education but were content to defer to the state when they were demanded to do so (Bélanger 2000). Schooling was not a significant priority with the initial settlers, although schools did appear in the larger towns. Yet even the modest growth in schooling that had taken place in New France was clearly stunted by Britain's military conquest in 1760. Despite the codification of a certain accommodation for the "French" way of life in the Quebec Act of 1774, education aimed at the French population lagged considerably behind that of the English. By 1790, the English population of roughly 10,000 was served by eighteen schools while the approximately 160,000 French had forty (Bélanger 2000, 13).

In 1787, the British Lord Dorchester tasked Chief Justice William Smith to head a committee to investigate ways to promote education in the colony. Smith was a Loyalist from New York State who was strongly opposed to denominational participation in education, a belief that clearly guided his final proposal for the establishment of a system of public schools free from official religious influence. Although opposition from the French Catholic clergy as well as a broader hesitation from London prevented the immediate installation of such a system, Smith's work did pave the way for the passage, in 1793, of An Act for the Establishment of Free Schools and the Advancement of Learning in this Province (Sissons 1959, 132). This in turn led to the establishment, in 1801, of the Royal Institution for the Advancement of Learning, which was, for all intents and purposes, the first public education system in the colony. Under the direction of the colonial government, the schools were officially non-denominational but were clearly a product of the British Protestant authorities and, in fact, the first president was none other than the Anglican Bishop of Quebec! The system did not actually begin in practice until 1818 when thirty-five schools opened, but by 1829 that number had grown to eighty-four (Magnuson 1980, 20). However, French Canadians, under the leadership of the Catholic clergy who renounced the schools, never did buy into it, and the vast majority of Royal schools remained English. By the mid-1840s, the system had essentially collapsed, and all the schools were shuttered.

Laws passed in 1824 (the Fabriques Act) and 1829 (the Syndics Act) provided more autonomy to local communities and their parishes and thus did eventually lead to the establishment of over twelve-hundred small French non-Royal public schools by 1832 (Milner 1986, 11). Interestingly, these acts were the product of a colonial assembly dominated by French Canadian followers of Louis-Joseph Papineau, a proponent of church-state separation and non-denominational education. The period between 1829 and 1836, when political turmoil led to the end of government funding for these schools, thus represented a rather unique time in Quebec's educational history: the relatively large numbers of French Canadians who enrolled their children in these short-lived state-controlled non-denominational public schools after 1829 did so despite the Catholic clergy's strong opposition to the emerging school system. Yet, somewhat ironically, things changed rather dramatically in favour of the Catholic Church with respect to education in the colony with the emergence and eventual defeat of the Papineau-led "Patriote" rebellion and the subsequent union of Upper and Lower Canada in 1841. Despite calls from Lord Durham, in his famous *Report*, to drastically improve upon the current educational system (and simultaneously use this improved system to aid in the overall goal of assimilation), and the practical efforts of Arthur Buller to establish a single, non-denominational public system for both French and English students, Canada East would move in a very different direction.

As Magnuson (1980, 28) has noted, the Catholic clergy in the colony had long sought full control over the education of French Canadian youth but had, since 1760, faced two important obstacles: the British Protestant leadership and the liberal-leaning, non-denominational preferences of the Papineau contingent that largely controlled the Assembly in the 1820s and 30s. The failure of the rebellions in 1837–8 led to a sharp decline in the influence of the French liberal class, thereby creating an avenue within society for the emergence of a more aggressive Catholic clergy now guided largely by the principle of ultramontanism. Advancing a conservative worldview founded on the infallibility of the Pope and opposed to any restrictions on the church by the state, the chief leaders of the Catholic Church in Quebec (most especially the ultra-montane Bishop of Montreal, Ignace Bourget) were no longer willing to defer to the state on matters of central concern. The 1840s therefore represented a new political opportunity for the Church. The autonomy of Canada East, combined with the demise of the Papineau faction, created an avenue for the Church to grab hold of Quebec's informal education system – a grip that would last for well over a century. That the ultramontane faction of clerics in Quebec would seek control over schools is surely not surprising given the Pope's thoughts on the importance of Catholic education:

> The mere fact that a school gives some religious instruction (often extremely stinted), does not bring it into line with the rights of the Church and of the Christian family, or make it a fit place for Catholic students. To be this, it is necessary that all teaching and the whole organization of the school, its teachers, syllabus and textbooks of every kind, be regulated by the Christian spirit, under the direction and maternal supervision of the church; so that religion may be in truth the foundation and crown of youth's entire training; and this applies to every grade of school, not only the elementary, but the intermediate and the higher institutions of learning as well. To use the words of Leo XIII: "It is necessary not only that religious instruction be given to the young at certain fixed times, but also that every other subject taught be permeated with Christian piety. If this is wanting, if this sacred atmosphere does not pervade and warm the hearts of masters and scholars alike, little good can be expected from any kind of learning, and considerable harm will often be the consequence."
>
> (Quoted in Boudreau 1999, 12)

The clergy moved quickly, pressuring the state on a number of fronts related to education, and were subsequently rewarded with a series of laws that were passed in the 1840s that granted significant control to the Church in this regard. This included the establishment of separate denominational (Catholic and Protestant) school boards in Montreal and Quebec City, the right of clerics to sit on school boards and teach without certification, and the codification of the principle of dissent – the promise that in towns outside of Montreal and Quebec City, the minority religious community possessed the right to their own school (Boudreau 1999, 31; Sissons 1959, 134–6). What is not so well known outside of Quebec is the vital role played by an English Protestant politician from Sherbrooke, Alexander Tilloch Galt, and the broader Protestant minority in the region: fearful of a French-dominated Assembly eventually clamping-down on Protestant schools, Galt was the key player in the national decision to enshrine this denominational arrangement in the British North America Act of 1867, thereby placing the newly emerged system beyond the reach of the provincial legislature (Milner 1986, 13).

However, it was not until 1875, with the National Assembly of Quebec again under pressure from the Catholic clergy, that the Catholic and Protestant Churches acquired essentially full control over education in the province with the abolishment of the Ministry of Public Instruction and the creation of separate Catholic and Protestant Committees who held power over the Superintendent of Public Instruction (Magnuson 1980, 43–5; see also Boudreau 1999, 18). This represented the beginning of what Manzer (1994, 52–3) has labelled the "Concurrent Endowment of Confessional Systems." This arrangement, wherein the state essentially took orders from the two Churches when it came to education, would last until 1964. Magnuson (1980, 38) has quite accurately described this period as, simply, "the triumph of clericalism" in Quebec. This is not to say that a system of schooling that was essentially controlled by the Catholic and Protestant Churches went wholly unchallenged over this period. As early as 1897, a bill was passed in the Legislative Assembly calling for the re-establishment of a Ministry of Education, although it was quickly defeated in the Legislative Council (Quebec's upper house at the time). The Catholic Clergy's strong opposition to the bill, including a telegraph direct from the Vatican warning that the Pope himself demanded its withdrawal, played a significant role in this defeat (Magnuson 1980, 47; Audet 1964). In the first years of the twentieth century, the Ligue de l'enseignement, an education-oriented group made up primarily of the business and intellectual elite of Montreal, called for an increased state role in the education system and the implementation of compulsory education laws – something that had been in place in Ontario since 1871. The clergy was quick to attack the Ligue, suggesting it was a dangerous, secular, and socialist organization whose demands for more state involvement in education would inevitably lead to the demise of French Canada as a nation (Magnuson 1980, 73). That this message largely resonated with the general population of the province cuts to the heart of the control the clergy did possess in the province.

Indeed, the ability of the clergy to successfully convince the majority of French Canadians during these years that a church-controlled education system was central to the survival of the French Canadian nation itself is perhaps the key factor in understanding the development of Quebec's post-Confederation system of education. At a time when basically all other Canadian provinces and American states were shedding church influence and building state-controlled systems, clericalism triumphed in Quebec. Government members seemed eager to reassure the church that they had little interest in upsetting clerical control. Magnuson points to a number of occasions where government officials, including premiers, went out of their way to dismiss secular education and praise close collaboration with the church (Magnuson 1980, 75). Indeed, long-time Union Nationale premier Maurice Duplessis, whose close political connections with the church have been well documented, frequently warned citizens that a vote for the opposition Liberals equated to a vote for the creation of a Ministry of Education. Such a message contained a substantial political punch. As Henchey (1972, 102) has noted, in the 1940s and '50s, to even mention such a ministry was "to evoke images of government control, statism, and the destruction of the rights of parents and the Church." This sense was perhaps best encapsulated by the famed Quebec intellectual Henri Bourassa, who deemed the state "an incompetent school master," too focused on material rather than spiritual concerns to be trusted with control over education (quoted in Milner 1986, 14).

Flipping the Script on Faith: The Quiet Revolution, the Parent Commission, and the Establishment of the Ministry of Education

As with almost everything else in Quebec, the Quiet Revolution led to significant changes in the education system of the province. An ideological revolution that had been percolating since the late 1940s and early 1950s in the liberal newspapers and periodicals of the growing educated francophone middle class, it exploded onto the political scene with the dramatic defeat of the long-ruling, conservative Union Nationale by the Jean Lesage-led Liberals in 1960. The Quiet Revolution ushered in a new, more confident, and outward-looking version of French Canadian nationalism that retained a connection to the French language but shed the traditional attachments to the Catholic Church. At the heart of this nationalism was a growing awareness of the economic power possessed by the minority anglophone population and the social power of the Catholic clergy. The election of the Liberals represented the key moment wherein the broad strokes of this new nationalism found concrete form in a government that was willing to utilize the state to take on these forces, place the province upon a path of modernization, and ultimately allow francophones to "retake" control of Quebec. As the infamous Liberal campaign slogan from the 1962 election on the nationalization of hydroelectricity declared, it was time the Quebecois, via the state, became "Maîtres Chez Nous," literally masters of their own house. Crucially, this sentiment embodied a wholly new outlook in the province where the state, rather than the church, would be understood as the foundational institution of the French Canadian nation. Clearly related to the rise of this sentiment was the rapid secularization that would take place in the province, resulting in the sudden decline of religion's influence across Quebec society that was without parallel in the rest of Canada (Christiano 2007; Gauvreau 2011). Combined, these factors quickly eroded the fundamental rationale for church-controlled education in Quebec that had governed majority opinion since the time of New France: that the church represented the central pillar of French Canadian nationalism. Given such developments, significant educational reform was inevitable.

Much has been written on the many ways in which the Lesage Liberals worked to embody this new nationalism. Although both the new governing ideology of the Liberals as well as the broader secularization of Quebec society would eventually lead to substantial reforms to the education system in the province, it was the actions of a key policy entrepreneur at this point, the Liberal minister of youth Paul Gérin-Lajoie, that truly kick-started the substantial educational reforms in Quebec. Throughout the 1950s, a growing chorus of critics were speaking out against the lack of state control over education. Not only had Catholic and Protestant controlled schools diverged in substantial ways, ensuring a very different educational experience for students across the province, there was also increasing concern that Catholic students outside of the elite private "classical colleges" were not receiving a quality education, especially in areas required for the modernizing economy such as management, science, and technology (Henchey 1972, 100). Responding to such concerns, Gérin-Lajoie successfully pushed for the creation, in 1961, of the Royal Commission of Inquiry on Education in the Province of Quebec, often simply referred to as the Parent Commission after chairman Msgr. Alphonse-Marie Parent. It is difficult to overstate how important the Parent Commission would be to the development of Quebec's education system going forward.

Tasked with investigating the system as a whole, the commission's first report in 1963 concluded that Quebec's lack of a central ministry responsible for education was a significant problem with respect to coordination and administration in the province. This was a radical suggestion given that the province had not had an Education Ministry for nearly a century. As mentioned earlier, the notion of creating one was very unpopular politically in the 1940s and '50s. In fact, even Lesage, in 1960, pledged never to create one should he be elected (Henchey 1972, 102). Yet Gérin-Lajoie responded to the commission's report by tabling Bill 60, An Act to Establish the Ministry of Education and the

Superior Council of Education. Passed in 1964, Bill 60 fundamentally altered the structure of the system by centralizing much of the responsibility for the education system under the state. Gérin-Lajoie was named Quebec's first contemporary minister of education. Although the official transfer of control over education from the Catholic and Protestant Churches to the state represented a monumental change in Quebec and was unsurprisingly opposed at first by certain members within the Catholic hierarchy, it is important to note that Bill 60 did not ultimately encounter a particularly fierce resistance from the Catholic Church. This is largely the result of two factors.

The first is directly tied to what Seljak (1996, 115) has labelled "the coincidence of the Quiet Revolution with the Second Vatican Council," and the broader confluence of characters involved in the Quebec educational reforms. In response to the Roman Catholic Church's embrace of aspects of modernity in the wake of Vatican II, especially in their affirmation of the modern state possessing a legitimate social role, many within the Church in Quebec found themselves reimagining their relationship to the government at the very same time the Liberals were declaring their intention to have the state replace much of the Church's previous role in society. The fortunate timing of this concurrence is seen most vividly in the role played by two individuals in particular, the archbishop of Quebec, Maurice Roy, and the archbishop of Montreal, Paul-Émile Léger. Roy and Léger were conversant with leading liberal French Canadian intellectuals like Pierre Elliott Trudeau, Gérard Pelletier, and Claude Ryan, and had been prominent figures in the reformist Second Vatican Council in Rome. Importantly, it was these men who largely represented the church in negotiations with the Lesage government over the state's plans to reform the education system. Staking out a more moderate position for the church with respect to relations with the state than had traditionally been the case, Roy and Léger paved the way for a relatively peaceful acceptance of Bill 60 on the part of the Catholic Church in Quebec (Milner 1986, 23; see also Dion 1967). As Seljak (1996) has argued, not only did this represent a monumental shift on the part of the Church, their decision to largely acquiesce to, rather than fiercely resist, the "revolutionary" social and political changes that were occurring in Quebec in the 1960s is perhaps the most fundamental reason why the Quiet Revolution remained essentially "quiet."

The second factor relates to the strategic approach of the Liberals themselves. Despite the fact that key leaders within the Church were moderating their outlook, the Liberals were cognizant of the fact that much of the French Canadian working class was not nearly as anticlerical as were the so-called "new middle class" of educated and urban francophone professionals who had propelled the Liberals to power in 1960. Indeed, the oft-quoted statistics on the precipitous decline of Mass attendance by Catholics in Quebec in the wake of the Quiet Revolution often mask the fact that this did not really begin to occur in a significant way until the late 1960s and early 1970s. Given this reality, the Liberals were careful to work closely with the church officials, most especially Roy and Léger, on these reforms. That Gérin-Lajoie, the government's point person on these negotiations, was a practicing Catholic also helped ease tensions between church and state, ultimately allowing for a deal to be reached (Rayside, Sabine, and Thomas 2017, 272–4).

It is certainly true that under the restructured system ushered in by Bill 60, the influential Catholic and Protestant Committees, who had essentially controlled education in the province since 1875, were reconstituted and had their areas of responsibility significantly curtailed. Henceforth, they would play an advisory role and be restricted to setting the curriculum for religious education in the schools only (Boudreau 2011, 213–14). But this was a much different outcome than that demanded by the more radical wing within the Liberal Party, which sought a completely secular education system and thus petitioned for an end to both denominationally organized school boards and all clerical influence over curricular matters (Wallner 2014, 164). This perspective was embodied most forcefully in the newly created Mouvement laïque de langue française, which favoured a secular approach to education that was organized solely around the principle of preserving the French language (Magnuson 1980, 119). The result was a bill that not only maintained the degree of religious influence in education demanded by the church (including denominationalism as its chief organizing principle), it further capitulated to the clergy's request for a reaffirmation of the right of private groups to maintain schools (Magnuson 1980, 108). It would be this language that foreshadowed a broader church-state agreement on the recognition and public funding of religious private schools in the province that would be formalized in 1968.

The Thirty-Year Faith Paradox: The Persistence of Confessional School Boards in a Rapidly Secularizing Province

Although Bill 60 represented a significant turning point with respect to the public education system of Quebec, the complete secularization of the school system was not just around the corner. In fact, despite the Parent Commission's recognition of the growing cultural and religious diversity of Quebec and its subsequent recommendation in 1966 that the state create a non-confessional school sector where numbers warranted, no such changes would materialize in the short term. A public education system grounded solely in Catholic or Protestant boards became even more problematic with the introduction of Quebec's Charter of Human Rights in 1975, which guaranteed equal treatment for all. Given the broader secularization that was occurring so rapidly at the societal level, the fact that Quebec's education system would remain tied to the antiquated confessional-based structure for more than three additional decades seems especially counterintuitive. Why did it take so long for Quebec to phase out clerical influence via confessionally organized school boards? One can point to three factors that preserved key aspects of the pre-Quiet Revolution status quo.

First, although the issue of clerical involvement in the education system remained contentious throughout the 1970s and '80s, the issue of language of instruction became far more so. Language overshadowed religion as the policy issue that needed to be solved. This was partly due to the fact that, despite the persistence of clerical influence after the creation of a Ministry of Education, the schools themselves were becoming increasingly secular. This was especially so for Protestant schools, but Catholic schools were also going through this transformation (Magnuson 1980, 119–21). Given the declining intensity of religious messaging within the schools themselves, the continuing existence of denominational school boards became less problematic to many. In fact, the Mouvement laïque de langue française, which had been a powerful opponent to clerical influence in the early 1960s, suspended its operations after the formation of an Education Ministry and the Parent Commission's recommendation that the province create a non-confessional board (Government of Quebec 1999, 3). But beyond the lessening interest in the question of religion in schools was the eruption of the language issue, which emerged into public view in 1967 with the so-called "Saint Leonard School Crisis."

The initial conflict centred on the ongoing preferences of Italian immigrants in the Montreal suburb of Saint Leonard to enrol their children in English rather than French courses (Cappon 1974). The Commission des écoles catholiques de Montréal responded to this trend with a plan to phase out English language classes, thus forcing the children of Italian immigrants into French-language courses, a decision that led to significant protests from the Italian community. Importantly, the televised protests between allophone immigrants and francophones in the community sparked a much wider debate in a province at a time when the majority francophone population was growing ever more sensitive to their declining numbers. The Union Nationale government of the day responded with the famed Gendron Commission, tasked with finding a solution to the concerns of francophones while simultaneously respect-ing the linguistic rights of non-francophone minorities. Yet, well before the final report was submitted, the Union Nationale passed Bill 63 in 1969, which spoke to the importance of preserving the French language but ultimately reinforced the rights of parents to choose the language of instruction in schools. The subsequent backlash from francophones to this legislation helped propel the Liberals to victory in the subsequent election in 1970. In 1974, the Liberals passed Bill 22, a somewhat half-hearted attempt to restrict access to English education for immigrants that failed to appease either side in the dispute and helped open the door for the election of the Parti Québécois (PQ) in 1976. In 1977, the PQ passed the infamous Bill 101, which continues to prevent the children of immigrants from enrolling in English language public schools.

There is little doubt that the amount of political energy consumed by the linguistic issue in the late 1960s and throughout the 1970s ensured that the issue of confessional school boards largely fell off the political radar (Interview with Jean-Pierre Proulx, 7 December 2016). However, a second, less well-acknowledged factor relates to specific battles at the school board level, especially in Montreal, in the 1970s and 1980s. As Milner has carefully documented, several groups of parents in Montreal remained focused on the issue of confessional school boards, convinced that the increasing cultural and religious diversity of Quebec's largest city was not well served by an education system governed solely by either Catholic or Protestant boards. In 1973 the elections for members of the Commission des écoles catholiques de Montréal (CECM), the Catholic school board in Montreal, were largely dominated by this issue and garnered significant interest from a variety of groups on all sides of the question (Milner 1986, 47–59). The most successful of these was a coalition of fifteen groups, led especially by the influential and well organized conservative Catholic organization the Association des par-ents catholiques du Québec (APCQ), who formed the Mouvement sco-laire confessionnel (MSC) to run and support pro-confessional board candidates throughout the city. Aided by the organizational prowess of the APCQ, the easily mobilized network of traditional Catholics, mean-ingful clerical support throughout the campaign, and some occasional fear-mongering that included references to the "totalitarian take-over of the schools" should confessional boards be phased out, MSC can-didates would win enough seats to control the CECM despite several polls taken at the time suggesting that support for the persistence of only confessional boards in Montreal was definitely a minority posi-tion (Milner 1986, 48–9, 56–9). A similar outcome occurred in the school board elections of 1977.

Speaking more broadly to the inability of those demanding school reform at the board level to achieve these ends in the 1970s despite having the majority of public opinion on their side, Milner (1986, 60–7) points to the well organized and cohesive nature of those anti-reform groups, especially the APCQ, compared to the more loosely connected groups who sought change. Just as important, however, was the political influence possessed by the network of groups who advocated on behalf of Protestant English education in Montreal (Milner 1986, 62–3). Often overlooked in discussions on the intermingling of religious and state forces around education issues in Quebec, Protestant educational leaders in the province, ever cognizant of their minority status, have always fiercely guarded their autonomy when it comes to education. Recall that it was the anglophone politician Alexander Tilloch Galt, not the Catholic clergy of Quebec, who was most active in pressing for the rights to confessional education in Section 93 of the Canadian Constitution. Despite the fact that Protestant-run schools in Quebec, for several decades, had essentially been secular in practice, the community was ardently opposed to nearly all the calls for reform that emanated out of the Quiet Revolution, fearful that English-only schools could eventually be phased out by an activist state animated by concerns over the preservation of the French language. Political connections with both the Union Nationale and Liberal Parties helped derail significant reform efforts in the 1960s and '70s. With the advent of the PQ in 1976, the group shifted tactics, relying more heavily on constitutional appeals to slow reform efforts (Milner 1986, 63).

This leads to the third, and perhaps the most obvious, key factor in the lengthy delay between the Parent commission's recommendations and the actual elimination of confessional boards in Quebec: Section 93 of the Canadian Constitution seemingly guaranteed the rights of denominational schools in the province, thereby rendering significant reform outside the purview of the provincial government. However, as Smith (1994, 204–6) has noted, the rights of denominational schools described in Section 93 were not as clear cut as is often assumed given that important aspects of the denominationally based education system in Quebec were finalized in the years just after Confederation, and were thus outside the provisions of the British North America Act of 1867. These ambiguities created differing views in Quebec on just what types of reforms were permissible. In the 1980s, in the wake of Bill 101 and the broader ways in which language, rather than religion, was becoming the key issue of division within the province, these differing interpretations were laid bare in a series of court rulings. It was the PQ that, in a 1982 White Paper, announced its intention to finally move forward with a plan to replace confessional boards with linguistic ones (Government of Quebec 1982). Aware that such a move raised difficult constitutional questions, the PQ began with a series of incremental reforms (one of which, related to the taxing power of boards, was eventually found to be unconstitutional) before introducing Bills 3 and 29 in 1984. The more well-known Bill 3 would create linguistic boards whereas Bill 29, in an attempt to comply with Section 93, retained denominational rights in areas of the province where they existed in 1867 (Buckingham 2014, 52). However, in 1985 the courts, citing the denominational rights listed in Section 93, blocked the PQs efforts in this regard.

In a testament to the growing support for the replacement of confessional boards with linguistic ones, the subsequent Liberal government also moved in this direction with Bill 107 in 1988. Similarly aware of the potential constitutional obstacles to reform, the Liberals simultaneously put a series of questions to the Quebec Court of Appeal in the form of a Reference Case. When the court returned a largely favourable ruling to the Liberals, supporters of confessional boards appealed the case to the Supreme Court. In 1993, the court ruled that the creation of linguistic boards was constitutional, but Protestants and Catholics retained the right to their own religious schools (Buckingham 2014, 53). In other words, the court was clear: the full and complete secularization of the public education system was simply impossible without an amendment to the constitution.

The Secularization of Public Schools in Quebec within a Faith Regime

Given the continuing decline of religious adherence in Quebec and the ever growing cultural and religious diversity of the province, it was becoming increasingly clear for a majority of citizens that complete secularization was required. In addition, not only were schools themselves largely abandoning religious content in their curriculums, the persistence of a denominationally organized system was clashing with Quebec's own policies aimed at cultural integration. Things began to officially shift when the government-appointed Commission for the Estates General on Education recommended "unlocking educational confessionality" to ensure "that all students can be taught the shared values that we as a society wish to embrace," and thus "continue the separation of Church and State" (Government of Quebec 1996, 55). Indeed, the report clearly recommended that the government of Quebec undertake the action required to amend aspects of Section 93 to allow for the abolishment of the confessional school boards and immediately replace them with French and English boards. Importantly, there was very recent precedent for such an approach. Newfoundland had, for more than a decade prior, been engaging in intense debates over the abolition of its denominationally organized education system, which would also require a constitutional amendment (see chapter 3). That such a step was already being seriously considered in another province provided much confidence to the current PQ government in Quebec to move forward with a similar request (Interview with Jean-Pierre Proulx, 7 December 2016).

PQ education minister Pauline Marois, a strong advocate of the secularization of education, moved quickly on the recommendation of the Estates General to seek an amendment to the Canadian Constitution Act of 1867 which would allow for the abolition of confessional school boards. Despite some objections from religious groups, Bill 109 received unanimous support in the Quebec National Assembly on 15 April 1997, an outcome that speaks to the wide support the proposal enjoyed throughout the province and across the political spectrum. In November of that same year, the House of Commons voted 204–59 in favour of Quebec's resolution and on 31 December, Section 93 was officially amended with the addition of a clause articulating that "paragraphs (1) to (4) of Section 93 so not apply to Quebec" (Young and Bezeau 2003, 2). On 1 July 1998, Quebec's Roman Catholic and Protestant school boards were replaced with French and English boards. The abolition of denominational school boards represented a significant shift that seemed inevitable since the 1960s. This itself, however, did not equate to fully secular public schools in Quebec. Indeed, Protestant and Catholic denominational public schools continued to exist and, especially on the Catholic side, religion was still interwoven into the curriculum. The PQ, no doubt in favour of eliminating this as well, trod somewhat more lightly on this issue, choosing to establish a task force in 1997 to examine the place of religion in schools and recommend an appropriate path forward given the increasing diversity of the province. The investigation was chaired by Jean-Pierre Proulx, a practicing Catholic and academic with much experience studying religion and education in Quebec. Despite the rapid secularization of Quebec society that had been underway for decades, the town halls hosted by the task force, as well as the broader public debates that emerged around the issue of religion in education at this time, grew quite heated, especially outside of Montreal (Interview with Jean-Pierre Proulx, 7 December 2016). Indeed, as several insiders admitted to the authors, the debate over deconfessionalization was one of the most difficult and divisive in Quebec's history.

The most pressing concern for many francophone Quebecois in predominantly Catholic regions of the province was the notion that Catholic education and tradition represented a core element of their identity (Boudreau 2011, 216–17). In fact, the Catholic Church in Quebec did much to push this notion, effectively altering their argument from one initially rooted in a defence of religiously inspired public education in general to one rooted in the idea that religion was a fundamental component of the traditional Quebecois identity and thus should not be quickly extracted from the schooling system (Interview with Jean-Pierre Proulx, 7 December 2016). Many opponents of the move to secularize education were emboldened by this argument and were quick to note that Catholic schools had existed since the founding of the French colony. This shift to an argument rooted in the desire to protect the traditional Quebecois identity obviously touched a chord with a wide swath of the citizenry who had grown up in a province long worried about cultural preservation. Other critics of the move to secularize the schooling system acknowledged that the persistence of Protestant or Catholic schools was unfair to non-Christians, but believed the solution was in extending the right to religious education to other groups, rather than curtailing the existing influence of Catholics and Protestants in the schooling system. A third stream of opposition also emerged, criticizing the Quebec state's continually increasing role in education at the expense of parents and the Church (Caldwell 2000). But each of these concerns, as well as the counter arguments in favour of secularization, essentially existed within the faith regime, rather than in a rights or choice regime.

Overall, Proulx's report highlighted the strong degree of polarization that existed in the province over this issue. On the one hand, the report concluded that a large minority of Quebec citizens favoured the continuation of some form of denominational education, despite the very low levels of mass attendance in Quebec. On the other hand, the report found that a slight majority preferred a secular school system (Government of Quebec 1999, 140–65; Milot and Proulx 1998). The final report of the task force, *Religion in Secular Schools*, released in 1999, was over two hundred pages long and acknowledged in great detail many aspects of the debate, including the positions of those opposed to secularizing the public system. Its conclusions, however, were clear: the status quo with respect to religion in Quebec schools was no longer appropriate for four reasons:

1. The current system is contrary to the principle that the state must remain neutral when it comes to religion in public schools.

2. It goes against the Canadian Charter of Rights and Freedoms and the Quebec Charter of Human Rights and Freedoms, both in principle and in practice, in that it discriminates against religions other than the Catholic and Protestant religions and potentially prejudicially affects freedom of conscience and religion.

3. It runs counter to the social and cultural goals of citizenship based on social cohesion and of the creation of a common civic space.

4. It no longer meets the social expectations for the majority of parents of all religions, nor does it meet those of teachers and principals. It therefore becomes a concept that is practically impossible to apply, given the lack of common will among the partners concerned.

(Government of Quebec 1999, 181)

The report made fourteen recommendations aimed at rectifying this situation. Chief among the recommendations for the Quebec government: abandon the practice of utilizing "notwithstanding clauses" to override aspects of the Quebec and Canadian Charters of Rights that were violated by the province's education system, revoke the denominational status held by public schools thereby creating a fully secular education system, and replace existing Catholic or Protestant religious instruction in schools with a new program aimed at studying religion from a cultural perspective (Government of Quebec 1999, 221–4). Despite opposition from certain quarters, the PQ, citing the importance of nurturing pluralism in Quebec schools, moved on the recommendation to abolish Catholic and Protestant schools in July 2000 when it introduced Bill 118: An Act to Amend Various Legislative Provisions Respecting Education as regards Confessional Matters. Additionally, long-running Catholic and Protestant chaplaincy services in schools were replaced with non-denominational spiritual care, a non-confessional advisory committee replaced the Protestant and Catholic committees that had long served in the Ministry of Education, and a Religious Affairs office was created to replace the deputy ministers of Catholic and Protestant faiths (Boudreau 2011, 218–19). However, the PQ was not prepared to end the practice of utilizing the notwithstanding clause. Bill 118 retained Catholic or Protestant instruction as the only denominational options within public schools, alongside the generic "moral instruction," and again included a notwithstanding clause to protect this scenario, which was clearly discriminatory towards non-Christian religions, from judicial challenge for another five years.

The PQ were defeated in the 2003 provincial election by the Jean Charest-led Liberals. Although the PQ had long been known as the party most dedicated to educational reform, especially as it pertained to the secularization of the system, the Liberals surprised many by continuing the march towards full secularization with the passing of Bill 95 in 2005 (Interview with Georges Leroux, 27 April 2016). This bill again renewed the notwithstanding clause that protected the existence of Catholic and Protestant instruction in public schools. However, the government explicitly limited this clause to a three rather than the five-year period while simultaneously announcing the creation of a new compulsory Ethics and Religious Culture (ERC) program that would replace the traditional streams of Catholic, Protestant, or Moral education options by 2008, thereby bringing Quebec's school curriculum in line with the Quebec and Canadian Charters of Rights. The introduction of the ERC program represented the Liberals fulfilling a central demand of the PQ-appointed, Proulx-led task force that had argued in favour of replacing religious instruction with the study of religion from a cultural perspective, with an emphasis on cross-cultural/religious dialogue. The importance of approaching religion from a cultural perspective in public schools has been understood for decades, within a popular stream of Quebec academia, to be a key to building social cohesion in a religiously diverse community (Interview with Fernand Ouellet, 21 June 2016; see also Ouellet 2000). The idea was also central to the contemporary calls for cultural understanding in the wake of the uproar in Quebec over "reasonable accommodation" for cultural and religious minorities which roiled Quebec society throughout the early 2000s, ultimately spawning the Consultation Commission on Accommodation Practices Related to Cultural Differences, chaired by the well-known academics Gérard Bouchard and Charles Taylor.

This is not to say the introduction of the ERC course was uncontroversial. Not only did the government find itself defending the policy at the Supreme Court on two separate occasions in relatively short order against separate charges that the course violated the rights to religious freedom of Catholic parents (*S.L. v. Commission scolaire des Chênes*, 2012 SCC 7 (CanLII), [2012] 1 SCR 235) and of religious private schools (*Loyola High School v. Quebec* (Attorney General), 2015 SCC 12 (CanLII), [2015] 1 SCR 613), a broad opposition emerged from three distinct perspectives (Interview with Georges Leroux, 27 April 2016). First, and perhaps least surprising, conservative Catholics across Quebec were opposed to the perceived "relativistic" approach to religion at the heart of the program which, for the first time in centuries in Quebec, openly questioned the truth of Christianity in public schools that had traditionally been Catholic (Farrow 2009). The "cultural" approach to religion at the heart of the ERC was especially hard to digest for conservative Catholics living in the far more homogeneous regions of Quebec beyond Montreal. Frequent allusions to "the rights of parents" to insist on a particular style of education, or at least to protect their children from a state determined to depict Christianity as simply one choice among many, were heard ("Quebec's Totalitarian Impulse," *National Post*, 24 June 2010; "Group Urges Parents to Keep Kids Out of New Religion Class; Loss of Christian Education Feared," *Gazette*, 26 April 2008; "School Course Violates Quebecker's Religious Freedom; Compulsory Ethics and Religion Studies Are Being Fought in Court," *Gazette*, 10 May 2009; "Quebec's 'Totalitarian' Take on Religious Education in High School," *National Post*, 12 December 2012). Indeed, an active member of a parent group opposed to the ERC lambasted the Quebec government in conversation with the authors, frequently citing the "state's intent to restrict the freedom of religious individuals by hijacking the role of the parent as the primary educator of their children" (Interview with B, 21 June 2016). The archbishop of Quebec, Marc Ouellet, who was serving as a cardinal in the Vatican, joined the chorus of opposition and even facilitated the writing of a carefully worded letter of general support for religious education and "parental rights" in schools from the Vatican that was widely understood as a critique of Quebec's ERC program in particular (Laval Congregation for Catholic Education 2009). The aforementioned Association des parents catholiques du Québec (APCQ), which played such a significant role in the debate over the persistence of confessional schools in the 1970s, were somewhat active in this segment of opposition to the ERC program as was a new grassroots movement comprised mainly of Catholic parents from outside Montreal, the Coalition pour la liberté en éducation (CLE).

A second strain of opposition to the course came from those in Quebec dedicated to the absolute secularization of the public sphere, including removing all traces of religion from schools. At the heart of this segment of opposition sat the Mouvement laïque québécois, which emerged in 1981, out of the same preference for secularization that had motivated the Mouvement laïque de langue française against the confessional public schools in the 1960s. Indeed, an observer close to the development and introduction of the ERC program confirmed that "a definite anti-religion sentiment, tracing its roots back largely to the traditional dominance of the Catholic Church in this province, is alive and well in Quebec, and was passionately opposed to even the mention of 'religion' in a public classroom" (Interview with Georges Leroux, 27 April 2016).

A third strain of opposition emerged from certain "nationalists" or "sovereigntists" who were not necessarily religious but felt a deep connection with Quebec's history and heritage, including its Catholic lineage. From the perspective of this group, often labelled as the "pure laine" (true natives of Quebec), the ERC program represented an unnecessary capitulation to the proponents of cultural and religious diversity rather than a commitment to continuing to instil "traditional" Quebec values and history into its students, a concern that was closely related to the broader concerns many in Quebec had expressed decades earlier about the threat the secularization of the education system would have on the preservation of the Quebecois identity. As Tremblay (2018, 291–2) has noted, this argument gained initial traction in the province in 2009 on the heels of a couple of PQ sympathizers issuing widely read public declarations against the ERC, claiming the program sought to "deconstruct the very foundations of the historical experience of Quebec and definitely embed state multiculturalism," an argument aimed at those in the province who had long feared a "Canadian-style multiculturalism" replacing Quebec's model of "Interculturalism" (Bouchard 2015).

Taken together, the opposition to the ERC program was not insignificant. Indeed, a good deal of debate ensued in Quebec newspapers and on local radio shows. The obvious connection between a new education program partially aimed to coincide with the increasing cultural and religious diversity of Quebec and the broader public debate over "reasonable accommodation" that had been brewing in the province since the early 2000s did much to elevate the controversy. Yet ultimately, the Liberals faced few serious roadblocks as they implemented the program. Despite Cardinal Ouellet's opposition, the broader contingent of the Catholic hierarchy in Quebec was far less hostile and, in fact, after initially criticizing aspects of the ERC concept, eventually signed a letter of support for the program that acknowledged, for the first time in its history, that it was the role of the church and the family, rather than the school, to instil religious values in children. Politically, certain members of the conservative Action démocratique du Québec (ADQ) party did occasionally express solidarity with the concerns of both the largely rural CLE as well as those nationalists who feared cultural dilution but, in the end, no party in Quebec dared make opposition to the ERC a central plank in its platform. Indeed, as one close political observer noted, "the vast majority of Quebec citizens were either supportive or indifferent to the ERC program. Those opposed made a lot of noise, but they were clearly in the minority" (Interview with Spencer Boudreau, 28 April 2016).

At the end of the day, the CLE was a very small organization and the APCQ possessed but a fraction of the membership and organizational capacity it did in the 1960s and 1970s. Similarly, the citizenry was not nearly as receptive to critiques from Cardinal Ouelett and the Vatican as it might have been fifty years earlier, speaking directly to Catholicism's loss of relevance in the province. In addition, that those opposed to the ERC split three ways: the ideological distance between the conservative Catholics and the nationalists on one hand, and the strong secularists on the other, made forming an effective political coalition virtually impossible. Thus, when the Supreme Court decided in Drummondville that the ERC course did not violate the right to religious freedom of Catholic parents, the last viable path to success for those opposed to the ERC was blocked.

For many, the installation of the ERC program represented the moment wherein the public education system in Quebec finally became wholly secularized (see, for example, Boudreau 2011; Fujiwara 2011). Indeed, for the first time in the province's history, religious officials were no longer in charge of any form of instruction. Yet, the broader debate over the implications of Quebec's commitment to *laïcité* that engulfed the province beginning in 2013 with the PQ's proposed Quebec Charter of Values and culminating in 2019 with the Coalition avenir Québec (CAQ, which absorbed the ADQ in 2012) passing Bill 21, An Act Respecting the Laicity of the State, raised arguments over the place of religion in public schools in a new way. Most obviously, the education-focused aspect of the *laïcité* debate centred on the issue of teachers and administrators wearing religious clothing in public schools. However, a lesser-publicized aspect of the *laïcité* debate, at least in the rest of Canada, centred again on the appropriateness of the ERC program as it related to the mandatory instruction, from a social scientific standpoint, on both Quebec's religious heritage and the comparative consideration of minority religions in Quebec. By 2016, leaders of both the PQ and CAQ – the two most aggressive proponents of a strict adoption of *laïcité* – raised concerns related to the religious culture component of the ERC and its positive association with the principle of pluralism that advocated, in their view, a blind acceptance of a Canadian-style multiculturalism that could potentially "dilute" Quebec's traditional heritage and identity (Tremblay 2018, 293–4).[1] Ultimately, this argument won out. In early 2020, the CAQ formally announced they would fundamentally revise and rename the existing ERC program, with the main objective being "to come up with new and enriching themes to completely or partially replace the content associated with religious culture" ("Quebec

Government to Abolish Ethics and Religions Course," *Canadian Jewish News*, 14 January 2020). In other words, instruction with respect to religion, even that delivered from a secular, comparative, social scientific point of view with the intent of tempering discord between majority and minority components of the population, would now be totally eliminated from public schools in Quebec. To the delight of both Quebec's radical secularists and the more traditional nationalists, a total and complete secularization of the public education system had been achieved.

Given the incredibly long history of church dominance over education in the province, this is obviously a very important policy outcome. Yet, that this change took until 2020, roughly sixty years after the arrival of the Quiet Revolution and the beginnings of the sharp decline of clerical influence in the province is, in many ways, the most perplexing development of all. But, as described above, a variety of factors conspired to delay what must have seemed to be inevitable to those who witnessed the passage of Bill 60 and the historic creation of a modern Education Ministry in 1964. In addition, as Milot and Tremblay (2017) have argued, the "accelerated transformation of Quebec's educational landscape between 1996 and 2008 reflects not only how educational priorities have evolved, but also appears to be a sociological indicator of Quebec society's relationship with fundamental rights and moral and religious pluralism." This is a key point to grasp. It is clear that Quebec is today a very secular province that reveres aspects of its history but also possesses little patience for the type of political and social influence possessed by the Catholic clergy of the past. On the surface it may seem less obvious, but a significant swath of the citizenry, led by an intelligentsia that has seemingly played an outsized role in public debate since the Quiet Revolution, is aware of and ready to embrace Quebec's increasing cultural and religious diversity. Indeed, this was the chief principle upon which the Proulx Report urged the state to fully secularize the public school system. No doubt this is not a unanimous position in the province, as the last decade has painfully shown, but we think Milot and Tremblay are correct when they point to the embrace of cultural pluralism by many in Quebec (and perhaps most importantly by elements within the Quebec state) as being an important factor in accelerating the educational changes that took place between 1996 and 2008, leading to the actualization of the promise of a secular system made in 1964. It also represents an interesting example of a long process of incremental change (especially displacement) after a powerful instance of exogenous shock to a political system.

The Partial Funding of Private Schools in Quebec

Today, Quebec funds private schools for operating expenses on a per-student basis at a rate of 60 per cent of the amount provided to a student attending a public school. In exchange for this funding, private schools are required to hire certified teachers, follow the government-approved curriculum, and abide by the limitations on English instruction in place since the implementation of Bill 101 in 1977. Private school enrolment in the province remains strong. In the 2019–20 school year, over 134,000 children were enrolled in private schools in Quebec, representing roughly 10 per cent of the entire school-age population (Macpherson 2022), a percentage that only slightly trails enrolment numbers in British Columbia. However, this percentage jumps to roughly 33 per cent when considering high-school aged children in Montreal ("Are Quebec's Private High Schools Creating a Segregated Society?" *CBC News*, 30 October 2017), a number that speaks to the particular importance of private education in Quebec's largest city. The fact that roughly a third of Montreal high schoolers attend private schools is wholly unique in Canada, but it is also the product of a long tradition of private education in the province. Or, as Magnuson (1993, 4) has argued, "in a society that reveres tradition, the private school has accumulated centuries of merit."

Stretching back to the Collège des Jésuites, established in 1635, Quebec has a lengthy history of private, often religiously affiliated, schools. Indeed, attending one of the several traditional Catholic-run "classical colleges" was, at least prior to the Quiet Revolution, considered the only viable route to a university acceptance for French Canadian youth (Burgess 1992, 86). Many such schools were the recipients, from time to time at least, of financial assistance from the state, running all the way back to the seventeenth century. However, such assistance was neither consistently or equitably provided (Magnuson 1993, 7). This changed with the introduction, in 1968, of Bill 56, An Act Respecting Private Education. This established the framework for recognizing, regulating, and funding private schools in the province. Unlike the introduction of public funding for private schools that occurred in the Western Canadian provinces, Quebec's Bill 56 was not the product of intense and strategic lobbying on the part of a policy entrepreneur in the traditional sense. Rather, the policy window opened for Bill 56 due to the historic compromise struck between the Catholic clergy and the Quebec government in the early 1960s that led to Bill 60 and the creation of a Ministry of Education in 1964. The negotiations over the shift in educational authority inherent in Bill 60, from the church to the state, have been discussed in detail above. One of the chief products of these negotiations was the inclusion of the following sections of the preamble in Bill 60:

> Whereas every child is entitled to the advantage of a system of education conducive to the full developments of his personality;
>
> Whereas parents have the right to choose the instruction which, according to their convictions, ensure the greatest respect for the rights of their children;
>
> Whereas persons and groups are entitled to establish autonomous educational institutions and, subject to the requirements of the common welfare, to avail themselves of administrative and financial means necessary for the pursuit of their ends.
>
> (quoted in Burgess 1992, 86)

This legislation saw the government of Quebec guaranteeing to the Catholic Church the right of private schools to continue to exist and furthermore, hinted that the public financing of these schools (at least to a certain degree) was legitimate. Interestingly, it was the Union National government of Daniel Johnson, rather than the Lesage Liberals (who suffered a surprise defeat in the 1966 election), who made good on the promise of the Liberals' Bill 60 with the introduction of Bill 56 in 1968. Yet the bill was supported by all the major political parties in the province, with Lesage, now leader of the Opposition, very vocal in his approval (Bezeau 1979, 25). The new law established two levels of funding for private schools: 60 per cent of the average cost of the per-pupil grant to public schools for recognized private institutions, and 80 per cent for those private schools deemed to be in the "public interest." It also laid out a variety of other technical regulations. This financial assistance was a boon to private schools in Quebec, which had seen enrolment numbers decline steeply in the face of the Lesage Liberals' intense promotion of public education following the passage of Bill 60. Bill 56 reversed this trend. Buoyed by state funding, French-language private school enrolments would triple within five years. English-language private school enrolments doubled (Magnuson 1980, 110–11).

There were certainly critics of Bill 56 from the beginning, dismayed that state dollars were being funnelled to private rather than public schools. However, it was not until the emergence of René Lévesque's PQ as a legitimate electoral force that the issue gained significant prominence. In fact, the PQ promised to eliminate funding to private schools in their successful 1976 electoral campaign. Yet this promise would go unfulfilled. As Magnuson (1993, 8) notes, many of the PQ cabinet ministers were products of private schools or had enrolled their children in them, leading to a lukewarm response to Leveque's campaign promise inside Cabinet. That said, the PQ did impose a moratorium on new private schools in 1977 and began to gradually reduce public funding in 1981. Since this time, the PQ has been the party in Quebec to consistently question the public funding of private schools; however, despite repeated threats throughout the party's existence, it has never moved decidedly in this direction. The Liberals, on the other hand, have tended to stake out a changeable and middling position, sometimes favouring cuts (the Robert Bourassa government of the late 1980s continued the PQ's pattern of gradual cuts, seeing per-pupil funding drop to nearly 50 per cent), and sometimes favouring increases (Liberal icon Claude Ryan, acting as education minster in the late 1980s, incrementally raised rates while the Liberal government of Jean Charest raised funding to the current 60 per cent, and publicly mused about additional increases on occasion).

Since the introduction of funding in 1968, the battle lines one would expect to be drawn, have in fact been drawn. On one side sit the various public-school teachers' unions, the PQ, and the broader union movement in Quebec. On the other, groups representing private schools in the province such as La Fédération des établissements d'enseignement privés (FEEP), The Quebec Association of Independent Schools (QAIS), and the Association of Jewish Day Schools. A recent survey found roughly 39 per cent in favour of government support for private schools and 52 per cent opposed (Mouvement L'École ensemble 2018). One of the more interesting things about this divide, however, is the near complete absence of religion as a direct point of concern in these debates. Indeed, nearly all opposition to funding hinges on notions of "elitism" in the private sector and the importance of directing scarce state resources to the public sector. Similarly, defenders of public funding for private schools most often refer to the importance of maintaining the tradition of private schools in Quebec, the principle of school choice enshrined in Bill 60, and the broader benefits of competition between the private and public sector. In other Canadian provinces, each of these arguments (with the exception of that related to the "tradition" of private schools) are often prominent in debates over public funding as well. However, in the rest of Canada, they are often accompanied by arguments related to the appropriateness of funding private religious schools. That debate over the funding of private religious schools is rare in Quebec is somewhat perplexing given the overtly secular status of society as well as the common notion that the bulk of Quebec's private schools are religious. Yet multiple respondents stressed to the authors that, despite the names of many schools, which speak to an obvious Catholic heritage, very few private schools in Quebec are, in fact, religious in terms of the content of instruction offered. Indeed, consider this comment by a senior member of FEEP, the organization that represents roughly 90 per cent of private school students in the province, on the uniqueness of private schools in Quebec:

> Every year there's a delegation of our team that goes to NAIS, which is National Association of Independent Schools in the United States. And we're always so surprised to hear how religious American private schools are. This is so different. They are talking about, you know, how to deal with homosexuality or transgender kids. And for us these are not religious questions. They are a psychological question, you know. What can we do for that kid? It has nothing to do with religion, we work with psychologists. We don't work with the clergy. And we thought, you know, some things are just – we are just in such a different world, you know, and sometimes it's difficult to discuss some issues with other private school organizations because our reality is very different from the composition of private schools in the rest of North America.
>
> (Interview with C, 8 December 2016)

There are, of course, exceptions to this pattern. Loyola high school in Montreal remains a prominent example of a traditional private school that has maintained its religious essence. There is also a limited number of Evangelical Protestant private schools in Quebec, in addition to the small number of religious schools that exist in the province to serve minority populations from the Jewish, Orthodox Greek, and Muslim communities. Funding for such schools has developed in a patchwork pattern, with certain Greek and Jewish schools gradually attaining separate agreements with the government after 1968, and a number of recent Islamic schools not receiving any funding because of a 2004 law that continues to prevent new private schools from receiving funding.[2] Public debates over the appropriateness of funding such schools do emerge from time to time in Quebec, most recently in relation to an aborted proposal by the Charest government to offer full funding to a selection of Jewish schools in 2005 ("Quebec Abandons Plan to Fund Religious Schools," *Globe and Mail*, 20 January 2005), but, given the small number of schools affected, these debates rarely ignite the passions of the average Quebecois.

---

2 For an in-depth description of Jewish Schooling in Quebec, see Rosenberg and Jedwab (1992) and Read (2018). For similar coverage of Islamic schooling in Quebec, see Sarrouh (2016), 180–221.

Though funding has been increased or decreased from time to time, and the 2004 changes imposed a limit to the number of schools, the foundation of the funding regime for independent schools has changed little since the passage of Bill 56 in 1968. It is true that, despite Bill 56 being the product of the historic compromise between the Catholic clergy and the state to transfer control over public education to the newly created Ministry of Education, the vast majority of Quebec's private schools are not nearly as religious as they once were. But, aside from some incremental changes in either direction, funding levels are not significantly different from what they were in 1968, nor is this likely to change in the near future. In fact, a path-dependent equilibrium has developed in Quebec like that in the Western Canadian provinces. Public opinion is largely divided; the major centre-left and left-wing parties threaten to reduce funding while the centre-right and right-leaning parties invoke the notion of "school choice" in defence of current rates; teachers unions take strong positions against the status quo while private school lobby groups, backed by a relatively high proportion of parents who send their children to private schools (especially in Montreal), pressure governments to resist such calls; groups such as the Mouvement laïque québécois demand an end to the funding of private religious schools while religious minorities stress the importance of defending their religious freedom. Yet very little changes and the network of partially funded private schools continues to embed itself as a key component of the overall education system in the province.

Conclusion

The development of Quebec's education system is quite unusual compared to other Canadian provinces owing most obviously to the incredibly long period of church control, followed by the radical shifts brought about by the exogenous shock of the Quiet Revolution, which transformed the province and the education system but kept the grounds of policy debate firmly within a faith frame. Cleary the Quiet Revolution lay behind this critical policy juncture which would ultimately alter the trajectory of education in Quebec from clericalism to a secular public system. Yet, also unique to Quebec, the full implications of this radical change in policy direction would only be realized incrementally – the exogenous shock to the education system that the Quiet Revolution represented had some immediate impacts but was fully worked out through a process of incremental change that eventually led to a secular public system and generous government support of private independent schools. Indeed, Canada's most secular province did not fully secularize its public system until 2008, or perhaps even 2020 if one counts the elimination of the ERC as total secularization, through a process best described as displacement.

It was also in the wake of the Quiet Revolution that Quebec's contemporary commitment to partially fund private schools was entrenched through a process that layered support for independent schools onto the evolving public system. Yet these decisions, too, were made in unique circumstances compared to those in the other provinces that offer support to independent schools. Rather than being the result of ongoing lobbying by particular policy entrepreneurs arguing on behalf of the "rights" of certain groups usually new to the political scene, or the importance of "choice" for parents, Quebec's decision to formalize funding for private schools was rooted in the grand compromise made between the Catholic Church and the state wherein control over public education was largely ceded to the government. In exchange for its compliance, the Church received assurances in the 1960s that it would continue to receive public funds to host its own private schools. Ironically, very few of those schools are today religious in a serious way, and most that are strictly religious in orientation are Jewish or Islamic schools rather than Catholic. For these religious minorities, arguments rooted in "religious freedom" continue to be made but for most other private school supporters in Quebec, the issue is one of "school choice" or, more frequently, the importance of maintaining the long-standing Quebec *tradition* of supporting elite, religiously affiliated private school education.

In comparative perspective, what stands out most about the evolution of Quebec's education system is how questions related to faith in schools have remained the key point of focus in debates over religious schooling in the province. That is, similar to Ontario, debates over religious schooling essentially continue to be ensconced within a "faith regime" rather than a "rights" or "choice" regime. Yet the way in which the majority of citizens have approached the debate over faith in schools has largely done a one-eighty. For significantly longer than any other province, the citizenry was content with total church control of education. However, in the wake of the Quiet Revolution, attitudes began to change en masse, leading to the state eventually implementing a number of reforms, including a constitutional amendment, aimed at eradicating any religious influence in the public system. But note how the issue of faith (and in certain cases its connection to Quebecois identity) rather than rights or choice has remained paramount in this evolution.

A similar point can be made with respect to the private education sector. Unlike the Western Canadian provinces, who share with Quebec a commitment to partially subsidize private religious schools, the decision to formalize this funding was essentially the product of a peace-offering granted to the Catholic Church during a period of significant transition wherein the state took over control of the public school system. Again, this was a decision made within a regime of "faith" rather than one of "rights" or "choice." Today, although arguments rooted especially in "choice" exist in Quebec, they are not nearly as commonplace, or as powerful, in Quebec as in Western Canada. Rather, the most persuasive, although not unanimously agreed upon, argument in favour of continued state support for religiously affiliated private schools in Quebec is rooted in the importance of "tradition" and "Quebecois identity" that is wrapped up in these largely Catholic-affiliated institutions. The evolution of Quebec's education system thus stands alone in Canada and appears to have reached a point of stasis from which it is difficult to imagine much significant change in the foreseeable future.

3 Faith's Resilience Creates Four Secular Systems in Atlantic Canada

Introduction

The Atlantic provinces are distinct from each other in their politics and political culture. New Brunswick's divide between French and English mirrors the larger Canadian reality in a way no other province does; Prince Edward Island is smaller and more rural than any other province; Nova Scotia has long been the economic and educational centre of Atlantic Canada; and Newfoundland stands apart from all three in its geographic isolation and late entry into Confederation. Viewed in contrast to the rest of the country, these provinces do share important similarities: they are poorer, secularized later and more slowly, have not seen significant inflows of immigration since the nineteenth century, are more rural, and are often seen to have more traditional political cultures. Though the NDP has met with success (especially in Nova Scotia) in the last twenty years, the region continues to be dominated by the Liberal and Conservative parties both federally and provincially (Wiseman 2007).

The school systems in each province are very similar in how they treat religious and independent schools today, but the Maritimes and Newfoundland have arrived at their contemporary governance regimes by different routes. In Prince Edward Island, Nova Scotia, and New Brunswick an informal nineteenth century compromise between Protestant and Catholic communities saw public schools in Protestant areas teach from a Protestant perspective and schools in Catholic areas teach from a Catholic one. Additionally, Catholic schools were often staffed by members of Catholic religious orders and located in Church-owned buildings. But these Catholic schools, because of their informal status, were not separate schools under Section 93 of the Constitution and so had no constitutional protection. When school amalgamation in the 1960s merged small schools of Protestant and Catholic flavours, the move to a more secular arrangement occurred with relatively little debate or protest (Manzer 1994, 2003). In the absence of a formal separate system or constitutional guarantees for Catholic schools, this transition meant that informal accommodation of religious identity disappeared very quietly in the mid-twentieth century. These provinces are classic examples of incremental change where drift and conversion (Mahoney and Thelen 2010) saw the evolution from a system suffused with religion and informally divided between Protestants and Catholics into a single public secular system over the course of the twentieth century. Unlike in the rest of the country, there seems to have been an absence of significant policy entrepreneurs promoting either rights or choice as alternative approaches to the problem. Once drift and conversion into a single public regime had occurred, it was quickly a politically stable status quo.

In Newfoundland, like Quebec, the nineteenth century political compromise saw no public school system created. Instead, the colonial government funded schools operated by churches. Initially government support was split between Methodist, Anglican, and Roman Catholic systems, but when Newfoundland entered Confederation in 1949 six religious school systems received constitutionally protected government support (Pentecostal schools were recognized in 1954, meaning seven denominations had constitutional protection for their schools from that point). This faith-focused regime was rooted in the organizational capacity of the churches, the deep poverty of the colony, and the absence of local governments that could provide government support for public school boards. While the Newfoundland government did gradually build its capacity to oversee and support education, the denominations (especially the Catholic and Anglican Churches), continued to be powerful political actors able to demand constitutional protection for religious school systems when Newfoundland entered Confederation in 1949. Though called into question from the 1960s onward, it was only when faced with a perfect storm of demographic decline, economic adversity, and institutional crisis in the late 1980s that Newfoundland's Liberal government moved to replace the province's denominational system with a single secular one (Galway and Dibbon 2012, 13). These reforms required a constitutional amendment – a result achieved in 1997 after two referendums. Like in the other Atlantic provinces, there was little appetite in these moments of exogenously driven change for a school regime built on either rights or choice principles. The result was a relatively sudden shift from a regime built on religious schools where their status was defined in faith terms to a single public system where no support was provided to religious or independent schools because their relationship with the government was defined in those very faith terms. In Newfoundland and Labrador, 1.6 per cent of students attend an independent school; the rate in Prince Edward Island is 2.2 per cent, in Nova Scotia 3.3 per cent, and in New Brunswick 1.3 per cent – the lowest in Canada (Fraser Institute 2022).

The Maritime Provinces

While the details differ somewhat between each province, the basic arrangement that Nova Scotia, New Brunswick, and Prince Edward Island arrived at in the mid-nineteenth century was one of de jure public support for non-sectarian but often functionally Protestant schools in most areas, as well as de facto public support in predominantly Catholic areas for Roman Catholic schools. Legislative frameworks for the government support of common schools were established in New Brunswick (1802) and Nova Scotia (1808) and for grammar schools in New Brunswick (1816) and Nova Scotia (1811) (Manzer 2003, 41). These schools were Protestant in practice at a time when Roman Catholics were effectively excluded from the franchise in these colonies (Garner 1969), but over the course of the first part of the nineteenth century they evolved into an informal arrangement where schools in Catholic areas operated as Catholic schools and those in Protestant areas operated as Protestant schools. This informal arrangement only partially overlapped with the linguistic divide at the time. Francophone Acadian regions were very poorly served with schools for much of the nineteenth century as the vast majority of both Catholic students and the Catholic hierarchy were English speakers from Ireland. Throughout the 1850s and 1860s there was substantial political mobilization on both sides of

Table 3.1. Key Dates in the Evolution of Atlantic Canada Education System

Date	Event
1802–36	Initial Education Acts in Maritime provinces
1867–1949	Confederation: Nova Scotia (1867); New Brunswick (1867); PEI (1871); NFLD (1949)
1871–5	New Brunswick Schools Act controversy
1933	Convention government in Newfoundland
1949	Newfoundland entrenches denominational education
1960s	School amalgamation in Maritimes
1967	Newfoundland Warren Report
1995–8	Newfoundland referendums, constitutional amendment, amalgamation

the question of whether or not Catholic schools ought to receive government funding as a matter of legislation. But, crucially, nowhere in the Maritimes did the informal support provided to Catholic schools receive formalized legislative approval (Silver 1997).

Ironically, the framing of Section 93 – its protection of separate schools "at the Union or is thereafter established" was a political accommodation to the Catholic bishops of Nova Scotia (Sissons 1959). In 1867, the bishops saw this concession as sufficient and expected that they would be able to gain provincial support for a formal separate system after Nova Scotia entered Confederation. This did not come to pass, despite serious political efforts in New Brunswick and Nova Scotia in the 1870s by Catholics to get such a system. Especially in New Brunswick, where the Caraquet Riots of 1875 were triggered by a dispute over a school board election that divided the town along religious lines and were linked to efforts at the federal level to disallow the 1871 New Brunswick Common school law, the religious divide did partially overlap with the French-English linguistic divide (MacNaughton 1947). But, the question was primarily fought out between the English-speaking elite of the province (Sissons 1959; Silver 1997). Despite these serious disputes in the 1870s, the informal accommodation of religion (meaning Protestant and Catholic claims) was reasonably stable from then on. There were rare episodes of contention, such as the Dartmouth School case in Nova Scotia in 1939–40 (Bérard 2005), but it seems that there was general acceptance of the form of accommodation reached in public elementary and (once they emerged) public secondary schools.

This very important difference between the Maritimes and most of the other provinces meant that all schools were formally public and non-sectarian from 1867 onwards. In the absence of a constitutional right to separate schools, an important element of the political context in the other provinces was absent. These public elementary systems were heavily influenced by the example of Egerton Ryerson in Upper Canada as colonial governments extended public support to elementary schools in the 1850s and 1860s. This situation, both before and after 1867, had been strongly opposed by the Catholic hierarchy, which sought public support for separate schools on the Ontario model. Despite significant lobbying and some political support, each provincial government in the Maritimes refused to move in such a direction. Instead, an informal and politically stable compromise was arrived at which was dependent on small elementary schools serving areas that were either homogeneously Catholic or homogeneously Protestant. Schools in Protestant areas were run very much along the lines of public schools in Ontario or the Western provinces, with days that started with the Lord's Prayer in its Protestant version, readings from the King James translation of the Bible, and provision for religious education after school hours by Protestant clergymen. Schools in Catholic neighbourhoods and villages, alternatively, would start their days with the Lord's Prayer in its Catholic version, readings from the Douay translation of the Bible, and would have time set aside before and after the school day for religious instruction by priests and religious brothers or sisters. Additionally, in many Catholic areas the schoolteachers would be sisters in Catholic religious orders paid a teacher's salary by the government and the school a Church-owned building leased to the local school district. In francophone districts, further, there was a good chance that all instruction would be in French (MacDonald 2000; Sissons 1959). In cities like Halifax or Dartmouth, the situation tended to be more changeable and mixed, but it was not out of the ordinary for schools staffed by members of Catholic religious orders operating on Church property to be classed as public schools (Bérard 2005).

What ended this practice of accommodation was not a secularization or debate over the embedded place of religion in the Maritimes. Instead, urbanization and programs of school amalgamation in the 1960s and 1970s made it difficult to maintain the old informal system that let Catholic and Protestant schools de facto operate within the public system. Manzer (2003), media reviews, and consultation with experts on Maritime politics (Interview with Don Desserud, 21 October 2016; Interview with Louise Carbert, 23 October 2016) found that there was little debate over these changes – they were administrative issues that generated concerns about the health of small communities rather than political ones that mobilized people on opposite sides of religious divides. There simply seems to have been no policy entrepreneurs seeking to maintain government support for religious K–12 schools. There was debate over government support for religious universities (MacKinnon 1995) and over the language of instruction (Behiels 2004), but these seem not to have touched on the religious schools at the K–12 level.

Contention over religious schools in the Maritimes, then, simply faded after the 1870s. Lacking constitutional entrenchment, there was little by way of rights to be debated. From the 1960s forward, Acadian nationalism made the critical debate about francophone schools the focus of rights debates in the Maritimes. We could expect that other features of the Maritime provinces have reduced pressure for the public support for independent or religious schools in the contemporary period. Having received relatively little immigration, the area does not have sizeable groups of people whose faith or cultural practices are not accommodated in the public system. The weak economy of the area and rural depopulation have hit the Maritimes hard in the last thirty years, meaning both that there are relatively fewer children in the education system and that the education system is persistently under-resourced, making it more difficult for claims rooted in choice to gain political traction. This has all added up to remarkably little pressure for government resources to go to schools operating outside the public system.

A final element at play in the Maritimes, and another holdover from the nineteenth century compromise, was that public support did go to church-associated academies, grammar schools, and colleges throughout the nineteenth century. These institutions, some of which had begun receiving public support in the 1830s when colonial governments focused on the education of local elites at what would now be called the high school level, were closely tied to churches. The more prominent of them evolved into small universities like St. Francis Xavier or Mount Allison. While functionally secular today, most retain something of their religious affiliations while also receiving state support. Others, such as Halifax Grammar School or Rothesay Netherwood in Saint John, New Brunswick, remained elite secondary schools but lost their government support and religious character. There are newer Christian schools in the Maritimes and a small homeschool movement, but neither group has lobbied much at all for provincial support and seem not to have been the subject of recent political controversy. In short, the contemporary situation in the Maritimes is the product of incremental endogenous processes of change. Change through displacement, as the public system transitioned from being Protestant to being secular, and change through conversion, as the amalgamation of schools did away with the historical informal protection for small Catholic schools, seems to have been particularly important.

Newfoundland and Labrador

Since 1997, Newfoundland has structured its school system in essentially the same way as the Atlantic provinces: as a secular public system divided between French and English language schools with a very small independent/religious sector operating without state support. This situation is stable and, although there have been other significant changes made to the province's educational governance in the last twenty years as the government amalgamated school boards (Galway 2014), the change to a single secular system with no support to independent schools has not been challenged. This is a shocking development, for before 1997 Newfoundland was the only province in which there was, strictly speaking, no public school system. All schools were denominational in character and churches were closely involved in the day-to-day operation of them. This situation had its roots in the initial granting of government funding to schools in the 1830s and had been constitutionally entrenched when Newfoundland joined Canada in 1949. Furthermore, it survived some remarkable exogenous shocks: the loss of self-government in the 1930s, the entry of Newfoundland into Canada in 1949, and significant attempts to change it in the late 1960s. Change, when it came in the 1990s, required the efforts of two premiers, with the public support of two referendums, and a constitutional amendment. As Galway and Dibbon (2012, 13) put it, it took a "perfect storm" of economic depression, secularization, demographic decline in the number of students, concern with an apparent achievement gap in academic outcomes, and ideational change in elite views of what education ought to be to create the circumstances for exogenously driven changes to the Newfoundland school system.

This dramatic change to a secular system took place in a way that trumped any potential for regimes of parental rights or choice. Only in Quebec do we have a comparable example of such dramatic change in how a provincial government treated religious and independent schools. In all of the other provincial regimes we examine, change occurred incrementally, and path dependence has been a very powerful force. Newfoundland stands very much in contrast to this: it is an example of dramatic change brought about when a window for policy change opened due to exogenous shock. The way this change took place makes it an important case, and so we examine the 1993–7 period at length here.

Newfoundland's organization of education was unique before 1997. Unlike in the other provinces, there was no public system and churches continued to be directly involved in the administration of schools right up until 1997 (a strong contrast to the Catholic separate systems of Ontario, Saskatchewan, and Alberta, where the schools were governed by boards elected from the Catholic community rather than having direct ties to the Church hierarchy). Academic and minister of education (among other roles) F.W. Rowe described the Newfoundland system:

> Perhaps the adjective most commonly used to refer to Newfoundland's education system is *unique* ... It is not a state system for two reasons: the state does not control it entirely, and the state does not provide all the money necessary to run it. On the other hand it cannot be called a church system. Through their various boards the churches own all the schools, yet the churches derive their rights from the state through the

legislation and depend largely on state grants both for construction and maintenance. Moreover, teacher's salaries are provided almost entirely by legislative votes.

(1964, 1)

This was a system with parallels only in Quebec: faith defined not just the political landscape and normative debate around education but also the institutional configuration of education in Newfoundland.

As in other provinces, the first schools established in Newfoundland were church based or small private enterprises. Church schools, often supported by donations from England, were almost the only schools outside of St. John's in the early nineteenth century and provided the only education accessible to the poor in that city. Private schools initially tended to be very small and run either by clergymen or by their wives. Targeting the colony's upper middle class, many of these private schools offered a curriculum mirroring that offered by English grammar schools. And, in a pattern that continued until late in the twentieth century, elite families tended to send their children to boarding schools in England, New England, or mainland Canada to be educated. Outside St. John's and a few other major towns, education did not penetrate very widely or very deeply into Newfoundland life. Early accounts identify a largely illiterate population cut off from schooling – the best access to education most children could hope for was Sunday school (which, at the time, taught academic subjects) (McCann 1988a; Rowe 1964, 1976).

Newfoundland gained representative government in 1832. In 1836, the colony's first Education Act was passed, providing modest government support to interdenominational elementary schools modelled on Ireland's national schools and governed by appointed school boards. This system was undermined, however, by the almost exclusive appointment of Protestants (particularly Anglicans) to these boards (McCann 1988a) and by the desire of the Roman Catholic and Anglican bishops to promote Church-run schools (Rowe 1964). The resulting tensions led the governor to "admit that in nearly every district of the island the children of either Protestant or Catholic parents had, at one time or another, been excluded from the benefit of schooling" in 1843 (McCann 1988a, 35). The 1843 Education Act responded to this dysfunction by splitting the government school grant between Protestant and Roman Catholic schools. Beginning almost immediately, the Anglican Church (and the elite of some other Protestant denominations) began lobbying for the Protestant grant to be subdivided so that each Protestant denomination would receive government support for its schools in keeping with its proportion of the student population. Heavily promoted by Anglican Archbishop Feild, this vision was controversial. Only in the 1874 Act did a Tory government introduce legislation that divided the Protestant part of the elementary school grant up between different Protestant denominations. Initially, recognized Protestant schools receiving grants were those of the Anglican, Methodist, Free Church of Scotland, Congregational Church, and Kirk (Church) of Scotland denominations (in addition to the already existing Roman Catholic schools). The Salvation Army was recognized as a denomination in 1892 and the Seventh-Day Adventist Church was recognized in 1921. Church mergers meant that, at the time of Confederation in 1949, government support for Roman Catholic, Anglican, United Church, Salvation Army, Congregational Church, and Seventh-Day Adventist Church schools was constitutionally entrenched. Pentecostal schools received the same status in 1954 (Rowe 1964, 94).

Secondary schooling was, until the 1950s, accessible only to a privileged few in Newfoundland. After an initial attempt at a state-supported non-denominational academy located in St John's failed in the 1850s, this part of the education system also developed primarily along denominational lines. State support went to the Roman Catholic (St. Bonaventure's), Anglican (Bishop Feild's), and Methodist-United Church (Prince of Wales) academies in St. John's. These were elite public schools on the British model that also acted as normal schools training teachers for the other schools on the island. As secondary schools spread across the island over the next century, they grew out of the existing denominational systems. Only in a few mining and industrial towns (where companies sponsored schools that were religiously integrated) did Newfoundland educational spaces operating independently from churches before 1949.

This is not to suggest that there were no voices arguing for a more public approach to education. Rowe (1964, 60) argues that government opinion in the 1840s supported non-denominational schooling. And, in the 1870s, the Orange Lodge was strongly opposed to the division of the government grant between Protestant denominations, seeing the change as a political opportunity for the Catholic Church. Finally, in 1895, the existing denominational systems took an integrated approach to educational standards when they created a Council on Higher Education, which set standard exams for high schools across the existing church systems. But the half century between 1870 and 1920 witnessed the entrenchment of a number of features of Newfoundland's educational governance that would remain present until the constitutional changes of the 1990s. Most visibly, clergy continued to be major political players in a way not seen in any province aside from Quebec. To some extent, this had cultural roots: Newfoundland was a society in which churches were very powerful social organizations. Church control of schools created a feedback loop in which they controlled schools because they had power and, at least in part, had power because they controlled schools. There was also a financial element. Rowe (1964, 69) explains that "with the Act of 1916, the government's role in education became preponderant and decisive. Hitherto, its chief role had been that of a contributor; now it assumed major financial responsibility." Only in the 1950s, and then only in some of the larger cities, did property taxes come to be used to support education. A poor colonial government simply could not offer widespread education without the financial and human resources that churches could deploy.

Two developments after the First World War confirm how strongly entrenched the denominational systems were. First, in 1920 the government established a Department of Education, a normal school, and eleven supervising inspectors. This was an important move towards the modernization and extension of the educational system (it was followed by the creation of Memorial University College in 1924). But, it was an extension that entrenched church governance in even the government part of the system as most decisions were overseen by a board of superintendents made up of the deputy minister of education and the superintendents of the three largest denominational systems. These superintendents were usually professional educators, but they were also church employees who continued as the de facto rulers of the system (McCann 1988b, 66) even after the creation of the ministry. Revised in 1927, this arrangement came to be regarded by the churches as "a Magna Carta of their rights and privileges, and when the Commission of Government took office six years later … they found the churches willing to fight tooth and nail to retain their privileges" (McCann 1988b, 68; see also Fagan 2004).

The second confirmation of the strength of this entrenchment of denominational education is illustrated by the experience of the Commission government. In 1933, threatened with bankruptcy, Newfoundland was forced to give up responsible government. It reverted to being governed directly by Great Britain through an appointed Commission of three British Civil Servants, three Newfoundlanders, and a British Governor. This system of government would continue until 1949. Losing independence is almost the ultimate shock to a political system, yet it is a shock that denominational education weathered despite the Commission's efforts to reform the existing system along the lines of existing British best practice. In 1935, the Commission announced a series of reforms that included the following:

compulsory education; the abolition of examinations for grades under eight; abolition of the offices of superintendent and assistant superintendent; the establishment of state schools in St. John's; and the possible abolition of out-port school boards ... These proposals amounted to a wholesale reconstruction of the denominational system, the first attempt in Newfoundland's history to make a frontal attack on the power of the Churches in education.

(McCann 1988b, 69)

The Roman Catholic and Anglican hierarchies, especially, mobilized quickly to resist these changes motivated both by principled opposition to the idea of state education and more mundane concerns about the possible fate of Church investments in school buildings. Despite the desire of both the Dominion office in London and the Commission to see a system of state schools, the Churches succeeded in creating enough pushback to stop the 1935 reform efforts. In 1937 and 1943 more limited reform efforts were also stalled by church opposition, although 1943 did see government aid extended to the integrated or amalgamated schools operating in some of the company towns.

Newfoundland entered the post-war period, then, with a very unusual political system, a discredited political class, powerful Churches, and a pressing set of questions about its political and economic future. Against this backdrop, Newfoundland had a National Convention in 1948 to identify possibilities for the island's future. The Convention identified three options: retaining Commission government, joining Canada as a province, or returning to independent dominion status with responsible government. A first referendum eliminated continued Commission government as an option while a second saw a narrow victory for Confederation with Canada. The referendums also saw Joey Smallwood, who would become the province's first premier and who would be in office until 1972, emerge as a populist political force. Education was not an explicit issue in the referendum campaigns, but religion certainly was. Though there were internal complexities, in general Protestants favoured joining Canada and Catholics favoured maintaining independence. Part of the opposition to Confederation on the part of Catholics was an argument "against material blandishments and in favour of the preservation, in isolation, of simple spiritual values" (Noel 1971, 257) strongly advanced by the Bishop of St. John's and Catholic newspapers. More concretely, there were fears that joining Canada would threaten denominational education and lead to divorce becoming legalized. Both referendum campaigns, but especially the second one, were marked by this deeply rooted sectarian divide (Gwyn 1968).

Smallwood, and the pro-Confederate side generally, were not averse to using the religious divide in their favour. They found that the Orange Lodge's anti-Catholic reaction, for example, created politically useful allies for them (Noel 1971). But they were keenly aware of the need to stop explicit opposition from the established Churches from becoming too strong. One way to avoid raising further opposition was to ensure that the existing regime of church schools was protected when the province entered Confederation. Furthermore, the terms of union worked out with Canada stated that divorce cases originating in Newfoundland would be handled as private bills in the Senate (as in Quebec) and the existing denominational structure of education would be constitutionally entrenched in Newfoundland.

Term 17 of the terms of union was the mechanism by which denominational education was constitutionally entrenched. This section, which applied to Newfoundland in lieu of Section 93 of the 1867 Canada Act, confirmed that

> the Legislature shall have exclusive authority to make laws in relation to education, but the Legislature will not have authority to make laws prejudicially affecting any right or privilege with respect to denominational schools, common (amalgamated) schools, or denominational colleges, that any class or classes of person have by law in Newfoundland at the date of union, and out of public funds of the Province of Newfoundland provided for education.
>
> (Penney 1988, 96)

Further, it confirmed that there was to be no discrimination between denominational schools or colleges in the disbursement of educational funding.

Term 17 created a constitutional setting very similar to what Section 93 had created in Quebec, Ontario, Saskatchewan, and Alberta. It was broader, as it protected the schools of denominations other than Catholics, but it constitutionally protected the public support of structures that tied education to religious belief and identity (Fagan 2004, 2012; Mulcahy 1988). But it also entrenched fragmentation in a system under severe, and multiple, pressures. Although Confederation, and the transfer payments that came with it, moderated the financial pressures on the provincial government somewhat, Newfoundland's school-aged population grew faster than that of any other province in the 1950s and 1960s. This meant that the educational system had to serve large numbers of students while also attempting to dramatically increase the number and quality of its teachers to the Canadian norm. With growing revenues and an expanding economy, these pressures could be managed without fundamentally reconsidering the structure of the system.

However, it was a system whose outcomes were not meeting the needs of Newfoundlanders or the expectations of politicians. This perception led the government to appoint a Royal Commission on Children and Youth in 1967. Usually known as the Warren Commission, after its chairperson Philip Warren, the commission was tasked with an overall review of Newfoundland's education system including Memorial University and post-secondary technical education. Though broad, its terms of reference explicitly directed it to not consider the denominational system. But, the commission found itself unable to respect these boundaries:

> We are fully aware that the churches have certain rights in education in this Province, including the right to operate schools, to select student teachers and arrange for their training and certification, to exercise general supervision over the content of the curriculum, to develop a curriculum for religious education, to receive and allocate certain grants, and to advise the government in matters of educational policy. Where there is no conflict between these rights and the rights of children, the Commission believes that the rights of the churches should be preserved. But if these rights infringe in any way on the unqualified right of every child to an education suited to his abilities and interests, then the state has obligation to see the appropriate changes are made in legislation. The state must respect the rights of parents to choose the type of education for their children, but at the same time it must see that minimum standards are provided in education in the interest of the common good. This Commission believes that the Provincial Government must consider the whole question of denominational education.
>
> (Newfoundland 1968, xv)

The commission found a school system that was struggling to grow rapidly enough to accommodate the youngest population in Canada, that was facing very significant shortfalls in student learning outcomes and graduation rates, and that often had unqualified teachers staffing one room schools lacking in modern amenities. It ended up recommending dramatic reforms of the Newfoundland school system from kindergarten through to university. With specific reference to denominational education, the majority report of the commission recommended "that the Department of Education be reorganized along functional rather than denominational lines" (70). This was a stance supported by submissions from the United and Anglican school systems, Memorial University, the

Teachers' Association, and a number of school boards (57). The report argued that "they [the Churches] should place less emphasis on controlling the educational enterprise, and more emphasis on developing and implementing programs of Religion Education for schools" (59).

While in agreement with the overall direction that the committee had taken, the three Roman Catholic members of the commission disagreed with its findings as they related to denominational education. They issued a minority report objecting to reorganizing the Department of Education. While agreeing that reform and organization of the education system was needed, the minority commissioners found that all the recognized religious denominations had publicly stated their willingness to cooperate with each other (Newfoundland 1968, 194). Paying tribute to the "selfless devotion of the Churches ... we may fully expect the progress in education that the greatly increased sums of money will now permit" (Newfoundland 1968, 194). To ignore this history and sacrifice, they argued, was not just a violation of the commission's terms of reference but opened the door to the overthrow of both the traditional rights of the Churches, "the rights of parents to educate their children in the faith of their choosing" (195), and would "OPEN THE DOOR FOR COMPLETE SECULAR EDUCATION" (195, emphasis in original). Instead, the Catholic commissioners argued that "modernizing the Department of Education can take place within the existing framework ... We submit that if the churches are relegated to an advisory position only, THAT IN A FEW SHORT YEARS, NOT EVEN THEIR ADVICE WILL BE SOUGHT!" (197). For the minority commissioners, the failings of the Newfoundland school system needed to be attributed to "our unhappy history, our lack of money, and our rugged geography" (197) rather than the denominational system.

The commission's recommendations on matters other than denominational education did trigger fairly extensive changes to the Newfoundland education system. It represents a moment where a group of policy entrepreneurs (the commissioners) did encounter an open policy window. Their recommendations addressed concerns that had been growing in the Protestant community about the inefficiencies created by the multiple system and, partially in response to the commission's report, the Anglican, United, and Salvation Army systems agreed to merge to create an Integrated System in 1969. The union of the three largest Protestant systems created something akin to a de facto public system in much of Newfoundland, for these schools tended to downplay religion in a manner similar to public schools in other provinces at the time; this represents an important moment of endogenously driven incremental change (Interview with Roger Grimes, 12 December 2016).

Furthermore, the Department of Education was restructured along functional lines as the commission had recommended. But, the government stopped short of confronting those who wanted to see denominational education continue (especially the Pentecostal and Catholic Churches) and even the commission recommended that religion continue to be taught in schools. Importantly, it also entrenched the views of two actors who would become key players in the constitutional changes of the 1990s. Philip Warren, after a time as president of the provincial Liberal Party, would become the minister of education in the early 1990s for the first part of the Wells government and would push changes to the system at that time (Interview with Warren, 7 December 2016). In the debates in the legislature following the release of the Warren Commission's report, Wells himself – a prominent MHA at the time – would argue that Newfoundland's education system was failing and that the denominational system was a significant part of its problems. The arguments that he made in 1968–9 (Gwyn 1968) were very much the ones that he would make as premier in 1994–5 (Interview with Clyde Wells, 8 December 2016).

The 1970s were a relatively quiet time in education politics in Newfoundland, in part because some of the pressure on the school system had been relieved by changes in the aftermath of the Warren Commission and in part because the retirement of Joey Smallwood in 1972 profoundly destabilized Newfoundland's political system. By the 1980s, pressure was once again beginning to build: the school-aged population was in precipitous decline, the population had begun a dramatic secularization, the province's economy collapsed, and the institutional credibility of the Churches was undermined by the sex abuse scandal at the Mount Cashel orphanage. These changes were a series of exogenous shocks that gave the notion of secularizing the system that Warren and Wells had been articulating in the 1960s (ideas by then shared by many others in the province) a real chance to gain traction.

The initial public argument for change to Newfoundland's school system came from the Newfoundland Teachers' Association in the form of a 1986 briefing paper entitled "Exploring New Pathways." In it, the association expressed a concern that "the system, however, as currently organized, has a serious and extensive flaw. That flaw is isolation by denomination." (NLTA 1986, 17). In a province that funded education at lower per-student rates than any other, the overlapping jurisdiction of school boards created inefficiencies and small schools that reduced the quality of education available to Newfoundland's children. Affirming the findings of the Warren Commission (24), the association called for a "Royal Commission with the broad mandate of examining the

administrative and economic disadvantage of the current denomination system and providing recommendations for improvement" (NLTA
1986, 25). Also of concern to the association, though not articulated in
the brief, was that a denominational system often created significant
problems for teachers. In some cases, for example, teachers of a different denomination than the school they were teaching in were fired.
In others, teachers who married outside of the denomination that
employed them felt that they needed to hide their marriage to protect
their employment (Interview with Roger Grimes, 12 December 2016;
Interview with Philip Warren, 7 December 2016).

The Teachers' Association brief landed in a provincial political system in crisis. Newfoundland's economy was in free fall, as was the provincial government's balance sheet. Demographically, the number of
children in the province was in sharp decline, and rural depopulation
was changing the distribution of those children – far fewer lived in the
outports and far more were living in St. John's and on the Avalon penin-
sula. By the early 1980s, public opinion had stabilized at a point where a
majority of Newfoundlanders (including a sizeable minority of Catholics) expressed discontent with the denominational system. While a slim
majority of Catholics supported the existing denominational system, it
was only among the small Pentecostal community that church schools
enjoyed overwhelming support. There was widespread concern that
schools were underperforming (Newfoundland and Labrador 1993).
While it would not become fully recognized until the mid-1990s and
the referendum campaign, Newfoundland was also a province that was
secularizing quickly (Interview with Clyde Wells, 8 December 2016).
Clyde Wells's election win in 1989, which ended seventeen years of
Progressive Conservative government, started the process of responding to these shocks by reforming educational administration. The Wells
Liberals were fiscally conservative and sought dramatic changes to
Newfoundland's government and economy (Hoy 1992; Interview with
Clyde Wells, 8 December 2016). On education, as discussed above with
reference to the Warren Commission, Wells had a long-standing per-
sonal commitment to education reform. Seeing education reform as a
priority, he appointed Philip Warren, leader of the 1968 Commission,
as his first education minister in 1989 (Interview with Philip Warren, 7
December 2016).

So, there was a premier and a minister of education committed to systemic change. The Conservative Opposition was divided on the issue
of religion in schools and chose to allow its MLAs to vote according
to their consciousness or according to the wishes of their constituents
(Interview with Loyola Sullivan, 7 December 2016). But the churches

were still important enough political actors, and the denominational system had enough public support, that the government pursued change at a deliberate pace. First, it appointed another Royal Commission. Chaired by Leonard Williams, an education professor at Memorial who had been a researcher on the 1968 Warren Commission, this commission's report, *Our Children, Our Future*, was released in 1992.

Like the 1968 Royal Commission, the Williams Report had a sweeping brief. Set against the backdrop of concern with Newfoundland's economy and society, the commission had, among other items, "a specific mandate of this Commission … [to] focus directly on the current denominational structure of our education system and whether it is contributing to fiscal and educational inefficiencies" (Newfoundland 1992, xv). Along with an extensive set of empirical studies, the commission sought reform that would enhance "equity, quality, freedom of choice, integration, responsiveness, accountability, and autonomy" (205). With reference to the denominational system, it evaluated four possibilities: retaining the existing form of denominational system, abolishing the system and replacing it with a secular one, retaining the denominational system and creating a new secular one, or modifying the existing systems to enhance interdenominational cooperation. Finding that the first three options were unworkable for a variety of reasons, the commission argued for the fourth, reforming, approach. These reforms would see the Churches continue to provide religious education in schools, establish pastoral care ministries to support children, and encourage cooperation between school boards and Churches in the provision of pastoral care (Newfoundland 1992, 236). Churches would continue to have an advisory role within the Department of Education (248). School governance would be decentralized, with more decisions being made at the level of the local school, and there would be a significantly changed role for school boards, which were to become religiously integrated and publicly elected.

These recommendations seem to have been broadly in keeping with the desires of the Wells government. After quiet negotiations with the denominations that were opposed to change (notably the Roman Catholic, Pentecostal, and Seventh-Day Adventist congregations), the government was open to an even more conservative approach that might have allowed for denominational education to continue in larger population centres while a fully integrated system operated in the rest of the province (Interview with Roger Grimes, 12 December 2016; Warren 2012; Interview with Philip Warren, 7 December 2016; Interview with Clyde Wells 8 December 2016). This would, though, require a constitutional amendment. Under the rules for amending the Canadian constitution, amending the clause protecting denominational schools in Newfoundland would require both the provincial and federal legislatures passing the amendment. Premier Wells felt that these changes would require popular support in a referendum to be legitimate, in part because of his experience with the Meech Lake constitutional amendment and partly because protection for the denominational school system had been approved through a referendum in 1949 (Interview with Clyde Wells 8 December 2016).

On 1 June 1995, Wells announced that there would be a referendum on 5 September "for the purpose of preparing a way to a single system of education by redesignating denominational schools to inter- or non-denominational schools" (Galway and Dibbon 2012, 34). The churches ran a well-financed and professionally organized campaign on the "no" side (Fagan 2004, 2012). Accounts differ as to whether the Liberal Party and the government were as well organized and as committed to arguing "yes" but the outcome in September was a very narrow 54–46 victory for the "yes" side in a referendum where only 52 per cent of the population voted (Warren 2012, 60). The Newfoundland House of Assembly passed a resolution calling for constitutional change, a request that the federal government of Jean Chrétien moved slowly on. The federal move to pass a bill amending the Constitution was further delayed when the Senate and the House of Commons passed slightly different bills on the topic in the spring of 1996. Reconciling this, amidst intense lobbying by both sides, took until December when the House of Commons rejected the Senate's modifications and passed its own bill. Implementation of these revised Term 17 terms was stalled when opponents of the changes won a judicial injunction in Newfoundland.

Premier Tobin (who replaced Wells in January 1996) and his education minister, Roger Grimes (Interview, 12 December 2016), decided to restart the process and to scrap Term 17 entirely (for an account that puts the fault on the government, see Fagan 2004, 2012; for one that emphasizes the role played by the Churches, see Warren 2012). At the end of July 1997, Tobin announced that there would be a second referendum to create a single public system, with provision for religious education inside it, on 2 September of the year. This time, the campaign mounted by the Pentecostal and Roman Catholic Churches was much less organized and much less resourced, while the government campaigned aggressively (Fagan 2012; Warren 2012, Interview with Tom McGrath, 9 December 2016). Tobin had the support of all members of the Liberal Party caucus and of the leader of the Progressive Conservative opposition (Interview with Roger Grimes, 12 December 2016; Interview with Loyola Sullivan, 7 December 2016). In the second referendum, the change side won with 73 per cent of the vote. The House of Assembly passed a motion calling for constitutional change two days later and, by mid-December, so had the federal House of Commons and the Senate. On 8 January 1998 the new Constitutional clause was signed in Ottawa allowing for the creation of a single public system.

Students started attending a single integrated system that fall. While the governance of the public school system in Newfoundland has undergone significant changes since then (Galway 2014), the imposition of a single public system did not create significant opposition (Interview with Steven Wolinetz, 5 December 2016). There remain a few private religious schools (Interview with Greg O'Leary, 6 December 2016) and a small public francophone board. But, overwhelmingly, Newfoundlanders seem to have been satisfied with the change (Interview with Roger Grimes, 12 December 2016) and there seems to be little appetite for government support to be extended to the private schools. In part, this seems to have been because of the overwhelming pressures placed on the stem. In part, it was because – by and large – students found themselves in the same schools with the same teachers come September. And, for those concerned with the place of religion in schools, a very careful and inclusive process of designing a new religious education program was rolled out (Interview with Bryce Hodder, 9 December 2016).

Conclusion

In all four Atlantic provinces, we see systems where the debate over government support of religious and independent schools has very much stayed focused on religious questions and understood as regimes of faith. While there were debates around rights with reference to francophone schools in New Brunswick and the rights of children to a good education was an important aspect of the 1968 Warren Commission's investigation of Newfoundland education, debates over rights did not replace religion as the primary feature of the educational regime. Similarly, there has only been the most muted discussion of choice in Atlantic Canada. Only in Newfoundland, where some policymakers saw the possibility of school choice in St. John's in the 1990s, was there any chance of a choice regime. Today, religious schools (and religious homeschoolers) are entirely private throughout the region. In this, Atlantic Canada is similar to Ontario, where the regime has been dominated by faith rather than rights or choice features.

The Maritime regime has been stable since the late nineteenth century, when Section 93 of the constitution was enacted in such a way that there was no constitutional right to government support for minority religious education because separate schools did not formally exist there. Until the 1960s, the public system allowed de facto accommodation of minority Catholic schools. These schools disappeared through amalgamation in the 1960s, seemingly without much political controversy (perhaps because of the emergence of francophone rights as the minority rights people would mobilize to protect). But this, combined with the gradual drift away from religious content in public schools throughout the twentieth century and the conversion of informal separate system as schools were amalgamated, resulted in a single secular public system in all the provinces through a process of incremental change.

Newfoundland and Labrador's contemporary education regime has been much more contentious, but the post-1997 settlement seems to have been stable for reasons akin to the sources of stability in the other Atlantic Canadian provinces. Religious identity was much more deeply entrenched in Newfoundland's educational regime when the province entered Confederation in 1949. As we have seen, it took a powerful set of exogenous shocks to create a policy window large enough for change to be forced through in the 1990s – change which had first been mooted in the late 1960s but which was too politically fraught then to be achieved. This big, formal change, driven by a series of exogenous shocks and promoted by powerful policy entrepreneurs, resulted in a sudden break with pre-existing practice when the system did change. Newfoundland, like Quebec, shows that even constitutional entrenchment is not a forever-fixed institutional anchor if pressures for change are strong enough.

4 Contention over Faith, the Shock of Rights, and Layered Choice in Manitoba

Introduction

Since the early 1990s, the funding and regulatory regime for independent schools in Manitoba has been similar to that of British Columbia and to post-1997 Quebec. It is also similar to the government support offered to independent schools in Alberta and Saskatchewan, though Manitoba does not have the fully funded separate system of those provinces nor the fine gradations in types of independent school. Instead, there is government support at 50 per cent of the operating grant for public schools provided to independent schools that teach a curriculum deemed equivalent to that in public schools and that agree to various reporting and transparency requirements. This funded independent-school sector includes a sizeable Roman Catholic system, schools of other faith groups (most notably, Mennonites and Jews), and various secular independent schools of both the alternative and prep school varieties. Additionally, there is a small group of non-funded independent schools, which are mostly religious and which turn down government support to avoid inspection and curricular requirements. This has been a politically stable compromise – while there have been recent disputes around LGBTQ rights and anti-bullying legislation, the fundamental architecture of the regime has not been the subject of much controversy since its introduction in the late 1980s. Today, 7.0 per cent of Manitoba students attend an independent school (Fraser Institute 2022).

However, the path by which Manitoba has arrived at this regime has been anything but smooth. Indeed, debates over religious and independent schools in Manitoba have been complicated, politically explosive, and nationally important in a way those of no other province have been. For a century after the province's entry into Confederation in 1870, Manitoba's education system was a crucible for debates about how to manage three critical (and mutually reinforcing) divides in Canadian life: that between settler and Indigenous communities, that between English and French speakers, and that between Catholics and Protestants. How schools should be governed and what they ought to teach were the critical issues in these debates and, until the 1960s, the English-speaking Protestant majority won battles to structure the school system in a way that it believed would make schools useful tools for assimilating non-Anglo-Saxon immigrants, francophone Manitobans, and status Indians and Métis. Religious identity and linguistic identity were closely intertwined during the nineteenth and first half of the twentieth centuries in Manitoba politics, with religious identity probably being more important as the Roman Catholic Church provided an institutional locus for the mobilization of the French/Catholic/Métis minority between 1870 and the Second World War (Crunican 1974, Lupul 1974). The connection between the Church and francophone Manitobans weakened after the Second World War, with the francophone community developing institutions and a lobbying strategy that emphasized language rather than religion (Behiels 2004, Hébert 2004). Similarly – though with less effect on education politics – the Métis community began to emphasize the ethnic or religious components of its identity, rather than linguistic or religious components, in the 1970s.

Those mobilizing for francophone schools, and eventually for the self-government of those schools, chose arguments based in constitutional rights. This strategy met with significant success in the 1980s and early 1990s through a combination of political and judicial tools and resulted in a significant rights aspect of Manitoba's overall educational regime. Though they considered rights claims as a possible model for their own lobbying, Catholics in the mid-1980s made a different choice. Working from an argument that had first been advanced in Manitoba in the 1959 Royal Commission on Education (the MacFarlane Commission) rather than returning to the Manitoba Schools Crisis and advancing rights arguments based on nineteenth century School Acts, they formed an alliance with other religious groups and existing (non-religious) independent schools to lobby using choice arguments. Made during the policy window opened up by court victories won by the province's francophone minorities, these choice arguments proved successful. This arrangement has remained more or less stable since the early 1990s.

We must recognize that the identities of policy entrepreneurs and the nature of the arguments they advance are much blurrier and more overlapping in Manitoba than in the other jurisdictions we examine in this book. With this caveat, there is evidence of the faith, rights, choice evolution at play in Manitoba that we find in other provinces even if the divides between the periods are not as clear. The development of the Manitoba regime of government support and regulation of religious and independent schools is deeply immersed in the province's own history and its diverse society. But, the Manitoba experience with religious and independent schools has both influenced and been influenced by other provinces. The 1870–96 school system was closely modelled on that of Quebec, while the English-speaking Protestants who overturned that system in the 1890s looked to Ontario for inspiration (Cook 1969; Morton 1969). The resulting political conflict – often referred to as the Manitoba Schools Crisis – was a powerful impetus for Alberta and Saskatchewan to have constitutionally entrenched, separate school systems when they became provinces in 1905. More recently, francophone mobilization from the 1960s forward was deeply influenced by events in Quebec and Ontario and the independent school sector has tended to look at the British Columbia system as a model.

Faith

In the provinces east of Manitoba, the extension of public schooling was carried out by pre-existing colonial governments. While what schooling looked like and the number of people involved changed throughout the nineteenth century in Eastern Canada, the identity of the state providing education was reasonably clear. In Alberta and Saskatchewan, although schools run by religious communities predated provincial governments, those governments were set up in a way that gave significant thought to how schools ought to be structured and operated as part of the foundation of the province. In British Columbia, the development of schooling and the development of the provincial government also overlapped,

Table 4.1. Key Dates in the Evolution of Manitoba's Education System

Date	Event
1869–70	Red River Resistance/Canada acquires Rupert's Land
1870	Manitoba Act
1890	Greenway government's Public Schools Act begins Manitoba Schools Crisis
1896	Greenway-Laurier compromise
1916	Public Schools made English-only
1959	MacFarlane Report
1965	Shared services introduced
1967	Francophone instruction allowed for half of school day
1980	Partial funding of independent schools introduced
1990	Letter of Comfort raises funding to current levels

but the early politics of education in British Columbia was considerably simpler and less contentious than that in Manitoba. At Confederation in 1867, what is now Manitoba was (as far as the Canadian and British governments were concerned) under the jurisdiction of the Hudson's Bay Company. There were schools, supported by churches, at various points in the territory but nothing that resembled either the local governments or extensive school networks of Eastern Canada. Outside the Red River colony, some small settlements around trading posts, and a few mission schools, education took place in traditional contexts just as governance took place within traditional settings such as the Métis hunts and parishes or First Nations. The acquisition of the North-West Territories by Canada in 1870 created deep divisions within the Red River population, divisions which rapidly came to be mirrored in Canada nationally. On one side were the francophone and Catholic Métis settlers of the colony, led by Louis Riel and supported by the Catholic Church and the Quebec government, who sought guarantees of bilingualism in the new province, recognition of traditional Métis land title, support for Catholic schools, and other minority protections. On the other side were Protestant settlers, mostly from Ontario, supported by the federal government, the newly appointed governor, and Ontario's provincial government seeking to establish the foundation of a more homogeneous government without minority protections.

Importantly for the future development of education, the Manitoba Act passed by the federal Parliament in 1870 did respond to some Métis concerns: it established a bilingual provincial government, protected public funding for Catholic separate schools (though it did not explicitly say that those schools would teach in French), and situated the federal government as the guarantor of schools already operating at the time (Buckingham 2014). It established a single Board of Education over dual Catholic and Protestant sections with power over moral and religious education. Teaching was conducted in either French or English, depending on the community. Given that French Catholics and English Protestants tended to live in different geographic regions, the two school systems had relatively little duplication. This governance system was modelled on the Quebec system of the day and seemed suited to a province with roughly equal numbers of (mostly anglophone) Protestants and (mostly francophone) Catholics. With the act being amended every year between 1873 and 1890, education became an almost constant political irritant in the new province. The political equilibrium that had underpinned the initial structure eroded as immigration from Ontario tipped the balance towards the anglophone Protestant side and internal changes within both communities made them less amenable to compromise (Morton 1969; Sissons 1959, 176). The protections for Catholic education enacted in the 1871 Act were removed by the Liberal government of Thomas Greenway in its Public Schools Act of 1890, when the government stopped public money from going to separate schools and required all ratepayers to pay public school taxes even if their children attended a separate school. This act also abolished Roman Catholic school districts and prohibited religious instruction and observance during school hours. Combined with legislation passed the following day that made the Manitoba government an English-only institution, it is difficult to understate the size of the political firestorm that the Greenway government created. This firestorm came to be known as the Manitoba Schools Crisis and was a central part of national politics from 1890 until 1912. It had important implications for how the Laurier government handled the establishment of Saskatchewan and Alberta as provinces in 1905 and overlapped with debates around francophone education in Ontario and about the power of the provincial governments more generally. It also remains the only Canadian political crisis of sufficient international interest to have triggered a papal encyclical, 1897's *Affari Vos*, which called for Catholic children to be given Catholic religious instruction. Though the political crisis was most focused on francophone issues, it also concerned the province's Jewish, German, Ukrainian, Mennonite, and Icelandic minorities and their right to instruct children in their own faiths and languages.

The federal government could have intervened directly in the case to disallow the Manitoba legislation, but neither the Conservative government (before 1896) nor the Liberal government (after) was willing to use that federal power of disallowance. Instead, the question was worked out judicially before the Supreme Court and Judicial Committee of the Privy Council (JCPC) and in electoral politics. In *Barrett* (1892), the JCPC "ruled that no protected right or privilege had been impaired as the Roman Catholic minority was free to maintain its own separate schools and so upheld the bylaw that required local taxation be collected for the benefit of public schools only." This decision was then appealed to the federal governor general under Section 22(2) of the Manitoba Act, an appeal challenged in *Brophy v. Manitoba*. Although the JCPC found that the appeal was justified and the Governor General in Council issued a remedial order calling for a return to the 1871 status quo, this order was ignored by the Manitoba government. In the absence of federal legislation to enforce 1871, there the matter sat until 1896 (Buckingham 2014, 40).

The issue was critical to the 1896 federal election, which saw the Liberal Party, led by Wilfrid Laurier, defeat the Conservatives, led by

Charles Tupper. Tupper had dissolved Parliament and triggered an election after his attempt to pass remedial legislation on the Manitoba schools issue had been filibustered. Though Catholic, with a strong base in Quebec, and under considerable pressure from the Roman Catholic hierarchy to intervene directly, Laurier refused to use the direct powers of the federal government to return Manitoba to the 1871 situation (Crunican 1974). Instead, his federal government and the provincial government of Thomas Greenway worked out a compromise in 1896. Under this arrangement, religious instruction was permitted during the last half hour of every school day and a Catholic teacher could be requested for every twenty-five Catholic pupils in rural schools or forty pupils in urban schools under the overarching aegis of a single public system. The compromise also allowed for instruction in languages other than English where numbers warranted (an invitation also taken up by Ukrainian, Icelandic, and Mennonite communities).

The bilingualism guarantee was removed in 1916 when, officially, instruction became English only, with the exception of some elementary schools in which an hour of French instruction a day was allowed (Sissons 1959). The 1916 changes in Manitoba shared much of their politics with Bill 17's contemporary enforcement of English-only instruction in Ontario but were also motivated by the perceived need to assimilate the large numbers of Eastern European immigrants that arrived in the province after 1896. The fear of the provincial government and the (now dominant) anglophone community was that the education would be splintered across a number of linguistic communities, preventing minority integration into Canadian life. At a time of sharp class conflict in Winnipeg, there were also fears that a failure to ensure integration would create room for a Communist movement. Importantly, these changes were never fully implemented with regards to the francophone community. While, officially, schools in French language districts operated only in English, in fact a system of informal accommodation grew up: most teachers in these districts were Catholics (often nuns or members of religious communities), and school inspectors turned a blind eye to the fact that almost all teaching was done in French (Behiels 2004; Russell 2003). This regulatory accommodation (Manitoba 1959) was somewhat similar to that of the Maritime provinces and seems to have been enough to ensure peace between the Catholic Church and francophone community, on the one hand, and the Manitoba government, on the other, for the following half century.

The Mennonite minority, especially that part of it that operated German-language schools, was less fortunate in the post-1916 period. A pacifist religious community, Mennonites had settled in Manitoba in 1873 partly because the federal government had promised them freedom from conscription and the right to run their own (privately funded) German-language schools. By 1919 – as a part of its move against bilingual education generally – the provincial government had forced these schools to close. In *R. v. Hildebrand* the Manitoba Court of Appeal found the federal government's 1873 guarantees *ultra vires* (beyond its legal authority) (Buckingham 2014), allowing the province to move forward. Many Mennonites left Manitoba, some for Saskatchewan (which was implementing English-only policies of its own) and some for South America. While not as politically critical as questions around francophone and Catholic education, the Mennonite experience did create a sizeable non-Catholic constituency for government support of independent schools of a sort missing in most other provinces at the time. It remains an important historical marker for the independent school community in Manitoba today.

Viewed theoretically, what we see for the first forty years of Manitoba's existence is a permanently open policy window with no settled consensus developing. Actors at both levels of government, the judiciary, and in what we would now call social movements were at odds with each other – in the absence of an entrenched bill of rights or a desire to observe the provisions of the initial education act – and stability on any other basis than the exercise of provincial power was impossible. The set of alternatives available (essentially, a single public system with some adjustment around the edges or an Ontario style separate system) provided little incentive for either side to compromise. Only political exhaustion and the intervention of the federal government allowed for an uneasy peace to be established in 1916.

By the 1920s, political controversy over religion and language in Manitoba seemed to have largely burnt itself out. While francophones and Catholics were unhappy with the compromise, they seem to have worked within the public system in rural areas through de facto francophone or Catholic schools and, in Winnipeg and other major centres, established a sizeable system of private Catholic parochial schools. Other religious communities, in particular Mennonites and Jews, established their own networks of private schools where and when they could afford them. The federal government had largely been pushed out of education governance. Religion and linguistic identity, for both minority and majority groups, were strongly linked. Both the Liberal and Conservative parties, then controlled by the anglophone elite, ensured that public support went only to a single public system at least partly on the argument that this "melting pot" model would ensure integration in a diverse provincial society. This also marked the end of political contention in a faith frame and the establishment of a relatively stable – albeit overwhelmingly Protestant and English – regime incorporating the political outcome of those struggles.

Rights and Language

This compromise – unofficial and local accommodations for linguistic and religious minorities set in an officially uniform public system supplemented by a sizeable network of private schools – was politically stable through to the late 1950s. The linkage of minority identity and school governance as a political issue in Manitoba occurred as part of the larger Canadian debate over bilingualism and multiculturalism. It was weighted with the religious background of the Manitoba Schools Crisis, and was followed by heated debates in the 1950s over the nature of mass education in the province (Buri 2016). Prompted by the Royal Commission on Education (the MacFarlane Report) of 1959, Duff Roblin's Progressive Conservative government (1958–67) moved to address both the issues of francophone education and school governance and public support for religious and independent schools through incremental changes. The (ultimately) successful challenge to this incrementalism by Franco-Manitobans and Catholic Manitobans (who made up the bulk of the private school community at the time) was grounded in a set of claims to rights that these overlapping communities saw as guaranteed by the 1890 remedial order. But, the two communities pursued different strategies for gaining self-governing schools (for francophones) and government support for independent schools (Catholics, in alliance with other religious groups and existing independent schools). Across both Conservative and NDP governments, these two groups had some traction with both politicians and public servants. However, francophones and the religious/independent school community chose to emphasize rights and choice differently and, as a result, pursued a different mix of litigation and politics. Francophone Manitobans emphasized their constitutional rights and, especially after the introduction of the Charter of Rights and Freedoms in 1982, pursued a strategy of litigation to defend those rights. The religious and independent school community, although it investigated launching litigation in pursuit of rights occasionally, emphasized choice arguments more and pursued political more often than legal action. At some junctures the independent/private school community benefited from the legal openings created by francophone activity. For the sake of clarity, we will first present the evolution of francophone self-governing schools and then that of the religious/independent school group as they pursued self-governing schools and government support.

The Progressive Conservative government of Duff Roblin (1958–67) saw reform of education as "the priority" when it came into office (Roblin 1999, 113). Though the preceding Campbell government had initiated a Royal Commission into education, which reported in 1959, it had otherwise allowed no change in the sector. Roblin, pursuing a fairly broad plan of modernization of Manitoba's government, did move on many of the Royal Commission's recommendations (though not its recommendation to fund independent schools) and, in 1962, promised to reintroduce French into all elementary schools. In 1967 the government amended the Public School Act to allow French instruction for 50 per cent of the day in some schools (Roblin 1999). This was followed by measures passed by the Schreyer NDP government in 1970 that authorized instruction entirely in French in some public schools. Over the course of the 1970s though, the francophone community came to hold the position that francophone education was not simply a matter of classes within regular schools, governed by public boards, being taught in French. Instead, it was important that francophone schools be self-governing and significantly autonomous so that they could serve their full role as community centres (Behiels 2004).

This was a broader question than just what education for francophone Manitobans ought to look like: it was debated concurrently with the question of whether all of Manitoba's laws back to 1885 were invalid because they had been passed only in English and how bilingual Manitoba government services needed to be. And, of course, all this played out against the background of national constitutional debates about the place of French and English in Canada (Doern 1985; Hébert 2004; Russell 2003). These questions were worked out through a complicated interplay of social movement activity, partisan politics, constitutional litigation, federal-provincial negotiations, and municipal politics, and – ultimately – the Supreme Court decision in *Reference re Manitoba Language Rights* in 1985. Once implemented, the principles of this decision gave both languages official status in the legislature and the judiciary, caused legislation that had originally been passed only in English to be translated, and provided provincial government services in French where the community was large enough.

With more specific reference to francophone schools, the question at issue was how far the rights of self-government based on Section 23 of the Manitoba Act would go and, after 1982, what the linguistic protections amounted to. Was education in French enough – as governments in the 1960s and 1970s had argued – or was it necessary for francophone schools to be autonomous and self-governing? Ultimately, it was the *Mahe* case (1990) that forced the provincial government to create francophone schools "where numbers warrant" (Behiels 2004). The Filmon PC government – more amenable to francophone claims than the Lyons PCs and less divided over the issue than the Pauley NDP – responded by creating a task force on francophone school governance (the Gallant Taskforce). The implementation process of the task force's recommendations was messy, with francophone organizations and the provincial government once again requiring a Supreme Court decision in a reference case to resolve their differences. But, the result was a single province-wide French-language school district that provided self-governing public schools to the francophone minority in Manitoba that began operations in 1994.

Independent Schools and Choice

In contrast to the high constitutional politics and the appeal to rights by the francophone community, the process by which independent schools (many of which were religious) received government support in Manitoba was defined by incremental change and policy layering. Though legal considerations and rights claims were an important part of these changes, political lobbying was the major avenue that independent schools pursued. More than in other provinces, it was an appeal that received favourable attention from all three major parties after it emerged with the 1959 *Report of the Manitoba Royal Commission on Education*, usually known as the MacFarlane Report. This report took care to examine the status of what it referred to as "private and parochial schools" where the "vast majority" were attending these schools because of the religious beliefs of their parents (175). The 9292 students who attended these schools in 1958 were exempt from attendance at public schools, provided that their school held an inspector's certificate stating that "the private school affords an education equal to the standard of the public schools in the province" (175). Recognizing the financial burden on families who sent their students to these schools while still paying public school property taxes, the commission reviewed the politically divisive history of the question and determined that it had received roughly equal numbers of submissions on both sides of the issue. It found that, in rural areas that were predominantly Catholic, Mennonite, or Hutterite, administrative mechanisms had been used to render the public schools "reasonably satisfactory" to the religious concerns of the community (178). As in the Maritimes, public schools in Catholic areas often hired Catholic sisters as teachers and were open to religious practices during the school day. In other areas, where these minorities were present in only very small numbers, the pragmatics of school size and financing meant that no accommodation could be achieved. The challenge was in those areas where minorities were size-able but the population diverse enough that the public schools could not be rendered de facto Catholic (or Hutterite or Mennonite). Such areas obviously included Winnipeg. As the commission saw it, the challenge was to "provide some measure of public support for private and parochial schools without injuring the public school system" (179). Full public support of separate schools was not recommended and, in fact, had not been requested by the communities themselves. Instead, the commission looked to the system of alternative (government sup-ported) schools in the United Kingdom to suggest partial support. It argued that such support was fiscally fair and prudent, in accordance with parental choice, and of benefit to social cohesion. To protect their independence, the commission recommended "no more regulation of these schools than is necessary to ensure that the education afforded in them is up to the general standard of the public schools" (180).

The commission made twenty-two specific recommendations con-cerning how to achieve these goals. The most important was that each school be required to incorporate and operate as a Private School Cor-poration within a single school district and be subject to that district's school inspector. There would be a "Private Schools Grant Commis-sion," composed of the Chancellor of the University of Manitoba, the Chairman of the Public Utilities Board, and a Justice of the Superior Court (one of whom would be a Catholic and one of whom would be a Protestant). This commission would pay a grant equivalent to 80 per cent of the provincial grant to public schools, the product of the general levy, and the provincial contribution to teachers' benefits proportional to the teaching carried out by these schools. Schools would have to provide to teachers "benefits which are, though not necessarily identi-cal, consistent with the benefits provided Public School teachers" (184). Finally, schools operating under these regulations would be eligible for "all educational aids and services, such as travelling libraries, etc. pro-vided by the Province to public schools" (184).

Coming at a time when Ontario, Saskatchewan, and Alberta did not yet fund separate high schools, this was a comparatively generous package, especially given the pressures that the post-war baby boom was already placing on the Manitoba education system and the politi-cal controversy at play over what Manitoba public education ought to be (Buri 2016). Though initially well received, the Roblin government chose not to act on the report's recommendations despite its election promise to abide by them (Stapleton and Long 1999). In Roblin's own accounting of his decision:

it was clear that even after seventy years, the Manitoba Schools Question was not entirely dead. The old shibboleths appeared. To accept the report as it was threatened to revive old animosities. This was deeply troubling. We cast around for some time to devise a policy to grapple with this issue. The separate school supporters, mostly Roman Catholics, felt their position was vindicated, and demanded action. Other forces, including some within my own caucus, felt otherwise. I concluded that direct action was not possible, but something had to be done. Our solution was to institute a system of shared services ... The plan had two great disadvantages. Public school supporters would be dismayed, fearing the gradual dismantlement of their system, and separate school supporters would feel prevented from achieving their expectations ... In any case, from a political point of view, we were pressing against the limits of our power ... Even so, within the government, this proposition was not a done deal. Caucus was distinctly uneasy, if not hostile to the proposal.

(Roblin 1999, 118–19)

Although public reaction to the change was "fierce" (Roblin 1999, 119), behind-the-scenes work in the legislature meant that the bulk of all three parties supported the proposal. What the Roblin government did introduce, in a 1965 amendment to the Education Act, was legislation that provided for publicly funded "shared services" to students attending private and parochial schools, subject to specific agreements between public school boards and private schools. These services included free textbooks, bus transportation, instructional services, and ancillary services – provided those services were physically provided to private school students in public school. This package was sufficiently attractive to the Catholic community that it stopped its efforts to petition the federal government to enforce the Remedial order of 1895, but it did not take the energy out of the Manitoba Association for Equality in Education (MAEE) (the broad lobby group that had been formed representing religious and independent schools). These shared service agreements tended to be awkward to administer and continually introduced episodic and localized tensions between public school boards and the private and parochial school community.

These localized tensions fuelled the efforts of the MAEE to expand the organization's membership beyond the Catholic community and to expand its set of policy arguments beyond the 1890 remedial legislation. This strategy accelerated after Joseph Stangl became president of the organization in 1968. Stangl's involvement in education, and particularly his work securing funding for Manitoba's independent schools, is very nearly a case study in policy entrepreneurship. A politically well-connected retired businessman and devout Catholic, Stangl's goal was to build a coalition that would advance Catholic claims to government support for Catholic schools in Manitoba in a way that would also gain public support for the schools of other faith communities. He rejected the fully funded separate model of Saskatchewan, on the grounds that it did not encourage sufficient parental involvement and commitment to schools. A sometime Liberal candidate, Stangl asked Catholics to support the Progressive Conservatives in the 1982 election because he believed that it was the Conservatives who were more likely to extend funding to separate schools. Despite his commitment to independent schools, he also served as a public school trustee and as president of the Manitoba Association of School Trustees. He was, in short, something of a master at building unlikely coalitions and finding unlikely partnerships (Stangl 2002; Stapleton and Long 1999) who one source described as the "spearhead of it all" (Interview with Susan Wilkeem, 24 August 2015).

Stangl's talent for coalition-building was particularly useful when the Roblin government was defeated by the NDP government of Ed Schreyer in 1968. Schreyer was known to look favourably on the idea of funding parochial and private schools. In the summer of 1970, the legislature passed a resolution 36–15 asking the government to "consider the advisability of granting financial assistance for the cost of instruction provided by qualified teachers in all educational institutions of the Province of Manitoba that offer a curriculum approved by the Department of Education" (Stapleton and Long 1999, 316). However, Schreyer's caucus was evenly divided on the issue and, despite concerted lobbying by the MAEE, the NDP simply delayed on the issue through the 1973 election and then throughout its second term until it was defeated by Sterling Lyon's Progressive Conservatives in 1977.

It was the Lyon government that introduced direct grants to private schools in 1980, a move supported by the Manitoba Association of School Trustees, the Manitoba Association of School Superintendents, and the Association of Secretary Treasurers. Support from these outside groups was motivated by their dissatisfaction with the difficulties of administering the shared service agreements. The funding model put in place by the Lyon government was initially satisfactory to the independent school community: the grant private schools received was 34.5 per cent of the provincial operating grant to public schools, which covered 16.9 per cent of the average cost in public schools. But by 1984 this coverage had fallen to 19 per cent and 14.3 per cent, respectively (Stapleton and Long 1999, 318). As some important independent schools were under significant financial pressure, the decline in government contributions created a strong incentive for the Manitoba Federation of Independent Schools (MFIS) to press for the 80 per cent support that the 1959 Royal Commission had called for.

This level of financial support was reinforced by the 1983 review of education finance in Manitoba entitled *Enhancing Equity in Manitoba Schools*. Written by Glenn Nicholls, Assistant Deputy minister of education, this report examined all aspects of education funding in Manitoba but focused almost exclusively on public schools and, especially, on the challenges facing small schools and small school boards. It did, in passing, mention the voucher system as a possible model for school finance (Education Finance Review Commission 1983, 31) and spent some time considering the 80 per cent support that the MFIS had asked for. Accepting that a policy decision had been made to support independent schools, the review concerned itself with the questions of how much and on what basis while referring to the following considerations:

a) Private schools in all provinces except Manitoba and British Columbia do not include separate (largely Roman Catholic) schools.
b) In British Columbia, independent school grants are based on 30 per cent of public school division costs. In 1982, this amounted to approximately $800 per pupil.
c) In Saskatchewan, for the first time, the average per-pupil grant received by public and separate schools in 1983 will be applied to independent schools.
d) The Alberta Government has just announced a full-scale review of aid to private schools. In 1982, the grant paid to independent schools was based on 75 per cent of the School Foundation Fund grant paid to public schools.
e) In 1983 in Manitoba, the 1982 grant to private schools of $435 per pupil was increased by the Consumers' Price Index of 10.2 to $480.
f) To be eligible for the current grant, Manitoba's private schools must hire qualified teachers and must provide the Manitoba program of studies. A private school liaison officer of the department of education must attest to the private school's eligibility for grants.
(Education Finance Review Commission 1983, 127)

The review recommended funding independent schools at the 80 per cent level on the basis of the block grant and the curriculum provided to public school divisions. Other forms of support or cooperation, such as student transportation or clinician services, would have to be worked out between schools and districts along the lines of shared service agreements.

The MFIS also hoped that the repatriation of the Canadian Constitution in 1982 would give it a stronger rights-based argument with which to advance its cause. The MFIS commissioned a legal opinion but was disappointed to discover that the new Constitution did not give independent schools a right to funding. However, the review did find that the Remedial Order of 1895 provided Catholic schools in Manitoba with a strong legal basis to argue for government funding for Catholic schools. This provided a legal "stick" that the independent school sector could use to threaten the government and offered it the opportunity to pursue a litigation-based strategy like the one the Franco-Manitoban community was pursuing at the time. And, in June 1986, the Catholic Trustees Association did file a petition with the governor general asking the federal government to pass legislation returning Manitoba to the pre-1890 situation. But this was part of a broader strategy, one that had as its goal government support for all independent schools in Manitoba, not just Catholic parochial schools. Stangl had been influential in arguing for this broad strategy and pointed to the success of the British Columbia Federation of Independent Schools (Interview with John Stapleton, 28 July 2015). In pursuit of this support, MFIS lobbied the government throughout the mid-1980s.

By 1987, this strategy had worked to some extent: the NDP government agreed to a one-time increase in public support and declared an "intention to move towards funding independent schools at 50 per cent of the grant provided to public schools" (Stapleton and Long 1999, 321). This commitment from the NDP was weaker, though, than what either the Progressive Conservatives or the Liberals were willing to offer independent schools. Both of these parties (led by Sharon Carstairs and Gary Filmon, respectively) made commitments to increase funding to the level recommended by the 1959 Commission (80 per cent of the average provincial grant or approximately 50 per cent of the average cost in public schools). Both parties also committed to cooperating with the federal government in a reference case to the Supreme Court on the Remedial Order Petition if the government and independent schools were unable to come to an agreement about appropriate levels of funding.

In any event, the Filmon Tories won the spring 1988 election, and their government implemented the contemporary system of funding and regulation of independent and private schools in Manitoba that is still in operation. Initially, this took the form of an increase to the grant to bring it up to the level of 40 per cent of the provincial grant for public schools. Over the next two years, the MFIS, government, and Manitoba Catholic School Trustees association negotiated the terms of a more permanent arrangement. This "Letter of Comfort," as it was called, was signed in June 1990. In exchange for withdrawing the Catholic petition to the federal government, it included a plan to increase the operating grant to all independent schools in the province to 80 per cent of the public level by 1997–8. This grant came with more stringent requirements on curriculum, financial accountability, governance, and student assessment than had previously been the case. It also clarified that grants could not be claimed for non-resident students and that new independent schools would have to operate without government assistance for three years before being eligible for government funding (Stapleton and Long 1999, 323). In 1994, this agreement was changed by mutual agreement so that rather than being 80 per cent of the provincial grant to public schools, the grant was defined as 50 per cent of the average expenditure per student.

This has proven to be a durable political compromise. Although the NDP, which might have been expected to oppose public money going to private schools, was in government from 1999 to 2016, there was no provincial level controversy over government funding for independent schools until controversies over LGBTQ status in schools and anti-bullying clubs broke out in 2012. Some interviews suggested that there had been minor tension when the party first came to power, but it was a relationship that improved as both sides worked on it (Interview with Lawrence Hamm, 26 August 2015; Interview with John Weins, 24 August 2015). The Ministry of Education, which supervised both funded and non-funded independent schools, had a reasonably good relationship with MFIS and with the schools that it supervised (Interview with E, 25 August 2015). This generally positive relationship at the provincial level between independent schools and the government was and is important, for it offset clear competition between public and independent schools at the local level and a sense of tension between some public trustees and their local independent school (Interview with John Weins, 24 August 2015).

Research interviews conducted in the summer of 2015 suggest that these positive relationships were important to maintaining the status quo arrangement through the controversy triggered by the NDP government's introduction of Bill 18, The Public Schools Amendment Act (Safe and Inclusive Schools) late in 2012 (the bill received Royal Assent in September 2013) (Interview with Robert Praznick, 25 August 2015). The bill defined bullying, including on social media or in other electronic forms, and required school boards to establish a human diversity

policy that would support students "who want to establish organizations or events on issues of gender equality, racism, disability, sexual
orientation and gender identities, and allow the creation of groups consistent with 'Gay-Straight Alliance'" (Kinahan et al. 2014, 189). It would
apply both to public schools and to funded independent schools. Both
the Progressive Conservative opposition and the MFIS opposed the
bill on the grounds that it infringed on religious freedom and that it
defined bullying in an overly broad manner (Evangelical Fellowship of
Canada 2013; Kinahan et al. 2014), but outspoken opposition was very
localized to the heavily Mennonite town of Steinbach. This issue was a
challenge for MFIS. It put the Federation at odds with the government
and created the risk of internal tensions between members schools that
were defined by a fairly conservative religious identity and others that
embraced a progressive religious identity or were secular. But these
dangers seem to have been mostly avoided. Since the bill's passage, it
seems that the independent school sector has had little difficulty com-
plying with its requirements, perhaps because non-funded independent schools (which tend to be the most religiously conservative and so
most likely to oppose it) were not subject to its requirements.

Conclusion

Manitoba's educational system has arrived at choice as a regime of supporting and regulating independent and religious schools very similar
to (and heavily influenced by) British Columbia's and akin to what Quebec would establish in 1997. Though Alberta and Saskatchewan's systems are more complicated and internally diverse, there are also strong
similarities between Manitoba's system and their independent school
systems. The system of partial government funding, combined with
significant government oversight and curricular compliance, has been
politically stable since the mid-1990s in Manitoba. As in British Columbia and Alberta, this system was the product of concerted lobbying by
a broad-based coalition of religious and independent schools successfully focused on choice, not rights or faith. Initially known as MAEE and
later as MFIS, this group was influenced by an important policy entrepreneur, Joseph Stangl, to expand beyond Catholic schools to include
both secular private schools and the schools of other faith communities.
The coordinated lobbying effort, which managed to avoid being tied to
a single political party, was also supported by the strong possibility that
the Catholic part of the independent school coalition had a claim to full
government support should the 1895 Remedial Order, implementing
Section 22 of the 1870 Manitoba Act, be reactivated. These efforts were

clearly helped by the success of the Franco-Manitoban community in winning court cases in pursuit of their similar claims to constitutional rights.

What is overwhelmingly clear in the modern period is that policy change in Manitoba happened incrementally, in a manner where layering was the dominant type of regime change. Shared services led to minimal government subsidies which, in turn, grounded claims from the MFIS for more substantial funding. Though politically controversial, after the 1950s, funding for independent schools did not seem to be an issue that created clear divides between political parties. Rather, it was divisive within parties. And both the 1959 Royal Commission on Education and the report of the review of education finance were supportive of extending government support to independent schools, suggesting that important parts of the educational bureaucracy were also supportive of the idea.

In the minds of all the actors was the historical memory of the politically explosive legacy of the 1890s Manitoba Schools Crisis, when the government of the day moved unilaterally to defund Catholic schools and limit French-language education (which was later ended entirely in legislation). This shock to Manitoba's political system created a national unity crisis and still stands as one of the most significant disruptions in the history of Canadian politics. It is, perhaps, not too surprising that Manitoba governments after the 1920s generally sought to minimize conflict on the education file and to avoid any instance of such dramatic change. The Manitoba Schools Crisis also left a legacy of unsettled constitutional rights that made the nature of arguments somewhat different from that in other provinces, especially those where funding for separate schools had been entrenched at Confederation and respected thereafter (Newfoundland, Quebec, Ontario, Manitoba, and Alberta). Because the constitutional rights of minorities were not observed in Manitoba, rights-based arguments were mixed in with those focused on faith and linguistic identity throughout the post-war period. And, in the 1980s, rights arguments were also mixed together with those that emphasized parental choice – the transition between different styles of arguments. Unlike the francophone community, however, those seeking government support for religious schools preferred to pursue a political path to a "choice" based regime rather than a legal "rights" based regime.

5 British Columbia's Sudden Embrace of a Regime of Rights and Choice

Introduction

Faith-Based Schooling in British Columbia is wholly subsumed under the broader category of Independent Schools, of which there were nearly four hundred operating in the 2019–20 school year, enrolling 13 per cent (88,470 students) of BC's entire student population (British Columbia Ministry of Education 2019a). BC does not have a publicly funded Catholic separate system like Ontario, Saskatchewan, or Alberta, nor are there faith-based "alternative" public schools in the province like those found in Alberta. In fact, the BC School Act insists that its public schools "must be conducted on strictly secular and non-sectarian principles" (School Act [RSBC 1996] c. 412, 76 (1)). As of 2019, there were 187 faith-based independent schools that receive funding from the BC government (British Columbia Ministry of Education 2019b), and it is estimated that between 65–70 per cent of students enrolled in the independent school sector attend faith-based schools (Interview with Peter Froese, 24 June 2015). Of the partially funded faith-based schools, over seventy are Catholic based, representing the largest component of faith-based schools in the province. There are also over fifty Protestant Christian schools in the province in addition to several Seventh-Day Adventist, Jewish, Islamic, and Sikh independent schools successfully operating. In fact, the largest independent school in BC is a Sikh school.

Prior to 1977, independent schools received no funding from the government, although certain concessions were made in the 1950s including tax exemptions and publicly subsidized textbooks and bussing. In 1977, the BC government legally recognized independent schools via the Independent Schools Support Act and offered direct public funding equivalent to either 9 per cent or 30 per cent of the per-student operating grant of local public school boards, depending on the particular school's willingness to meet certain accountability measures, follow the government-approved curriculum, and employ certified teachers. In 1989, public funding was increased to either 35 per cent (Group 2 schools) or 50 per cent (Group 1 schools) of the per-pupil grant provided to public schools. The vast majority of faith-based schools fall within the Group 1 category, although there is also a handful of small faith-based Group 3 schools, primarily Mennonite in orientation, that receive no funding. Total public funding provided to Group 1 and 2 schools amounted to roughly $335 million in 2018–19 (British Columbia Ministry of Education 2019b).

Given the relatively high proportion of students who are enrolled in independent schools in BC, and the high level of public funding Group 1 schools receive relative to levels of public aid found throughout the rest of Canada, it is perhaps no surprise that noted BC historian Jean Barman (1991, 21) has marvelled at the degree to which "non-public schools have come to be perceived as an integral component of [BC's] system of education" in both concrete legislation and general attitude. Indeed, both the BC Social Credit and Liberal parties, who have together largely dominated BC politics going back to the 1930s, have "actively encouraged non-public schooling as an option for British Columbian families," at least since 1977 (Barman 1991, 22; see also Fallon and Paquette 2008).

This is a particularly striking outcome given the fact that, unlike all other provinces in Canada, BC's early education history was significantly shaped by a strong aversion to any form of publicly funded faith-based education. BC's 1872 Free Public Schools Act explicitly stated only non-denominational schools would be funded by the public purse. Although certain pockets of religious British Columbians, most especially BC Catholics, protested fiercely against this stance for several decades, the province stood alone in Canada as a jurisdiction unwilling to offer any financial assistance to faith-based schools for over a century. Essentially since its beginnings, BC has been one of Canada's most secular provinces, and its early approach to education was shaped by a strong preference for a clear separation of church and state. More recently, its governments, largely reacting to pressure from human rights tribunals and the courts, have emerged as one of the country's leaders in advancing LGBTQ rights within their education system. Yet, its independent schools are today some of the better funded in Canada and have further enjoyed a significant degree of autonomy with respect to the issues around sexual orientation recently. What explains this paradox? How does a province that refused to legally recognize, let alone publicly fund, faith-based schools for a century very quickly become one of the leaders in Canada in supporting them?

Table 5.1. Key Dates in the Evolution of British Columbia's Education System

Date	Event
1849	First School in Fort Victoria – A joint venture between the Hudson's Bay Company and the Anglican Church
1860	First non-denominational schools established
1865	BC Catholics begin to lobby for state support for Catholic schools
1865	Act Respecting Common Schools prohibiting sectarian schooling within the common system passes in Colony of Vancouver Island.
1871	British Columbia joins Confederation.
1872	Free Public Schools Act explicitly states only non-denominational schools would be funded by the public purse.
1951	Maillardville School Strike. BC government agrees to subsidize textbooks for independent schools.
1966	Creation of Federation of Independent Schools Associations (FISA) in British Columbia
1977	Independent Schools Support Act introduces partial funding to independent schools.
1988	Royal Commission on Education (Sullivan Commission)
1989	Independent School Act increases public subsidies to independent schools.
2002	Standing Committee on Education calls for more market-driven initiatives in education system.
2006	Corren Agreement signed

This chapter aims to explain this sharp divergence in the policy trajectory of the province's governance of independent education in BC that occurred in 1977. On one hand, this is a story that highlights the power of path dependence both before 1977, wherein the province resisted calls to fund religious schools for over a century, and again after 1989, when the province last made any significant changes to the funding formula for independent schools. Outside of this twelve-year period, very little has changed with respect to the governance of religious schools in BC. On the other hand, understanding the dramatic shift in policy that occurred in 1977 requires grasping both the immediate political context of the time and, more importantly, the broader exogenous factors that placed incremental pressure on the education policy subsystem in post–Second World War BC. These included the growing diversity of the province, the changing mores of the citizenry, and especially the emergence of a key policy entrepreneur whose endorsement of a particular strategy did much to shift the debate over the funding of independent schools in BC from one centred on the appropriateness of the secular state subsidizing religious education to one evaluating the claim that parents ought to have the right to choose the type of education their children receive. It is difficult to overstate how important this transition was in terms of garnering the public and political support required for the introduction of government support for independent schools in 1977.

In successfully altering the terms of the debate in this way, the entire axis of the governance of religious schools in the province transitioned from a regime of "faith" to a regime of "rights" in a way that strongly mirrors the experience of Alberta but is wholly different than that of Ontario. The regime of rights that emerged was rooted in the notion of a parent's "right to choose" spelled out in the United Nations 1948 Declaration of Human Rights, rather than any right rooted in the Constitution of Canada. Inherent in the notion of a parent's "right to choose" as it is understood in BC was always a focus on "choice," which has allowed for an easy transition into the contemporary regime of "choice" that has largely structured the contemporary debate over religious schooling in the province since the early 2000s under both Liberal and NDP governments. Much less visible than in other provinces were rights arguments focused on linguistic minorities or (since there were none) pre-existing guarantees of support to religious groups.

Historical Foundations: Barring Faith from Schools

As Calem and Fleming (1988, 54) note, the early schools of British Columbia "did not distinguish the public from the non-public sector with any great precision." The first school in the province was built by the Hudson's Bay Company (HBC) in Fort Victoria in 1849, and it was soon followed by additional schools for the children of HBC employees. Such schools tended to be run by the Anglican Church but were partially funded by the HBC. Several Catholic schools would emerge in the following years as well, financed by Church authorities and parental fees. By the late 1850s, some schools were even receiving support from the colony, although most were not. The dominant schools at the time were clearly those Anglican-run, British-style institutions serving the upper classes of the Hudson's Bay Company. The discovery of gold in the Fraser River in 1857 altered the trajectory of the region, including attitudes toward schooling. Tens of thousands of new faces flooded into both Fort Victoria and the colony of British Columbia throughout the 1860s from the American frontier and from central and eastern Canada. In both cases, these were groups of predominantly non-Anglican settlers who were immediately at odds with the established "self-contained and self-confident social order centred around the original Hudson's Bay families" (Barman 1986, 245). The new arrivals found articulate leaders in prominent newspaper men Amor de Cosmos and John Robson, who utilized their newly formed publications (the *British Colonist* and the *British Columbian* respectively), to insist on a more democratic society. An important commitment for this group was a common system of non-sectarian education available to all. (Calem and Fleming 1988, 54; Barman 1986, 245–6; Cunningham 2002, 9–13). The central thrust underlying this demand for a common school system was this democratic and class-based opposition to the dominant, Anglican-based upper crust of society. But there was also a desire to avoid the "religious feuds" engrossing the eastern provinces (Van Brummelen 1996, 103), a latent anti-clericalism (McNally 1999, 10), and an American-based belief in the importance of the separation of church and state. Indeed, it was a collection of American settlers motivated by the writings of Horace Mann, a fierce proponent of public, non-sectarian education, who set up the first non-denominational system of common schools in Victoria in 1860. Although financial difficulties would force these schools to close in 1864, the attachment to them by the bulk of Victoria citizens would spark an even louder public outcry for a proper common system going forward (McNally 1999, 76).

A central spokesperson for this common school movement was John Jessop, a devout Methodist schoolteacher who had studied under Egerton Ryerson in Ontario. Working alongside De Cosmos, Jessup held public rallies in support of establishing such a system in BC, rallies that triggered debate in the Legislative Assembly of the colony of British Columbia in 1864. The decisive tipping point seems to have come from the newly appointed governor of the colony, Arthur Kennedy, who, in 1864, made his support known for a non-sectarian system encompassing all children: "Don't you think that in a country like this, where men are thrown much together, it would be better that they should be educated together?" (quoted in Barman 1986, 248). Popular mobilization and the governor's support led to passing of the Act Respecting Common Schools by the Colony of Vancouver Island in 1865, which prohibited sectarian schooling within the common system. The colonies of Vancouver Island and British Columbia were united in 1866 and three years later the combined legislature passed the Common School Ordinance, affirming the existence of a single non-sectarian education system. In 1872, one year after entering Confederation, John Jessup, now BC's first superintendent of schools, ensured passage of the Free Public School Act. This act could not have been clearer on the question of faith-based schooling: "All Public Schools under the provisions of this Act shall be conducted upon strictly non-sectarian-principles. The highest morality shall be inculcated, but no religious dogma or creed shall be taught" (quoted in Manzer 1994, 59–60). The debate throughout the region had been and continued to be wholly centred on the question of the appropriateness of government support for religious education and the answer in the province was unequivocal: "no."

Although BC was the only province to enter Confederation with a system of public education that explicitly forbade denominational schooling in both theory and practice, it would be an exaggeration to suggest religious instruction was prohibited as well. Jessup, a devout Methodist, was not opposed to such instruction and, in fact, the 1872 Act encouraged the use of an opening prayer as well as lessons on the Ten Commandments (Cunningham 2002, 14). Furthermore, Jessup insisted on a province-wide set of textbooks that "all assumed a literal interpretation of the Bible and a belief in orthodox Christian doctrines" (Van Brummelen 1986, 19). In other words, the early "non-sectarian" public schools of BC were, in essence, Protestant Christian based. Similarly, as Calem and Fleming have noted, the 1872 Act did not "question the legitimacy or, for that matter, the desirability of non-public schools" (1988, 54). These factors lend credence to the interpretation of BC Catholic Bishop Remi De Roo, who followed Barman by suggesting that it was opposition to "the Anglican monopoly [over education in BC] that resulted in no funding for independent schools," rather than a broader anti-religious sentiment (Cunningham 2002, 15). By 1877, it was therefore clear that the implicit goal of the series of acts concerning common schooling in BC from 1865–72, had been achieved: all of the Anglican-run schools, now firmly outside of the public system, had collapsed (Van Brummelen 1996, 104).

Catholic-run schools fared better. BC's relatively small Roman Catholic population kept a limited number of Catholic-run schools afloat, although financial difficulties were always present. In response to such difficulties, prominent Catholics did lobby for government support. In 1865, in the heat of the debate over the creation of a non-sectarian common system in Victoria, a pamphlet championing the right of parents to educate their children in the Catholic faith was published in the hopes of achieving the type of publicly funded separate Catholic system found elsewhere in Canada. John Robson, editor of the popular *British Columbian* newspaper, quickly responded by chastising the authors for suggesting their faith was uniquely suited to contribute to the moral improvement of society and thus deserved special treatment (McNally 1999). The position articulated by Robson was essentially the position that emerged victorious in the legislative debates held prior to the colony joining Confederation. This fact ensured that Section 93 of the British North America Act, which protected denominational schools in existence at the time of Union, was irrelevant to British Columbia in

1871: denominational schools did not exist in law, therefore were not owed support from the province.

Nevertheless, throughout the 1870s and early '80s Catholic leaders continued to press for a funded separate system, including several petitions forwarded to the BC Legislative Assembly, but to no avail. In fact, Catholic bishops officially suspended political activity in 1883 (Cunningham 2002). As McNally notes, not only was a clear anti-clericalism present in the debates over public schooling in the 1870s, "by the mid-1880s it was clear to all but the most obtuse that British Columbia was a thoroughly secular society and destined to remain so; organized religion would certainly be tolerated there, but little more could be expected" (McNally 1999, 84). This realization did not, however, suppress the Catholic lobbying of the BC government on the issue for very long, and there were a variety of failed attempts to achieve some level of government support by Catholic school supporters over the next several decades. Such efforts, however, were consistently rebuffed by governments beholden to ongoing financial concerns, a somewhat latent "Gentleman's anti-Catholic sentiment" in the words of a BC education historian (Interview with Thomas Fleming, 14 August 2015), and, above all, a strict adherence to the notion that public money was for public schools, period.

This was a path-dependent situation that created a regime of faith that was embodied by the stark contrast between completely independent religious schools and a funded public system that remained stable throughout the first half of the twentieth century despite intermittent Catholic lobbying. Then, in 1951 an initial crack in the "public money for public schools" position emerged when independent schools were provided textbooks by the BC government at no charge for the first time. Within six years, the government also agreed to pay the costs of dental and health services in Catholic schools, passed legislation meant to enable publicly funded transportation for students attending non-public schools, and agreed to provide municipal tax exceptions to independent schools (Downey 1986, 307–9). These changes foreshadowed the significant shift in policy that occurred in 1977 when the Social Credit (SC) government of Bill Bennett dramatically altered course and offered public funding to non-public schools. The magnitude of this shift was not lost on the government. Education minister Patrick McGeer, the politician most responsible for pushing the legislative change forward, noted that the Independent Schools Support Act would "remove the discrimination which has characterized our approach to the financing of education for the first 105 years of this province's existence" (quoted in Cunningham 2002, 189). How does one make sense of such a sharp turn, abandoning a policy that had been in place for over a century? A quick, and ultimately unsatisfactory answer, would be to simply reply that the SC government had come to realize that public opinion itself had turned on this question (as, in fact, it had). But of course, the real question then becomes why had public opinion shifted? This is a much more complicated question that requires an examination of the changing demographic, social, and political context of the province going back decades.

The Creation of FISA and the Introduction of Public Subsidies: Replacing a Regime of Faith with a Regime Combining Rights and Choice

The political activities of Catholic school supporters ebbed and flowed somewhat but, on the whole, remained aimed at pressuring the government over the issue of "double taxation" for the bulk of the twentieth century. Simply put, Catholic lobbyists complained that Catholic parents were forced to fund the public system via the tax system while simultaneously having to fund their own non-public schools. Adding to their sense of grievance was the fact that public schools were exempt from municipal taxes whereas Catholics schools were not. In the early 1930s, Catholic school supporters were approached by representatives of the Private Schools Association (the body representing elite independent university prep schools), which also faced the issue of double taxation. Hoping that a combined effort to lobby government would prove more successful than past solo efforts, this group was ultimately rebuffed by the Catholics, who preferred at this point to continue their lobbying efforts on their own (Cunningham 2002, 31–2).

A more consequential mobilization began in 1951 when two Catholic schools in the largely francophone community of Maillardville followed through on threats to close their doors in protest, thereby inundating the surrounding public system with an unexpected influx of students. Although this move put a severe strain on the public system, the government refused to change course on the issue of funding for Catholic education and, by the fall of 1952, the two offending schools backed down in defeat and reopened. According to Downey (1986, 310–13), the ploy won the Catholic schools very little sympathy from either the government or the public at large. However, broader factors related to demographics, cultural mores, and even the Catholics willingness to compromise, would shape the debate over public funding for independent schools in unexpected ways over the following two decades.

Central to this story is the post–Second World War population boom in BC in general and the increasing diversity it created in the province.

Between 1941 and 1981, the population of the province tripled. Importantly, the majority of these newcomers were from continental Europe, and many subsequently brought with them a desire to educate their children in schools steeped in their particular culture and religion. Thus, the non-Catholic independent school population increased rapidly as a variety of conservative Protestant, Jewish, Seventh-Day Adventist, Mennonite, and Dutch Calvinist institutions emerged throughout BC. Between 1945 and 1978, 65 new independent schools were created, bringing the total to 180, enrolling around 24,000 students (Fleming 2010, 235). Of these newly arrived groups, none were more important to the movement seeking public aid for independent schools than those from the Dutch Calvinist tradition. Mirroring the events in post–Second World War Alberta, the roughly 20,000 Dutch immigrants brought with them a firm commitment to the type of publicly funded Christian education that existed in their home country (Barman 1991; Van Brummelen 1996). Not only did they work quickly to establish their own independent faith-based schools, they also organized a sector-wide effort to lobby government for funding. This group would soon become the Society of Christian Schools in British Columbia, a driving force behind the eventual creation of the Federation of Independent Schools Association in BC (FISA BC). Indeed, several individuals who would go on to play important leadership roles within FISA during its ultimately successful quest for public funding, including the first executive director Gerry Ensing, were a product of this tradition. Like arguments made by the Dutch Calvinist immigrants in Alberta, the essence of their plea for public funding for independent schools in BC was the notion that in a truly democratic society, a parent's right to send their children to a school of their choice must be protected (Cunningham 2002). Interestingly, in 1951, H.G.T. Perry, a former BC Liberal education minister, expressed solidarity with these concerns in a letter to the editor that placed the growing debate over the funding of independent schools within the broader context of the rights of minority groups (Fleming 2010, 234–7). Although Perry was certainly in the minority at this point in the political class, this style of argument, first introduced in the province by Dutch immigrants, became, and continues to be, the central mantra of the independent school movement in the province.

Led most assertively by the Dutch Calvinists, this new, sizeable non-Catholic pocket of the population that was committed to faith-based schooling outside the public system had the potential to shift the political conversation on public funding in post–Second World War BC. But it was not until the Catholics agreed to work together on this issue that the tide really began to turn. The motivations behind the Catholics' openness to cooperation, which reached its climax with the creation of FISA in 1966, were twofold. First, in the wake of the second Vatican Council in 1962, a newfound emphasis on cooperation and reconciliation between Catholics, Jews, and Protestants emerged worldwide, including in BC. Second, those Catholics most involved in government lobbying efforts shifted their focus from a battle waged upon the principles of religious freedom to one based upon democratic pluralism and minority rights. This Catholic turn is clearly articulated in a key speech made by Bishop Remi Joseph De Roo in Chilliwack in 1963. Outlying his newfound appreciation for an argument the Dutch Calvinists had already been making in the province, De Roo noted:

> The Catholic School question is not a religious issue. I think we Catholics may be largely to blame for our failure, to date, to make this case clear. Even today we will all too frequently hear references to the question of private and parochial schools in terms of "religious war." As long as we allow the question of Catholic schools to be treated as a "religious" or "church" issue, we are doomed to failure ...
>
> I suggest, then, that the solution to the school question is to be found not in the realm of religious issues but rather that it should be considered as a matter of democratic principle – the freedom of parents to educate their children in conformity with their convictions, as long as these convictions are not contrary to the common welfare.
>
> (De Roo 1963, 5)

That Catholics in BC coalesced around a message that emphasized democratic pluralism rather than religious liberty in the fight for public funding represents a key moment in BC's evolution. In the abstract, this shift represents the point wherein the regime of faith that dominated school governance in BC since the mid-nineteenth century gave way to a regime that combined "rights" with "choice" a full generation before choice emerged as important in other provinces. More concretely, for the first time in BC's history, a clear path towards concrete collaboration among disparate independent school groups who sought financial assistance from the state had appeared. The precise events that led to the formation of FISA in 1966 from four different groups representing Catholics, Dutch Calvinists, other faith-based schools, and a collection of secular independents has been thoroughly detailed by Cunningham (2002) and Froese (2010). Most pertinent to this study were the initial decisions made by the newly formed organization around both the tactics utilized and the central message employed while pressuring the government to have independent schools formally recognized in law and appropriately funded by the state.

The central message espoused by FISA in its early years was encapsulated in their first brief presented to BC's Social Credit government in 1967. FISA opened the brief by noting that, by educating nearly 26,000 students, the independent school sector was saving the government over $11 million annually based on the per-pupil cost of public schooling, in addition to over $27 million in capital costs. Yet, these schools were without status in law and the vast majority were in imminent danger of closing due to financial pressures. Building from the UN's Declaration of Human Rights statement regarding the child's right to an education and the parent's right to choose the kind of education, FISA demanded immediate legal recognition as well as funding equivalent to that provided to public schools. This request was supplemented by philosophical arguments that paralleled those first made by Dutch Calvinist immigrants in the 1950s and that were later adopted by Catholic officials in the 1960s: it would form the foundation of FISA's position going forward. The key arguments revolved around parental rights, democratic pluralism, and the benefits of competition within the education sector:

> It is the right and duty of the parents to choose the kind of education which will transmit their own values and standards to their children ... [b]ut a choice becomes impossible unless financial support is available ...
>
> A multiplicity of philosophies in education exist in democratic societies ... the government must refrain from subsidizing a single system which inevitably promotes a single outlook ... Democratic systems, on the other hand, must foster effective pluralism ...
>
> [H]ealthy competition is productive of maximum benefit as it is to all human endeavour. Excellence in education cannot be legislated in being, but local comparisons of the achievements of different schools will have the effect of spurring all to educational excellence.
>
> (Federation of Independent Schools
> Associations 1967, 3–4)

With respect to FISA's tactics, a two-pronged approach was employed that included both the direct lobbying of BC MLAs and cabinet ministers and a broader public education campaign on the quality education independent schools provided, the amount of tax dollars they saved the government, and, most importantly, the legitimacy of the rights to exist and receive public funding such schools should possess within a pluralistic society. Prior to 1966, debates related to the recognition or funding of independent schools were not on the general public's radar. The issue was rarely, if ever, mentioned by the press, nor had any of the central political parties in the province developed specific policies on the issue. A small handful of backbench MLAs from both the Liberals and Social Credit had expressed some mild support for independent schools but the extent of the long-governing Social Credit's official stance on the issue was captured by their dominant leader W.A.C. Bennett's oft-mentioned quip that "public money was for public schools," an argument he had used repeatedly when fending off requests from Catholic representatives in the 1950s. Within a year of FISA's formation, the issue of funding independent schools was raised within the legislature by a sympathetic pair of backbenchers only to be immediately drowned out by howls of opposition from leaders of both the NDP and SC, with Premier Bennett thumping "the loudest and longest." For Cunningham, Bennett, who would lead SC to seven consecutive electoral victories and serve as premier for an astounding twenty years (1952–72), was easily the most significant roadblock faced by those lobbying on behalf of independent schools. A "one-man government" that had exhibited a tinge of anti-Catholic sentiment at times, Bennett "was deaf to philosophical arguments that contradicted his belief in a single, non-sectarian school system that provided the same education for everyone" (Cunningham 2002, 89–93).

In the midst of this period of BC politics, FISA's first executive director, Gerry Ensing, led a broad public relations effort as well as a more targeted campaign aimed at MLAs. Working to build familiarity and trust with politicians of all stripes while simultaneously educating them about the services provided by independent schools was clearly important to FISA but the organization understood very early that they were playing a long game with respect to attaining the policy changes they demanded. Reflecting some years after funding was granted in 1977, Ensing explained how FISA realized that "legislation would only be changed if we, as a federation, would change the political climate in British Columbia to allow that kind of change to take place" (Ensing 1980, 9). Thus, in addition to traditional lobbying, FISA launched a significant public awareness campaign that utilized media interviews, op-eds, and letters to the editor, an annual information booth at the Pacific National Exhibition, town-hall style forums across the province, and even the installation of large billboards outside various independent schools highlighting the lack of state funding received despite the educational services they performed. Ensing was the undeniable leader and public face of this campaign, but the broader organization played a significant role as well. FISA ensured that designated representatives throughout the province (totalling around one hundred) were well educated on the issue and capable of effectively engaging the media and politicians in their home communities as well as educators and administrators at various educational conferences throughout BC. FISA also maintained strong connections with the parents of independent school children, primarily through a newsletter, and constantly reminded them to write letters to politicians and newspapers (Cunningham 2002, 108–11).

Within a few short years, concrete progress within the legislature in response to FISA's efforts was becoming apparent. By 1970 a FISA poll suggested that at least thirty-four MLAs supported legally recognizing independent schools, up from ten in 1968. Early that same year a SC backbencher, supported by a handful of Liberal MLAs, put forth a private member's bill requesting this recognition, although it was strongly opposed by Bennett and died on the Order Paper. In 1971, the BC Liberals became the first party to pass a resolution officially supporting the recognition and funding of independent schools, with an increasing number of members within the NDP and SC similarly softening their stance (Cunningham 2002, 112–15, 125). Importantly, public awareness of the issue and, most significantly, support for independent schools, continued to grow in response to FISA's efforts. In 1972, a commission sponsored by the BC Parent-Teacher Foundation sided with FISA's arguments and concluded that the public system's monopoly should be replaced (Cunningham 2002). By 1976, a poll commissioned by the BC Teachers' Federation (BCTF, which, ironically enough, was fiercely opposed to FISA's agenda) revealed that 57 per cent of citizens felt independent schools should be either fully or partially funded by the state, whereas only 37 per cent were outright opposed. Among those aged 19–34, support grew to 64 per cent (Federation of Independent Schools Associations, 1976a).

These small victories for FISA were occurring within the context of a much larger shift in the politics of BC. In 1972, Dave Barrett's NDP toppled Bennett's SC party, thereby removing from power a conservative premier who had steadfastly refused to budge on the independent school issue despite the rather obvious movement occurring below him. In fact, Cunningham (128) suggests that Bennett's inflexibility on the independent school issue may have been one of the important factors that led to his defeat (although surely the broader contention that his government had grown tired seems to hold more explanatory power).

Nevertheless, Premier Barrett did signal to FISA the potential for some movement on the issue, although this did not come to fruition, perhaps mostly because of the party's strong relationship with the BCTF. In 1973 W.A.C. Bennett retired and his son Bill Bennett was selected as the new SC leader, a significant development given the younger Bennett's clear endorsement of the legal recognition and funding of independent schools. At the same leadership convention, the party adopted this position as well and, at the drop of a hat, a remarkable 180-degree turn had occurred within the BC SC party. Although occurring four years prior to partial funding being implemented by Bill Bennett's Social Credit government, this precise shift in 1973 represented the true moment of victory for FISA. The policy window for change that had begun to swing at the 1973 convention opened wide when Social Credit returned to government in 1975.

In January of 1976 the Ministry of Education, now headed by former Liberal MLA and fierce advocate for the funding of independent schools, Patrick McGeer, requested FISA's input on the question of funding. FISA replied with a brief entitled "The Independent Alternative": it rehashed the arguments from the 1967 brief that suggested funding was a requirement of a democratic and pluralistic society, including a quote from John Stuart Mill's *On Liberty*, that noted the "unspeakable importance [of] diversity in education," before providing a more detailed proposal for how such a system could be introduced and monitored (Federation of Independent Schools Associations 1976b). The Throne Speech of 1976 contained a public promise to review the issue of independent school funding, McGeer quickly established a Non-Public School Committee to work on the legislation, and by December of that year the Independent Schools Support Act was being drafted, to be introduced and passed in the legislature as Bill 33 in 1977 (Cunningham 2002). The act did not follow all of FISA's requests, but it did provide a per-pupil grant equal to 30 per cent of the per-pupil operating cost of a public school in the same district to independent schools that had been in operation for at least five years, were not promoting intolerance or violence, had adequate facilities, employed certified teachers, followed the basic tenets of the provincial curriculum, and participated in learning assessments. Those independent schools unwilling to follow the last three conditions were eligible for a 9 per cent per-pupil grant. In the 1977–8 school year, ninety-nine independent schools qualified for the 30 per cent rate and two for the 9 per cent rate. Interestingly, over sixty eligible schools, most being small Christian schools, refused to seek funding at this point, ultimately fearing government control (Cunningham 2002, 215–16).

Although Bill 33 represented the watershed moment in terms of the introduction of funds for independent schools for the first time in BC's history, FISA would, over the next decade, strengthen its presence as the central advocate for independent schools and continued to make the case for increased funding rates (Barman 1991, 21). In fact, the SC government had quietly assured FISA that the levels introduced in 1977 were "intended only as a minimum," although a dramatic increase to as much as 80 per cent funding was understood as being politically risky (Cunningham 2002, 230–1). Agreement among FISA's various sub-associations on the appropriate level of funding from their vantage points was not easy to find. The bulk of Catholic representatives aspired to 100 per cent funding levels their counterparts in Alberta, Saskatchewan, and Ontario had long received, whereas several other groups feared the increased accountability and subsequent loss of autonomy should the funding level rise at all. In 1985, FISA members compromised on a request to a maximum of a per-pupil grant equal to 50 per cent that was provided to public schools (Cunningham 2002). The SC premier at the time, Bill Vander Zalm, a devout Christian and strong supporter of independent schools, responded to FISA's requests by granting a small funding increase in 1986. More significantly, he established a Royal Commission on Education in the province in BC (the Sullivan Commission), which would focus most heavily on aspects of the public system but would also render an important verdict on the independent school sector in the province. This, in turn, precipitated updated legislation and increased funding.

FISA submitted a seventy-page brief to the commission and encouraged several independent school supporters to provide positive testimony as well. The essence of FISA's message delivered to the commission remained nearly identical to the important briefs presented in 1967 and 1976: justice within a democratic and pluralistic society requires that governments take seriously a parent's right to choose the kind of education they desire for their children (FISA 1988). The Sullivan Commission subsequently responded with an incredibly positive assessment of the legitimacy of independent schools in BC, leading to the SC government's decision in 1989 to pass the Independent School Act, a piece of legislation that received significant input from FISA. Central to the act was a recategorization of independent schools and a funding increase in accordance with that requested by FISA that remains in place today. As of 1989, independent schools that continued to adhere to provincial guidelines around curriculum, assessment, and teacher certification would be classified as Group 1 schools and would receive a per-pupil grant equal to 50 per cent of that of local public schools so long as their operating costs did not exceed those of neighbouring public schools on a per-pupil basis, a stipulation designed to prevent wealthy elite-style independent schools from receiving the highest level of funding. Rather, such schools would now be classified as Group 2 schools and would receive a 35 per cent grant. In 1989, a third category of funded schools existed but has since been scrapped. Today, Group 3 schools, which are not required to meet the Group 1 requirements, and Group 4 schools, which cater mainly to non-provincial students, receive no funding.

Making Sense of the Entrenchment of "A Parent's Right to Choose"

Clearly the SC electoral victory in 1975 was the key political moment with respect to the introduction of funding for independent schools. For the first time in BC's history, a political party that was publicly support-ive of funding for independent schools was in power. It was thus only a matter of time before a policy path followed for over a century was to be abandoned. Yet, it is far too simplistic to suggest that such a significant policy shift can be explained by a single election. In fact, Downey (1986, 320–1) suggests that there are four contributing factors that explain the shift leading to Bill 33 being passed in 1977: the leadership of newly minted SC education minister Patrick McGeer (who had long champi-oned the issue), the lobbying efforts of FISA (and the lack of an effective counter lobby by the BCTF), the internal division on the issue within the opposition NDP, as well as the shifting "mood of society." We concur with this brief assessment and wish to use the following paragraphs to expand further on these key factors as well as how they interacted in order to generate a school governance regime structured around the notion of a parent's "right to choose" rather than one focused on the question of a secular government subsidizing religious education. This combination of "rights" with "choice" has parallels to what the other Western provinces would arrive at in the late 1980s and early 1990s. But BC stands out as an early adopter at least in part, we suggest, because the two categories were so closely combined, and there wasn't a distinc-tive period of transition between them.

FISA is critically important to this policy story and, like the Chris-tian Action Foundation and the Societies for Christian Education in the Alberta case, are a textbook example of a "policy entrepreneur" willing to devote considerable resources, often over long stretches of time, in the hope of a future policy outcome (Kingdon 2003, 122–32). Created in the mid-1960s out of a diverse range of independent school interests, the organization immediately began a process of traditional government lobbying and broader public awareness work that can be tied directly to the emergence of Bill 33. As Barman has noted, the passage of this bill, "underlined the extent to which a small but determined vested-interest group could set public policy" (1991, 15). Indeed, in response to FISA's work, both the public at large and a large swath of BC MLAs grew to be more supportive of the notion of support for independent schools. But the reasons behind FISA's success in this regard go beyond the simple fact that they exerted such effort. Rather, their tactics and the content of the message they espoused were especially effective in that particular period of BC's political history.

With respect to tactics, the simple act of ensuring a unified voice representing over 90 per cent of the independent school sector in the province represented a significant step forward in terms of becoming a vital player within the education policy community. Prior to this unification, a number of solo efforts waged by representatives of Catholic, Calvinist, and secular elite prep schools had failed to rouse any meaningful response from government. As the SC education minister at the time of FISA's founding told Gerry Ensing, "I doubt whether our government's policy will change overnight, but it is certainly significant to see you people here representing all the independent schools" (Ensing 1980, 9). The actual work of FISA on this file, in terms of both lobbying and public awareness, seems to have been very well designed and executed. The overt decision to remain non-partisan in these efforts, and to conduct persistent, respectful, diplomatic, and low-key lobbying and public awareness grounded in significant research and carefully structured arguments that avoided questioning the quality of the public-school system also proved important (Downey 1986; Cunningham 2002). Two former deputy ministers of education interviewed for this project agreed with this broad assessment, both recalling that their respective ministers appreciated FISA's professionalism and competence. This approach stands out as unique compared to the overt partisanship and political gamesmanship practiced by the BCTF, FISA's chief adversary within the education policy community of the province, over the past decades (Fleming 2011). In fact, one former deputy minister of education suggested to the authors that the decision to initially fund independent schools was at least partly related to the SC government's intense dislike for the BCTF who had, in the early 1970s, overtly supported the NDP party (Interview with I, 13 August 2015).

FISA's decision to resist framing the issue of a lack of funding for independent schools as one of religious freedom being denied, despite the fact the vast majority of independent schools were faith based, is incredibly important to understanding the policy change that occurred in 1977. As long-time FISA executive director Fred Herfst recalls:

[FISA] decided right from the beginning to frame the issue as an educational one rather than a religious one. In other words, it was not framed under the notion of "we want religious freedom," it was framed under the notion of "parental rights to direct the education of their children." And that parental right should involve the right for parents to choose ... the kind of education that they wanted for their children ... [This decision] made it possible for FISA to form and have both the faith-based and the non-faith-based schools work together because you were working on a principle that all could support. And that was really a crucial, crucial move ... It was the '60s and the '70s, there were entire cultural mores that were changing, leaning toward individual autonomy and choice ... and I think that mindset spilled over into all sorts of areas. The word "choice" became very, very formative. That was the very fertile soil in which it became possible [for citizens] to consider alternatives.
(Interview with Fred Herfst, 10 August 2015)

Barman (1991) and Downey (1986) similarly conclude that the growth of diversity in the province in the 1950s and 1960s and the related increase in openness to pluralism in general and both individual and minority rights in particular during the 1960s and 1970s played a significant role in lessening public and political opposition to funding for independent schools. That FISA struck this precise chord with a message emphasizing pluralism and the right to choose for minority groups rather than "religious freedom" was a stroke of genius that ensured the faith regime that had dominated the debate over the funding of religious schools for over a century was overtaken by a "right to choose" regime in the province. As educational historian Thomas Fleming notes, despite the fact that the overwhelming beneficiaries were faith-based schools, Bill 33 was clearly understood at the time to be a secular bill (Interview with Thomas Fleming, 14 August 2015). In a testament to this interpretation, consider the language employed by SC premier Bill Bennett, defending the passage of Bill 33 in the legislature some years later:

I think one of the fundamental things in rights and opportunities in a democracy is that the minds [of our children] and education not be controlled by monopoly by the state. One of the best opportunities we have to make this country grow and to ensure its success is to have alternative education systems so that our children will be equipped in various

ways ... They will be given the opportunity to choose the education
system of their choice.

(quoted in Cunningham 2002, 146)

Similarly, consider the manner by which the 1988 Royal Commission on Education (Sullivan Commission) responded to the issue of independent schools as framed by FISA. Calem and Fleming (1988) summarize the arguments put forth by FISA and its supporters to the Commission as follows:

[P]arents "have a prior right to select the kind of education they believe appropriate for their children," and that it is up to the state to furnish tangible assistance in making this choice possible. Choice is thereby understood as enhancing parental participation in children's schooling, and the consequence of such engagement is viewed as beneficial to public and non-public sectors alike. Beyond this expectation, parental choice is also considered to be an absolute good which helps promote justice for all, and which enriches the general public good in a democratic society. Additional lines of this argument hold that no system or service that is entirely monopolistic in character will remain motivated to provide the kinds of educational experiences a pluralistic society demands.

It is difficult to overstate how clearly and completely this line of argumentation convinced the commission. Speaking to the question of public aid for independent schools, the commission's final report noted the diversity of the province, "perhaps the most inescapable and salient fact of British Columbia life in the late 1980s," before concluding:

With this recognition of diversity comes the need for choice – choice that centres on learners and parents, choice that is located at the level of the individual school district, the individual school, and where possible, the individual classroom. In a society that seeks greater measures of differentiation and greater acknowledgement of diversity, choice is of paramount consideration, the Commission believes. It speaks in a direct way to individuals participating in the educational decisions that affect their lives and to the empowerment of youngsters, their parents, and the school professionals who serve them. Choice, the Commission maintains, invigorates the responsibility that must pertain at every level of schooling, from the parents at home, to the child at school, through the teachers, administrators, and governance officials, and, finally, to the senior officials in the Ministry of Education and to the Minister of Education as the highest educational official in the provincial system. Choice likewise presumes a faith in people's abilities to decide wisely and a capacity to trust that they will do so. It presumes freedom of opportunity to decide; it entails responsibility for the consequences of such action. In framing a perspective on the issue of support for independent schools, the Commission recognizes the importance of diversity and choice and their value as sound educational principles.

(British Columbia 1988, 201–3)

Based on this reasoning, the commission subsequently recommended that the level of public aid to independent schools be raised from 30 per cent to 50 per cent of the per-pupil grant provided to public schools, a recommendation that the BC government quickly implemented in 1989 and that remains in place today.

Finally, beyond the importance of FISA tactics and the framing mechanism employed, one cannot understand this substantial policy change that occurred in 1977 without highlighting the shifts within the broader political climate of BC, beginning with the NDP toppling W.A.C Bennett's long ruling SC party in 1972, the accession of Bill Bennett to SC's leadership, his eventual electoral victory, and finally the defection of prominent Liberal MLAs and longtime proponents of independent school funding, Patrick McGeer and Garde Gardom, to the SC party (Downey 1986, 316). In fact, a former advisor to McGeer has speculated that Bill Bennett's support for the extension of funding to independent schools was part of a back-room deal to entice McGeer to cross the floor (Interview with Jim Carter, 25 June 2015), although McGeer himself, whom Bennett would eventually name education minister, denies this. Back-room deal or not, it is clear that the presence of McGeer within the SC party was a crucial factor in this story. Indeed, it was McGeer who, in the mid-70s, "became the chief architect of Bill 33 and the strategist who maneuvered the new policy through society, through the Opposition, and through the Legislature" (Downey 1986, 320). In this way, McGeer himself can be understood as an additional policy entrepreneur in this story, although his role in working to couple the policy, problem, and political streams was not nearly as significant as the efforts of FISA.

The Independent School Sector and Contemporary BC Politics – The Entrenchment of School Choice

Since the 1989 decision to increase the level of funding for independent schools, BC's approach to the sector has settled into an extended period of stability. To be sure, the BCTF has remained steadfastly opposed to the partial funding of the independent schooling sector and the BC NDP, which has strong ties to the teachers' union, raised the issue from time to time throughout the 1990s. But, as one former senior BCTF member recalls, NDP premier Glen Clark, although not wholly comfortable ideologically with the funding of such schools, was adamant "about not wanting to politically take on the independent school consistencies" in the late 1990s (Interview with H, 11 August 2015). Subsequently, NDP leader and premier Ujjal Dosanjh did quietly implement changes to how the per-pupil funding of students enrolled in independent schools was calculated in 2000, which resulted in a net loss of roughly $5 million annually to independent schools (FISA 2002). FISA was quick to react, launching a public awareness campaign and encouraging independent school supporters to write letters in opposition to the move. This grass-roots mobilization led to over 20,000 letters of opposition arriving on the desk of the education minister and hours of talk-radio programming across the province dedicated to the issue, which led the NDP to ultimately back down and reverse the funding changes (Froese 2010, 39–40; Cunningham 2002, 261–7).

In 2001 the BC Liberals swept into power and remained there until July of 2017. Their tenure was a very positive one for independent schools in BC. Although funding levels did not increase, the Liberals worked closely with FISA on nearly all matters of educational policy related to independent schools, a process that culminated in the creation of a new post – the Parliamentary Secretary for Independent Schools – which provided FISA with a point person within Cabinet. The most recent policy win for FISA came in 2015 with the Liberals agreeing to its request to strip BC municipalities of the power to tax playgrounds, fields, and parking lots owned by such schools ("Tax Exemption Planned for BC Private Schools," *Times Colonist*, 31 May 2015). This period of Liberal rule also saw independent schools emerge victorious in a number of battles involving government-mandated programming that addressed sexual orientation in positive ways.

The unique demographics of BC have produced many educational conflicts between LGBTQ activists in and around the distinctly secular and progressive city of Vancouver and the evangelical Christian "Bible Belts" (the area around the Lower Fraser Valley including the communities of Surrey, Langley, and Abbotsford) that surrounds it (Smith 2004; Walton 2006). These conflicts have often involved educational questions. Although two Supreme Court cases (*Trinity Western University v. BC College of Teachers* [2001] and *Chamberlain v. Surrey School District no. 36* [2002]) have gained the most notoriety, the most important case with respect to the education system in BC may have been the product of a Human Rights complaint against the government that was settled out of court. In 2006, the BC government signed what has widely been dubbed the "Corren Agreement," the settlement of a Human Rights complaint launched in 1999 that charged the Education Ministry with discriminating against homosexuals by failing to depict them in a positive light within the approved curriculum. The 2006 settlement addressed this complaint by committing to a review of the entire curriculum to ensure the LGBTQ community was depicted in a positive way, introducing new rules preventing parents from removing their children from courses that addressed sexual orientation, and creating a new course (Social Justice 12) that would specifically address, among other things, issues around gender identity and sexual orientation. These changes pushed BC to the forefront of Canadian provinces when it came to addressing issues around sexual orientation within the education system.

As expected, certain public schools and school boards within the Lower Fraser Valley strongly opposed these developments for religious reasons but the Liberals stood firm and refused their requests to opt out. However, the government was far more lenient with respect to independent schools. Roughly 65 per cent of the schools represented by FISA are faith based and a significant portion of those were very concerned with the Corren Agreement. FISA contemplated seeking intervener status in the Human Rights hearing in 2005 on behalf of these schools but ultimately decided against it. This was partly due to the lack of consensus between religious and secular schools that made up its membership but, much more interestingly, was also due to the BC government's private assurance to FISA that it would defend their interests in the case (Interview with Peter Froese, 24 June 2015). When FISA did raise the concerns of many independent faith-based schools with the government following the announcement of the agreement in 2006, the education minister responded with a letter confirming that the government would not require faith-based independent schools to teach lessons that conflicted with the tenets of their faith (Interview with Doug Lauson, 24 June 2015).

Similar concessions were made to faith-based schools between 2007 and 2012 when anti-bullying policies were made mandatory and expanded upon for all educational institutions in the province, public and independent. Despite a strong push from the BCTF to include specific language that highlighted the need to protect LGBTQ students, the Liberal government responded instead to arguments from FISA and others that argued against a policy that highlighted any one particular group of students. Indeed, the final wording of the Level 1

Training Manual for BC's ERASE Bullying program made clear its goal was that "Every child in British Columbia feels safe, accepted and respected regardless of gender, race, culture, religion or sexual orientation." For the BCTF and the broader community of LGBTQ activists in the province, the refusal by the BC Liberals to move beyond such a statement and specifically highlight the need to protect LGBTQ children was a clear win for FISA. A former BC deputy minister of education has acknowledged FISA's role when explaining BC's approach to this issue:

> FISA has had good access to the Liberal government. They are positioned well philosophically with this government around choice. They can be a bit of a thorn in the side, but you know ... they're a professional body with professionals running it.
>
> On the human rights issue, the province was persuaded to avoid getting into a place where we start recognizing this aspect of this community, and this aspect of that community. We wanted to be entirely respectful to all. [But] any school who was not recognizing this would get their licence lifted. So FISA, it's over to you ... you figure it out. But if you don't, and you get sued, and they come after you, don't expect us to help you, because we're going to be on the side of the lesbian, gay, and transgender group. You have got the human rights legislation you wanted ... so show us. You demonstrate to a judge that you're acting properly and if you can't demonstrate that to a judge then shame on you and I hope they lift your licence.
>
> (Interview with I, 13 August 2015)

The influence FISA maintained with the BC Liberals was due to their consistent lobbying efforts, the large independent school constituency they represent, and alignment on the core principle of parental choice. Of course, the notion of "choice" had been central to debates over independent schools in BC well before the Liberals came to power. The BC Liberals embrace of "choice" in education, however, had distinct philosophical roots. Much like the Alberta Progressive Conservative party in the mid-1990s, the BC Liberals entered government in 2001 with a sense that the education system had grown inefficient and unresponsive to the needs of both student learners and the emerging marketplace. In 2002, a Standing Committee on Education produced a report elaborating on these fears and arguing for the implementation of more market-driven incentives within the existing system as a way of improving student outcomes (Fallon and Paquette 2008). In response, the Liberals fully commitment themselves to the principle of "school choice" in the neoliberal sense of the term, altering the per-pupil funding formula for public schools and eliminating catchment areas thereby allowing parents the capacity to choose what school their children could attend (Fallon and Paquette 2008). Interestingly, the deputy minister of education overseeing these changes was Emery Dosdall, the same individual who had strongly encouraged school choice in Alberta as superintendent of the Edmonton Public School Board just a few years prior. As the president of FISA acknowledged, the Liberals "have been very open to collaboration because of their own philosophical embrace of choice. If you believe in choice, you will support all forms of schooling, and this includes independent schools" (Interview with Doug Lauson, 24 June 2015).

That said, in 2016 the Liberal government did reverse course and now requires all schools, both public and independent, to include specific protections for gay, lesbian, and transgender students in their anti-bullying policies, a decision that FISA has decided not to challenge ("BC Schools to Add Protections for LGBTQ Students in Anti-Bullying Policies," *Globe and Mail*, 8 September 2016). Such a decision by FISA may be related to the results of a 2016 poll that found roughly two-thirds of BC citizens opposed the public funding of private religious schools ("Two of Three B.C. Residents Oppose Governments Funding Religious Schools," *Vancouver Sun*, 14 June 2016). It is conceivable that an organization with a long history of strategically framing the issue of funding for independent schools as one of parental choice rather than religious freedom would see the results of such a poll as a sign to tread carefully on the issue of addressing sexual orientation. Indeed, a high-profile public spat with the government on such an issue in one of Canada's most secular and progressive provinces may very well generate a broader anti-public funding campaign – an outcome FISA surely wants to avoid.

Such speculation aside, it was surely a matter of more immediate concern for FISA that in July 2017 an NDP-led minority government was sworn in. There has always been a vocal faction within the NDP that is opposed to public dollars for independent schools on ideological grounds. And the BCTF, which continues to be strongly aligned with the NDP, remains adamantly opposed to public funding for private schools (BCTF 2017). Yet we conclude that it is unlikely an NDP government will alter the level of funding independent schools receive at any point in the near future. There are a few reasons for this. First, politically, the independent school sector represents a sizeable constituency (13 per cent of all children schooled in BC), that crosses a wide range of communities including the large and dispersed Catholics, the

Evangelical Protestant "Bible Belt" of the Fraser Valley, the variety of diverse ethnic communities throughout the Lower Mainland, as well as the wealthy prep-school supporters and middle-class parents who support secular alternative educational philosophies. Given the size and diversity of this coalition, in addition to FISA's professional and battle-tested leadership, its history of employing successful lobbying and pressure tactics, and its well-worn seat at the middle of the table that is BC's education policy community, it seems unlikely that any government would see a political winner in a move to roll back the most significant gains the sector has realized. This could be especially tricky for the NDP given that several of their MLAs send their children to independent schools and some past party leaders are graduates of non-public programs. As one former BC education minister noted, "there's been a pretty strong political consensus around it being appropriate to fund, generally speaking, at the 50 per cent level, and it has not been for many elections now the source of debate in electoral competition. In fact, it would be politically foolish to reopen something that has been the object of political consensus for this long" (Interview with George Abbott, 23 September 2015).

Second, the NDP, alongside most bureaucrats within the Education Ministry, have come to fear the potential fiscal costs associated with the defunding of independent schools. In other words, there is a sense that, should the government defund them, the majority of Group 1 schools would face financial ruin and quickly be forced to raise tuition substantially or close entirely. In either scenario, it is likely that thousands of students would flood into the public system where the government would be on the hook for per-pupil funding at a rate double that given to independent schools. Add to this the capital expenditures for additional classrooms and facilities required to house these students (independent schools receive no public subsidies for such expenses), and it becomes clear that any government that dares rescind public funding from independent schools will potentially lose money in the transaction. In other words, the BC NDP seems to grasp (as do most provincial governments that offer funding to non-public schools), that the funding of such schools is actually a fiscally responsible arrangement – every student that graduates from an independent school is a student that has been educated for less than half the price of a public school graduate.

Finally there is the question of political optics for any government daring to respond positively to a central request from the BCTF. In short, the teachers' organization has very little public credibility at the moment. For some ideological opponents, the "social justice advocacy" the organization has overtly embraced throughout its history is problematic.

For a broader swath of the citizenry, however, the 2000s represent a period of unusual instability in the public schooling sector headlined by an ongoing series of feuds between the Liberal government and the BCTF, culminating in short strikes in 2005 and 2012 and a months-long strike in 2015. Fairly or not, the BCTF has received a lion's share of bad press related to these work stoppages that, especially in 2015, severely interrupted student progress. As one former deputy minister of education within the Liberal government noted, "Every time BCTF went on strike or did something obnoxious, we'd get spiked enrolment in independent schools. The biggest feeder, the biggest single driver of people in independent schools is BCTF" (Interview with I, 13 August 2015). Clearly this statement seems tinged with anti-BCTF sentiment in general but the broader message, that incessant labour instability in the public school sector has driven more and more parents towards the independent sector, is an important factor in this story.

Conclusion

Initially, British Columbia stood alone as the only province intent on ensuring a strict divide between church and state in its schooling regime. Like the rest of Canada, the regime of "faith" dominated the debate over funding religious schools but, unlike the other provinces, the answer to the appropriateness of such funding was "no." The result was an education system built upon a single network of non-denominational public schools and a smattering of wholly unfunded independent schools. This arrangement lasted for over a century, despite the frequent pleas of BC's Catholic community, who long sought funding for Catholic-centred schools approaching the levels found in several other provinces. However, in the 1970s, BC's educational system faced a critical policy juncture that resulted in exogenously triggered regime change. In 1977, the BC government authorized the allocation of public funds for qualifying independent schools, an allocation that rose to contemporary levels in 1989. Underlying this policy shift was a broader transition from the long-running faith regime to one centred more fully on rights, especially the rights of parents to choose the type of education their children received. This transition did much to deflate the controversy that had long surrounded the issue of funding religious schools in an adamantly secular province by wholly reframing the issue as one related more so to the requirements of democratic pluralism in a diverse society.

The period between 1977 and 1989 saw a series of incremental changes, mostly policy layering, as the details of this new regime were worked out. An important element of the success of independent schools at gaining more government support during this time was the professionalism, focus, and comparative unity of FISA, the independent school sector's umbrella lobbying group which enjoyed substantial influence with the educational bureaucracy and with the government. This change can be categorized primarily as layering, as the regime established in 1977 was gradually made more generous. Since 1989, a second period of policy inertia has largely descended upon the issue of funding independent schools, best understood again as the product of path dependence. Politically important opponents of government funding for independent schools exist in BC, exemplified most clearly by the BCTF's ongoing campaign in opposition to this funding. However, the teachers' union's central foil in this policy battle, FISA, has shown itself to be an effective defender of the status quo, despite not possessing the same tangible resources of the much larger BCTF. FISA's strength in this regard, in addition to the more general costs (both fiscal and political) a drastic policy change to an area affecting over 13 per cent of students in BC would endure, suggests that even the recent electoral demise of the strongly "pro-school choice" Liberal Party does not seem to point to any serious policy changes on the horizon with respect to the funding of independent schools. That said, mirroring changes witnessed in many of the provinces we have examined, a policy area that does seem susceptible to change is that related to the autonomy of faith-based schools, especially with respect to instruction on sexual orientation and gender identity. Indeed, since 2016 all independent schools are required to comply with the same standards followed by public schools with respect to specific measures aimed at protecting LGBTQ students within their anti-bullying provisions, an outcome FISA had quietly fought against for the preceding decade. Yet this seems like an area FISA is content to concede so long as the broader funding formula remains in place. Given that the dominant regime in BC is currently that of "choice," we expect this commitment to independent schools to remain in place for the foreseeable future.

6 Incremental Change and Policy Layering in Saskatchewan

Saskatchewan's religious school regime is similar to Alberta's. The vast majority of students attend the public and separate (Catholic) systems, there is a self-governing francophone system that is part of the public system, and public support is also provided to multiple categories of independent and associate schools, many of which are religious. Saskatchewan groups these independent schools into a number of categories that receive different levels of funding and follow more or less closely provincial curriculum and teacher accreditation rules: historic high schools (which receive a grant worth 70 per cent of per-student funding provided to public schools), registered independent schools (which do not receive government funding), qualified independent schools (which receive 50 per cent of the provincial per-student funding), and associate schools (which are funded at 80 per cent and are overseen through agreements with local school boards). Historic high schools tend to position themselves as elite prep schools (even if they retain some religious affiliation and character), registered and qualified independent schools include both religious and non-religious schools, and associate schools must be religious. In 2019–20, 2.8 per cent of Saskatchewan students attended one of the various types of independent schools (Fraser Institute 2022) and 22.1 per cent attended the publicly funded separate system (Fraser Institute 2017).

Surprisingly, though Alberta is usually seen to be a conservative polity and Saskatchewan a social democratic one (Wiseman 2007), the evolution of these two provincial regimes show remarkable parallels over the last century. Both – at their establishment in 1905 – had government support for separate (Catholic) systems constitutionally entrenched as the federal government of Wilfrid Laurier tried to avoid the strife over religious schools that had plagued Manitoba. This was only partially successful, for political contestation over language education and Catholic schools was heated in Saskatchewan after the First World War.

But this strife died down by the 1930s and the extension of full funding to Saskatchewan's Catholic high schools in 1964 by the Co-operative Commonwealth Federation (CCF) was an uncontentious and bipartisan affair (Alberta's had been receiving full public funding since 1905).

Beginning in the 1960s, other groups began to lobby for government funding in both provinces, grounding their claims in both rights (especially the francophone minority) and choice (groups that sought public support for their independent schools). And in both, the contemporary system for funding independent, associate, and/or charter schools emerged in the late 1980s and early 1990s, as policymakers were influenced by ideas of choice and with some pre-existing funding for religious schools. In the last decade, both provinces have seen skirmishes between the government and Catholic and independent schools over LGBTQ issues and anti-bullying clubs in schools. That the sixty-year time difference in the funding of separate high schools did not affect the overall trajectory of the system can perhaps be explained by another important feature of the politics of both provinces. At least after the 1920s, the politics of religious and independent schools was comparably quiet. In Alberta, this can be attributed to that province's pattern of one-party dominance. By contrast, Saskatchewan has had a pattern of competitive and often ideologically polarized party politics. But, funding for religious and independent schools did not clearly divide political parties in Saskatchewan. Instead, parties were internally divided on the issue but tended, especially in government, to support the status quo (Interview with Richard Holdern, 2 April 2018; Interview with Pat Atkinson, 28 July 2015). Lobbying for resources was often done quietly by community leaders with good connections to both government and opposition. And, even after governments had made relatively significant policy changes, the opposition (whether Liberal, CCF/NDP, or Saskatchewan Party) chose for reasons of its own to not voice significant opposition or, once in government, to reverse the changes.

Table 6.1. Key Dates in the Evolution of Saskatchewan's Education System

Date	Event
1870	Rupert's Land transferred to Canada
1875	NWT School Bill
1905	Saskatchewan Act and provincial status
1917	English-only legislation
1963	Funding extended to separate high schools
1964	Funding extended to historic high schools
198x	Modern independent school funding regime established
2020	*Good Spirit* decision overturned on appeal

Unlike other provinces, where the existing regimes seem fairly solidified and not likely to change at the time of writing, Saskatchewan's regime has just finished facing a significant exogenous shock to both its structure and to its quiet style of politics. In *Good Spirit School Division No. 204 v. Christ the Teacher Roman Catholic Separate School Division No. 212* (2017 SKQB 109 (CanLII)), usually referred to in the press as the Theodore case), a 2017 Saskatchewan Court of Queen's Bench decision, the court found that the government could not provide funds for children who were not baptized Catholics to attend separate schools. In response, the provincial government and separate school association appealed to the provincial Court of Appeal and the provincial government also passed legislation, invoking the Constitution's notwithstanding clause in creation of the School Choice Protection Act, to maintain the status quo. Given that roughly a third of children in the separate system are not baptized Catholics, a situation where such students would not receive government funding would be a real shock to the separate system. While the Theodore decision did not directly address the other types of independent schools that receive public support in Saskatchewan, the principles it articulates may affect the other schools as well (Eidsness, Steeves, and Dolmage 2008). By invoking Section 33 of the Charter of Rights and Freedoms in the School Choice Protection Act, the provincial government has ensured that the issue of separate school funding and religious equality will come up in five years when the bill is renewed. In February 2021, the Supreme Court of Canada declined leave to appeal this decision, rendering the School Choice Protection Act moot and protecting the status quo.

The pattern of change in Saskatchewan has been one of incremental layering. Though there have been moments where a fundamental reordering of government support for independent and religious schools has been raised in Saskatchewan, policy action has never been taken to roll back support to a definite category of school. Instead, the government has consistently chosen to extend funding and add new categories of schools, usually without having come under significant political pressure. In sequence, this has allowed schools founded in faith, in rights claims, and in choice to each receive government support under a unique funding regime that has evolved in an additive and incremental way over time.

Faith

Debates about the political place of religious schools were important to the early politics of Saskatchewan. Religious tension between Catholics and Protestants overlapped with linguistic tensions between the francophone and anglophone communities from the beginning of European settlement in the province (Eager 1980; McLeod 1968). In Saskatch-ewan, which experienced very high levels of immigration before the First World War, this public-separate (Catholic) division overlapped with ethnic divides in the province so initial debates focused on the status of separate Catholic schools. Three stages in the development of this aspect of the system can be identified: the period before Saskatch-ewan became a province in 1905, when the system was broadly similar to Quebec but under significant pressure as immigration changed the demographics of the province; between 1905 and the 1930s, when the system – now running on Ontario lines of separate, publicly funded ele-mentary schools for Catholics who also supported a network of private high schools – was at the centre of political controversy; and between the 1930s and today, when the separate system has become relatively entrenched.

The first efforts (the 1875 NWT Act and the 1884 School Ordinance) to create a territorial school system were similar to Quebec's dual system (Eager 1980; McLeod 1968). Under this arrangement, the first school in every district would be public but would be either Protestant or Catho-lic depending on which group was the majority in the area. If there were sufficient adherents of the minority faith in a district, then a religiously defined separate school could be created for them. This created a system of Roman Catholic and Protestant public schools and Roman Catholic and Protestant separate schools throughout the Northwest Territories. These schools were overseen by a territorial Board of Education made up of two Protestants, two Catholics, and the Lieutenant Governor, who usually operated, like in Quebec, as separate Protestant and Catholic sections. Churches initially had fairly direct involvement in these sec-tions but, as the territorial government grew, churches became more removed from the operation of government supported schools (though they continued to operate mission, residential, and private schools) (Noonan 2006). In 1892, these dual sections were replaced by a single Council of Education, with the same membership, but with a jurisdic-tional arrangement that moved more power to the territorial govern-ment. Schools continued to be allowed to conduct religious instruction for a half hour a day and instruction continued to be in both French and English, as decided by the local district. In this way, the school system retained substantial flexibility (Scharf 2006).

As in Manitoba, this division of schools initially matched the popula-tion makeup of the part of the Northwest Territories that would become Saskatchewan. However, very substantial immigration between 1885 and 1911 made the balance between Protestants and Catholics difficult to maintain. The provincial elite came to be Protestants from Ontario who strongly believed that schools needed to operate in English and work to intentionally integrate immigrants into a non-denominational Christian civil religion. With the example of the changes initiated by the government of Manitoba, and strongly assimilationist policies being pursued by the government of Ontario at the same time, politicians in Saskatchewan seeking a single (or "national") school system had powerful examples to look to. Alberta and Saskatchewan's Catholic minorities desired constitutional protections for separate schools. The question of how to manage religious minorities in the new provinces was of national political importance. The Laurier government had to answer it while respecting the positions of both the Catholic and francophone elite of Quebec and the Protestant and English-speaking elite of Ontario. And, it had to do so while avoiding the political explosions triggered by the Manitoba Schools Crisis. In short, there were powerful incentives for the federal government to find a compromise.

The Laurier government did this by clarifying in Section 17 of the Saskatchewan Act 1905 (and in the matching Section 17 of the Alberta Act 1905) that Section 93 of the BNA Act applied to the new provinces, with the clarification that schools recognized under the 1901 Ordinances of the Northwest Territories would continue to be recognized and that nothing in the new acts should be read as restricting religious instruction in either public or separate schools. As Saskatchewan had not yet begun the government funding of high schools, this legislation – as in Ontario – entrenched public support for separate elementary schools.

Arriving at this foundational compromise had important political implications both provincially and nationally. At the provincial level, political parties were just beginning to form in 1905. Saskatchewan Conservatives, led by the former premier of the Northwest Territories Frederick Haultain, had opposed the Laurier compromise in the 1905 provincial election. For Haultain and the Conservative party, this opposition was publicly grounded in the position that the entrenchment of separate school rights in the province's constitution amounted to an infringement on provincial jurisdiction over education. But, many in the party were also closely tied to the anti-Catholic Orange Lodge and held strongly to the belief that a single school system was critical to the integration of a diverse population into the new polity. What became the provincial Liberal Party, led by the province's first premier F.W. Scott, was happy to accept the compromise enacted by the federal government and to generally leave the issue closed – even to the point of disavowing any connection to the support offered to them by the Catholic Bishop of Saint Boniface late in the campaign because of the Liberal's support of Catholic schools (Eager 1980; Langley 1950).

Laurier's actions on the school question in Saskatchewan (and Alberta) triggered a crisis within the federal Liberal Party. At issue was the first draft of the Saskatchewan and Alberta Acts which, in addition to the provisions mentioned above, included a clause that would have guaranteed that proceeds from the sale of land set aside to support education be shared "equitably" between separate and public school systems. Laurier himself understood, probably incorrectly, that this was a continuation of existing territorial practice. Those who supported him saw it as a way to ensure that separate and public schools were equitably supported across all three sources of government funding: provincial grants, property taxes, and Dominion Lands sales. Opposing Laurier's ideas was a group centred around Clifford Sifton, the minister of the interior and the most important Liberal in Western Canada. Sifton saw the Dominion Lands clause as a departure from, rather than a continuation of, existing practice, and he resigned from Cabinet in February 1905 over the issue. To some, his resignation signalled a split in the Liberal Party over the question of separate schools in Western Canada. Laurier managed to avoid this crisis by removing the Dominion Lands clause from the final draft of the bill. As in all the other provinces, concerns about the protection of francophone schooling were conflated with Catholic schooling, although the 1905 debates seem to have focused on religion (McLeod 1968). This removed the question of separate schools from the federal level and largely ended debate over separate schools in Alberta as well. But, in Saskatchewan, as in Manitoba and Ontario, funding for separate high schools would continue to be an issue for another quarter century.

The 1905 Saskatchewan Act created the constitutional reality of entrenched funding for separate elementary schools and the political reality of support for those schools from the provincial Liberal Party and opposition to them from the provincial Conservatives. The Liberals were the party identified with the support of Catholic (and other) minorities and the provincial Conservatives were associated with English-speaking Protestants and a preference for a single system of "national schools" (Lipset 1950). In the 1908 and 1912 elections, separate schools and the language of instruction issue were not terribly important. But, both language and religion were important issues in 1913–17, overlapping with parallel debates in Manitoba and Ontario and fuelled by the nationalism of the First World War. 1913 had seen legislative debates over the allocation of corporate income taxes between public and separate schools as well as on whether individual ratepayers were able to choose which system to direct their support to. By 1916, the Conservatives were making much of the poor standard of English teaching in the schools of Mennonite, German, Ukrainian, Doukhobor, and French Canadian communities after a report by E.H. Oliver called attention to the issue (McLeod 1968, 135). Education was also a major issue in the 1917 election, though their commitment to English-only education prevented the Conservatives from succeeding in ridings that were not predominantly anglophone. Though electorally successful, the Liberal government of Martin did pass legislation in 1918 restricting instruction in languages other than English to the first grade, which could be taught in French, or to an hour a day of French, in an attempt to forestall this pressure (McLeod 1968). Paired with legislation passed the year before that required attendance at a government-recognized school, minority communities in Saskatchewan were faced with a difficult choice. Some groups of conservative Mennonites chose to emigrate to Mexico rather than accede to pressure from the provincial government to send their children to public English-speaking schools (Bergen 1990; Klaasen 1970).

The early 1920s saw the linked issue of religion and language in schools simmer in Saskatchewan, but it became heated again during the 1928 election. The Conservative Party, led by James Anderson, took the line that integration into a diverse society required a single public school system, operating in English, that could assimilate Catholics and European immigrants into a single English-speaking polity that embodied what they referred to as British values. Anderson had been a senior official in the Department of Education before entering politics, with special expertise in the integration of new immigrants (the subject of his PhD dissertation), and a deep commitment to a single system of "national schools" as the best way to achieve this integration. Campaigning with the veiled support of the Ku Klux Klan, the Conservatives made opposition to separate schools an important issue during the 1929 campaign. After winning the election, the Conservatives amended the School Act, banning religious garb and symbols in any public school (Noonan 1998, 45). Unable to deal with the Depression, Anderson's government was defeated in 1934. The Liberals, who governed until 1944, seem to have returned to their preferred approach on the separate school question of supporting the status quo and allowing significant local flexibility on questions of language and religious instruction. And, although the CCF made reform of the education system a major goal after it won office in 1944, its changes did not affect or politicize separate schools. Instead, its reforms focused on the amalgamation of school boards, creation of comprehensive high schools, and improvement of teacher training.

Though most political attention was focused on the separate system, it is also important to note that a group of private schools were founded early in Saskatchewan's history which continue to be an important part of its independent school landscape. Initially known as junior colleges and now referred to as historical high schools, these schools were established by churches throughout the province and provided the only high school instruction in some areas. Some also provided the first year or two of a BA degree. Through the twentieth century, some junior colleges became part of the university system either through federation agreements with universities (Saint Thomas More College, Luther College, and Campion College) or through provincial purchase (Regina College, which became the University of Regina). Most Catholic junior colleges became separate high schools after full funding was extended to Catholic high schools in 1964 but some closed. However, the seven of these junior colleges that remain in independent operation make up the uniquely Saskatchewan category of "Historic High Schools" (Anderson 2003; Holdern 2013). They began to receive modest government financial support in 1965 and have received fairly substantial grants since 1991, officially as a continuing recognition of the service they provided to the province when there were few other places offering high school or university courses.

Rights

After the Anderson government, the question of government support for independent schools, separate high schools, and French-language schools largely dropped off the political radar in Saskatchewan until the 1960s. When these questions re-emerged, the initial focus was on the issue of funding for separate high schools. That this was a question was an artefact of the 1907 High School Act. Unlike in Alberta (where separate high schools existed in 1905 and thus received public funding beginning then), there had been no separate schools offering high school classes in Saskatchewan in 1905, and so there was no clear constitutional protection for them. When the provincial government created the category of public high schools in 1907, it created a distinct category of school board to regulate high schools and a different system of tax support for them. This meant that many communities had a public elementary school board, a separate elementary school board, and a public high school board. Religious high schools, of which there were thirty-two in operation by the 1960s, were entirely private.

For some denominations, especially Lutherans and Mennonites, this arrangement was satisfactory as it ensured that their schools could operate free from government interference. But for Catholics this was an unsatisfactory arrangement that they had fought against in 1907 and considered raising again in 1928–30. There had been some preliminary meetings between the government and the Catholic hierarchy in 1939 with an eye to preparing a reference decision on the question, but the issue had been "dropped" by the Catholic side (Weber n.d., 19). It was brought forward again in the late 1950s, when a "Brief on Parental Rights in Education" was presented to W.S. Lloyd (the long-time minister of education in the Douglas CCF government and, from 1961–4, premier) by the Catholic Schools Section of the Saskatchewan School Trustees Association (SSTA 1959, 1963). This brief, and the Catholic commentary around it, clearly grounded their demands on the government for full funding for separate high schools in rights arguments. They found support for a rights-based claim to public support for separate high schools in the "BNA Act, the School Ordinance of 1901, and the Saskatchewan Act of 1905" (3). But support for this vision of education could also be found in natural law and in the Universal Declaration of Human Rights, which protected parental rights in education (5). Practically speaking, their campaign was driven by the increasing demand for secondary education and the dramatic increase in resources that would be required to meet the needs of the baby boom generation.

This brief was formally presented to a committee of Cabinet by the Trustees Association on 4 June 1959. Discussion focused around the question of why these issues had taken so long to be raised by the separate school community, whether separate schools had taught high school level classes before 1905 (probably not), and the effects of school centralization on the separate system. In his address to the Catholic Trustees summarizing the meeting, the president of the Catholic Trustees Association, J.T. Schuck, was at pains to identify the "close spirit of cooperation and harmony that existed between ourselves, the Department of Education and the S.S.T.A. ... [and that] No one really wants a legal battle over the mechanics of law" (Schuck 1960).

In 1963, during the CCF government of Woodrow Lloyd (a former education minister), separate school funding again emerged as a political issue. In an exchange in the legislature between O.A. Turnbull, the minister of education, and Ross Thatcher, the Liberal leader of the Opposition, the question was posed whether the "government [had] received requests for school grants from private or denominational high schools or from any organization on behalf of such school" (February 20 p. 1–2 vol. 5 fifth session fourteenth legislature). Turnbull's response was that the ministry had been receiving such requests for a number of years and had taken a number of specific actions in response (though he did not specify what those responses were in the house). In 1964, Thatcher supported the government's throne speech promise to extend government funding to separate (Catholic) high schools. But, he asked that it go further arguing that

> the Liberal Party supports the principle of financial aid to private high schools of all denominations ... It is a well-known fact that for some years most private high schools in Saskatchewan, whether they be Mennonite, whether they be Lutheran, Anglican, or Roman Catholic, have found themselves in serious financial difficulties. They must depend almost completely on fees and donations for support because they receive little or no public monies. We think that today in Saskatchewan, the private high schools are doing a sound, outstanding, educational job. They are teaching the same curriculum and operate under the same standards as our tax-supported high schools. In general, they are inspected by the departmental high school superintendents and their students, as I understand it, write the regular examinations. Today the supporters of these private schools are obliged to support the public education system and in addition pay for the education of their children in the private schools. To us, this seems unfair ... Our main objective is to assure the children of Saskatchewan equal opportunities for good education and justice to the Saskatchewan taxpayer.
> (Thatcher sixth session fourteenth legislature 1964, 47)

The dividing line between the two parties on the schooling issue, then, was the extent to which funding ought to be extended to non-public high schools, with the CCF arguing that it ought to go only to Catholic separate high schools and the Liberals arguing that public support ought to also be extended to the other independent high schools in the province. In a narrow sense, then, it is not too surprising that the CCF's extension of funding to separate high schools in 1964 – right before the government triggered an election – caused so little controversy or debate. Indeed, though the CCF introduced funding for the separate school sector, it was the Thatcher government that introduced legislation clarifying how the governance of separate high school boards would operate.

But, in a broader sense, this bipartisanship towards government funding to independent and religious schools is very puzzling. The CCF and the Liberals had a deeply oppositional relationship and operated in a party system defined (in their minds) as a struggle between democratic socialism and free market capitalism. The province had just undergone two years of deep division over the introduction of Medicare and the ensuing doctors' strike. And yet, on the question of funding for separate high schools, there was agreement between the parties – surprising if we consider the debates of the 1920s and 1930s in Saskatchewan and the explosion of controversy when funding was extended to separate high schools in Ontario in 1985. But it was a classic example of policy layering: the extension of full funding to separate high schools created a policy window for the independent high schools in the province to lobby for government support. In 1960 there were thirty-two private high schools, thirteen of which would – after 1962 – become part of the fully funded separate system. About ten of the others, under significant fiscal pressure, lobbied the Liberal government of Ross Thatcher for public support and, when the Liberals won the 1964 election, this lobbying resulted in a grant of $85 per student per year towards operating expenses and a refund of 10 per cent on capital repairs or new projects. The private schools that received this grant fluctuated somewhat in numbers but would be grouped together as the "historical high schools" in the 1980s (Holdern 2013). Funding these schools opened up a common ground between the faith communities that had formed them and a more secularly oriented choice approach to school funding in the 1990s.

The mid-1960s also saw the emergence of francophone claims that were very much rooted in rights arguments. There was incremental progress towards self-governing francophone schools in the 1960s and 1970s, but it wasn't until the *Mahe* decision in 1990 that courts clearly found a right to self-governing schools for francophone minorities outside of Quebec. Initially, the government of the Northwest Territories had been bilingual in its courts, its legislative assembly, and – with a local option – in its schools. As English settlers quickly became more numerous, however, the government moved to change this. In 1892 the territorial government switched to an English-only Assembly and greatly restricted the teaching of French in public schools. As detailed above, this discord quickly became caught up in debates over the funding of Catholic separate schools (Julien 1995). Religion quickly subsumed language, and it was in Roman Catholic areas that instruction continued to be in French. However, by the turn of the century, francophones were a minority even within the Catholic community, meaning that this protection was not terribly effective when the government moved seriously against minority languages in 1917. In 1912, the francophone community in Saskatchewan had begun organizing as L'Association culturelle franco-canadienne de la Saskatchewan (ACFS). Francophone education was always an important part of that organization's mandate, but it was not until the 1960s that much progress was made on extending French-language instruction in Saskatchewan schools beyond its then current maximum of grade one and an hour a day in more senior grades (Julien 1995).

In 1965, francophone students in Saskatoon's Catholic system went on strike, calling to receive some religious education in French. The government's response was to set up the Tait Commission and, by 1968, create "type A" and "type B" schools that taught in French. These rights were extended through the 1970s, partly in response to the national dynamic created by the Royal Commission on Bilingualism and Biculturalism. By 1978 the province allowed for Area Minority Schools that could offer programs in any minority language but which depended on school boards granting permission for them to operate. Many boards declined to provide such schools or to provide French-language education only through French immersion programs or in bilingual settings. This made many in the community concerned that this way of delivering francophone education was setting kids up to be assimilated into the dominant language (Julien 1995, 121).

As in other provinces, this concern drove the francophone community to press for self-governing schools. Early progress on francophone self-government had been driven through legislative processes and, especially for such a small minority group, met with considerable success. But in the mid-1980s, when the ACFS really began to focus on self-governing schools, the Conservative government of Grant Devine refused to extend provincial support. Consequently, Saskatchewan's francophone community turned to the courts for relief between 1984 and 1986. In this, they benefited from the 1982 Constitution's entrenchment of language rights in education and the concerted efforts of francophone minorities across Canada to use the courts to press for recognition of their rights. Ultimately, the issues around self-governing francophone schools were resolved with the *Mahe* case in 1990 and quickly implemented by the incoming Romanow government (Julien 1995).

The rights arguments most visibly promoted by the francophone minority were administratively influential in ways that affected the progress of other groups and helped trigger a reassessment of Saskatchewan's school system in the late 1980s and early 1990s. This reassessment represents a policy window that, ultimately, would entrench choice as an important principle in Saskatchewan. Following *R. v. Jones* and early Charter decisions on francophone issues, Saskatchewan policymakers were keenly aware that any regulation of independent and religious schools would have to comply with the evolving Charter jurisprudence grounded in commitments to rights.

Finally, an important issue of rights and educational governance was before the courts in Saskatchewan as this book was being written. In

Good Spirit v. Christ the Teacher, a 2017 Court of Queen's Bench decision also known as the Theodore case, the trial court found that the provincial government's funding of non-Catholic students to attend separate schools violated both Section 2 and Section 15 of the Charter of Rights and Freedoms, could not be justified on the grounds of the *Oakes* test (that the violation of rights could be "demonstrably justified in a free and democratic society"), and were not protected from Charter scrutiny by Section 93 of the 1867 Canada Act or Section 17 of the Saskatchewan Act. The decision argued that only students who were baptized Catholics could be funded to attend separate schools while protected by Section 93 and Section 17. This decision has been appealed by both the separate school board association and the provincial government. In a March 2020 decision, the Saskatchewan Court of Appeal overturned each of the grounds of the initial decision, finding errors of legal interpretation. It was appealed to the Supreme Court of Canada, which denied leave of appeal in February 2021. This meant that the status quo situation of provincial funding of separate schools, and functionally open admission to those schools, could continue.

Parallel to this legal situation ran an interesting and dynamic political situation. In an almost unprecedented step, the provincial government passed legislation at the same time as it appealed the initial decision. Bill 89, The School Choice Protection Act, invoked the Canadian Constitution's notwithstanding clause (Section 33) and the notwithstanding provisions of the provincial Human Rights code to maintain the status quo with regards to funding separate schools. The government's primary justification for using this legislation was that there was the threat of substantial disruption in the education system (given the judgement's one year implementation period) and that it represented an infringement on parental choice. Surprisingly, the government's use of the notwithstanding clause did not trigger significant political opposition. Buckley Belanger, the sole NDP MP who spoke at the bill's second reading, was careful to articulate his party's support for Saskatchewan's publicly funded school system, both Catholic and public. The NDP opposition supported the government's appeal of the ruling, seeing clarity on such an important issue as an important public good, but opposed using Section 33 before the appeal was decided (Belanger, 15 November 2017, 2928 of Hansard, second session twenty-eighth legislature), especially as a stay of judgement had been granted in April (Beck, 7 May 2018, 4223). And, though the case had been appealed to the Supreme Court at the time of 2020 provincial election, the opposition did not make the situation a political issue.

Choice

Saskatchewan also extends public support to a number of other categories of schools, many of which are religious. Though some of the categories of the support date back to the 1960s, it has expanded most noticeably in the last thirty years, driven forward by choice-based arguments. The most established of these schools are the historical independent high schools (Anderson 2003; Holdern 2013; Braun 1991). Today, there are seven of these schools, most of which retain some religious affiliation but are predominantly identified as academically elite schools. They have their origins in the period before the Second World War, when many rural areas lacked the population to support public high schools and no government support was given to separate high schools. These needs were met by what, in 1960, was a network of some thirty-two private denominational high schools. After funding was extended to separate high schools in 1963, these private denominational schools fell in number to twelve by 1976 and then to eight by the 1990s (Noonan 1998). They continue to be funded by the government recognition of their role as historic "schools of necessity." Though they retain some residual religious affiliation, their primary character today is as the self-defining academically elite schools in the province. Their government funding grew more generous and more standardized in the 1990s as part of the review of the private school sector detailed below, but the place of the historic high schools in Saskatchewan's school system has been fundamentally stable.

The extension of government funding to other independent schools was the result of a policy window that opened in the 1980s for a number of reasons. Legally, as in other provinces, funding for francophone schools and court decisions mandating their self-government created important rights arguments. Administratively, Saskatchewan's minister of education was leading a wholesale review of the provincial curriculum. Politically, the 1982 election victory of Grant Devine's Progressive Conservatives brought to power a party that was firmly committed to reforming the public sector and which had a definite bent towards choice-based, promarket solutions. This created an environment where there was general discussion of school governance and funding in Saskatchewan. But the most direct factor was the growing number of private Christian schools. This created a category of private schools in the province that did not fit in well with existing legislation but which had very close political relationships with the Devine government. It was perhaps somewhat natural, then, that the new government sought to regularize their status, as well as that of homeschoolers (Interview with

Chris Gerrard, 1 August 2018). This created something of a policy problem: how was the government to ensure that the children attending these schools were receiving a quality education? Finally, the passage of the 1982 Constitution and the entrenchment of individual rights in the Charter of Rights and Freedoms created some uncertainty around whether governments could compel attendance, especially by those who opted out of the public system for religious reasons. Eventually tested in Alberta in the *R. v. Jones* case, this issue was closely followed in Saskatchewan.

Though the Saskatchewan government's consideration of the question of private or independent schools occurred at the same time as the changes to francophone education discussed above, the two issues did not overlap very much. Similarly, the question of separate schools was not in any way linked to the question of independent schools. They seem to have been treated as three different issues, and the separate school question as one with no real need for change (Interview with Chris Gerrard, 1 August 2018). Thus, the private school sector was understood to be the existing historic high schools, a handful of Seventh-Day Adventist schools that – though small – had also been around since the 1920s, and a sizeable number of Protestant Christian schools that had grown up since the 1970s. Talks between the Christian school community and the Department of Education had begun in 1983 about how to regularize the position of the newer generation of private Christian schools. Issues under consideration included compulsory attendance, post-secondary recognition of private education, and whether private schools should pay property taxes to municipalities. Also being discussed was shifting the system from one where private schools functioned as corporate entities and parents would ask the government for permission to enrol their children or establish a new independent school, to a system where parents would report their intent to operate or enrol their children in such schools. An important jurisdictional issue was that existing legislation had independent schools supervised by their local school boards – a troubling situation for them as local boards were often seen to be in competition with independent schools (Interview with Chris Gerrard, 1 August 2018).

The 1986 election, a significant curricular overhaul across the public system, and the ongoing *Jones* case in Alberta all delayed meaningful movement on the file. So, the first significant public approach to these problems was the 1987 *Review of Private Schooling in Saskatchewan*. Written by Gordon Dirks, who was working as a public servant and bible college administrator in the 1990s and who would later move to Alberta and serve in 2014–15 as minister of education in Jim Prentice's

Conservative government, the report acknowledged intellectual debts to Ontario's *Report of the Commission on Private Schools in Ontario* and Alberta's *Study of Private Schools in Alberta*. Dirks's report found that the historic high schools were receiving a grant equal to 58.8 per cent of the grant provided to public and separate schools (Dirks 1987, 27) and a grant of 10 per cent for any capital construction. The historic schools, as well as other private schools, also received in kind public support in forms such as shared use of libraries, driver training, and gifts of textbooks. Outside of the historic high schools, Dirks found a very unclear regulatory framework for private schools that left them in an unsatisfactory limbo. Thus, his conclusion was that they should be regulated, that homeschooling be allowed to continue, and that a clearer regulatory framework for both be set up. He also recommended that the province clarify that private schools were to be exempt from municipal property taxes, and that they receive a per-pupil grant of $50 per pupil per year (the historic high schools would continue to be funded at a higher level). Finally, the report advocated that Saskatchewan follow a recommendation of the Shapiro Report in Ontario and create mechanisms for the creation of Associate Schools that could affiliate with their local public or separate board and then receive substantial public funding.

This report was followed, in the fall of 1990, by the *Report of the Minister's Advisory Board on Independent Schools: Final Report to the Minister of Education*, which advised on the implementation of Dirks's recommendations. This was a much more extensive exercise deliberately designed not only to give the government direction but also to build a stable and workable consensus on those recommendations among stakeholders in the system. At the same time, the minister of education established an Independent Schools Branch in the Department of Education, made legislative changes to refer to private schools as independent schools, and amended the relevant acts exempting them from municipal property taxes. At the time, the independent schools saw exemption from property taxes as more financially lucrative for it than any grant scheme the government was likely to enact while those opposed to government support of private schools saw even very small grants as the start of a slippery slope towards extensive government funding. Thus, direct provincial government funding was quickly moved off the table. The branch's first director, Chris Gerrard, had been the minister's advisory board secretary and, before that, president of the Saskatchewan Association of Christian schools (Interview with Chris Gerrard, 1 August 2018). The report recognized that the system was under pressure because of new rights to education for the disabled in the Charter of Rights and

Freedoms, court decisions involving the francophone community, and extensive revisions to its core curriculum. Not mentioned in the report, but very significant political issues at the time, were the financial pressures facing the provincial government and the significant rural depopulation that was occurring (Pitsula and Rasmussen 1990). The report was guided by nine principles provided by the minister of education:

1. That the government of Saskatchewan has a compelling interest in the education of all Saskatchewan children, of which the primary vehicle is the public education system in its two dimensions, the public schools and the separate schools.
2. From either a historical, legal, or practical perspective, independent schools have the right to exist in Saskatchewan.
3. The Government has an interest and the responsibility to put in place a legislative and regulatory framework for the operation of independent schools in Saskatchewan.
4. In order to operate legitimately in Saskatchewan, independent schools will be required only to be registered and not licensed.
5. The costs of operating independent schools will continue to rest with parents who choose this form of education for their children. There will be no new operating grants beyond those currently provided to the historical high schools.
6. By their very nature, independent schools are similar to public schools in some respects and different in others.
7. Independent schools must provide a quality of education comparable to that of public schools.
8. Independent schools must abide by generally accepted teaching principles with respect to academic content, teaching pedagogy, teacher training, and child development.
9. Independent schools must not promote values which conflict with the rights, freedoms, and moral principles upon which our society is based.

(Saskatchewan 1990, 3)

These principles were broadly in line with the recommendations of the Dirks Report, except that the minister (and by extension, the advisory board) rejected Dirks's recommendation that some funding be offered to independent schools except for those schools which met the same requirements as the historical high schools. The upshot was a recommendation that four categories of independent school be recognized in regulation: historical high schools, alternative schools, accredited schools, and registered schools. Later, as the recommendations of the report were being transformed into regulation, a category of Associate School was also enacted – this kind of school receives 80 per cent of the funding of a public school, is supervised by the local board, must teach the provincial curriculum, and must employ provincially accredited teachers.

Even during the severe financial crisis of the mid-1990s, the NDP government did not seriously consider removing government funding from independent schools despite the party's electoral alliance with teachers' unions, deep commitment to the public system, and an extraordinary set of financial constraints (Interview with Pat Atkinson, 28 July 2015). With reference to the historic high schools, this seems to have been a result of an important part of caucus having had positive experiences as students or as parents of students (Interview with Richard Holdern, 2 April 2018). With reference to the more recently recognized independent schools, the government's position was more a commitment to ensuring that individual students, whose parents had chosen to have them educated outside the public system, were still receiving a good quality education. They were Saskatchewanian students who still deserved the basics of a good quality education (Interview with Pat Atkinson, 28 July 2015).

This schema was modified by the Saskatchewan Party government of Brad Wall in 2012 which created a new category of "qualified independent school." They receive provincial support at 50 per cent of the rate provided to public schools, provided "operation as an independent school for a minimum of two years, the utilization of Professional "A" teachers, the implementation of Saskatchewan curriculum, participation in the provincial accountability framework, adhering to ministry directives and policies, financial reporting, among other criteria" (Saskatchewan 2018, 6). The same changes also equalized funding for associate schools across the province at 80 per cent of the per-student rate of public schools. Though a significant amendment, this seems to have occurred with relatively minor opposition from the NDP – perhaps because the government was able to portray the funding as new money rather than a reallocation of funding within the education envelope. In the spring of 2022, again with little political debate, another category of "certified independent school" was created which would receive 75 per cent of the per-student rate of public school (Saskatchewan 2022).

Gay-Straight Alliances have been a simmering issue in both independent and private schools since about 2012 in Saskatchewan, with the NDP and important voices in the education establishment arguing that Alberta's example should be followed and made mandatory. To date, the government has rejected this approach in favour of regulations which require that schools facilitate a Gay-Straight Alliance club should students request it. This difference has not created major political controversy – perhaps because no compelling test case has come forward, perhaps because this more informal approach seems to be working reasonably well, or perhaps because progressive voices in the education sector have been focused on improving the situation of Indigenous students.

Conclusion

The evolution of the relationship between independent and religious schools in Saskatchewan and the provincial government is an almost classic case study of incremental change through policy layering within a policy regime. Once the deeply divisive issue of (Catholic) separate schools was settled early in the twentieth century as a result of federal government action – a classic exogenous shock – changes have been uncontentious, incremental, and have emerged out of a relatively tightly knit group of interested parties. By the 1960s, most changes were either politically non-controversial or were situations where both major parties were internally divided. Previous regimes of state support for religious schools have not been removed but, rather, added onto as new policy entrepreneurs have gained support for their specific schools and added characteristics of "rights" and "choice" to a foundational regime of "faith." One result of this pattern of change is that, though the independent school sector is tiny in Saskatchewan, the multiple different categories of schools and their different relationships with the provincial government make for a complex web of slightly different regulatory schemes and accountability relationships. Since the 1980s, this has contributed to the non-partisan nature of the independent school issue – both political parties have parts of their electoral coalition that have close ties to one or another category of independent school and so are hesitant to move against the status quo, whatever the status quo may be.

By threatening to disrupt the separate school system with a legal logic tied to a secular vision of a "faith" regime, the *Good Spirit* case had the potential of becoming an exogenous shock to the system like the one the Newfoundland financial crisis of the early 1990s or the Quiet Revolution in Quebec created for school systems in those provinces. The original decision would have threatened the integrity of the separate system and might have drawn independent schools into the resulting policy aftershocks. The Saskatchewan Party government's threat to use the Constitution's notwithstanding clause to defend the status quo raised the political stakes a great deal, even if it never became operational because of the Supreme Court decision. But the failure of the NDP to make a substantive political issue out of that threat, and the government's successful legal defence of the status quo, closed this potential moment of exogenous shock. Instead, the legal struggle around *Good Spirit* has confirmed the stability of the foundation of Saskatchewan's layered system. As this book was in production in the summer and fall of 2022, a scandal hit four independent schools in Saskatchewan. Serious allegations of physical and psychological abuse, the use of students for political campaigning, and the maltreatment of queer students have been laid against them; class action lawsuits are also being pursued. Three of these schools have been placed under provincial administration. There have been serious questions about how it is that such misconduct – which is alleged to have continued for at least a decade at one school – escaped government oversight mechanisms. Whether this scandal leads to a reconsideration of the Saskatchewan regime is, at this time, unknown.

7 Layering Faith and Choice in Alberta

Introduction

Alberta's contemporary education system offers the widest array of publicly funded schooling options in Canada, including several alternatives grounded in faith traditions (Banack 2015; Hiemstra 2017; Hiemstra and Brink 2006). Alberta has maintained a fully funded separate (essentially Catholic) system that parallels its public system since 1905, is the only province to offer fully public charter schools, and allows public school boards to host fully funded alternative schools that can maintain a distinct cultural, linguistic, pedagogical, or religious approach. Although the Calgary Board of Education has specifically prohibited religion-based alternative schools since 1983, over half of all school boards across the province (led most assertively by the Edmonton Public School Board) offer a variety of fully funded faith-based options under this format. In addition, Alberta offers accredited private schools, the majority of which are religious, between 60–70 per cent of the Per-Pupil Basic Instruction grant awarded to public schools, a funding level that was raised as recently as 2008. As of the 2020–1 school year, over 38,000 students attended private schools (representing roughly 4.3 per cent of all school enrollment in the province) and just shy of 175,000 students attended separate schools (representing roughly 24 per cent of total school enrollment) (Alberta Education 2022).

Finally, since 1988, the province has loosened the restrictions on homeschooling and is the only province to offer a per-student grant to participating families thereby allowing those so inclined, the vast majority for religious reasons, easy access to an educational experience completely removed from the traditional school environment. In addition to supporting these various avenues of education, Alberta has consistently provided religious schools considerable autonomy with respect to course content and pedagogical approach, so long as the broad parameters of the Alberta Education curriculum were followed. Most recently (and controversially), this has involved significant leeway on instruction around sexual education and orientation in ways that correspond with the religious teachings of the school in question, although this has recently begun to change.

Clearly the initial commitment to fund a separate Catholic system placed the province on a path-dependent trajectory with respect to Catholic education. The broader level of support that non-Catholic religious schools have received since 1967, both in terms of funding and autonomy, seems to fit well with the perception that Alberta has, for several decades, been an especially religious province. Indeed, not only was Alberta famously led by two prominent evangelical Christian radio personalities through the mid-twentieth century, William "Bible Bill" Aberhart, premier from 1935–44, and his protégé Ernest Manning, premier from 1944–68 (Banack 2014a; 2014b), a clear strain of religious-based social conservatism emerged in the PC party under premiers Ralph Klein and Ed Stelmach in the 1990s and early 2000s, culminating in what essentially amounted to a fifteen-year battle against the extension of a variety of rights for the LGBTQ community (Lloyd and Bonnett 2005; Rayside 2008). Yet, as this chapter will argue, although the overall evolution of this system of educational governance is attributable to a variety of systematic and case-specific factors, the degree of religiosity in the province is not central to this story. In fact, the Alberta government's initial decision to offer partial public aid to private schools in 1967, which was layered atop the existing policy of fully supporting Catholic separate schools, is better understood as a product of the strategies employed in the 1960s by the private school lobby, led by a group of outspoken Dutch Calvinist immigrants who had mostly arrived in the province in the wake of the Second World War, and the broader political culture of the province they operated within, than of the ideological preference or religious leanings of the government of the day. The particular strategies employed by the faith-based school lobby continued to aid in their various victories under the Progressive Conservative government, which ruled the province from 1971 until 2015. However, broader factors related to both self-interested electoral calculations and especially a general commitment to "school choice" – rooted, in turn, in a wide embrace of the ideology of neoliberalism in the 1990s in the province – are also of immense importance when seeking to understand how Alberta's intricate network of schooling options has come to be. Finally, it is impossible to come to grips with the evolution of Alberta's educational system without alluding to the province's broader populist political culture (Banack 2016; Laycock 1990; Stewart and Sayers 2013; Wesley 2011; Wiseman 1981, 2007), encapsulated most simply in the widespread belief across the citizenry in the intellectual and moral capacity of the "common person." For the education sector in particular, the popularity of such a sentiment has ensured that a parent's "right to choose" the type of schooling their children receive has been treated as a paramount concern in nearly all debates related to education in the province going back to the mid-1960s.

The following sections flesh out in much more detail the evolution of Alberta's approach to religious and private education in order to identify the precise factors that have propelled the province toward its current position. Following the broader pattern established in this book, this begins with an exploration of the historical period wherein the "faith" regime was central to the development of the educational system. At the heart of this regime were a variety of debates related to the appropriateness of publicly funding religious education – debates that proved relatively favourable to the province's Catholics, who were granted full funding, but less favourable to other religious groups. This is followed

Table 7.1. Key Dates in the Evolution of Alberta's Education System

Date	Event
1882	First publicly supported school in Edmonton
1884	Ordinance Providing for the Organization of Schools in the Northwest Territories
1892	School Ordinance
1905	Alberta Joins Confederation, separate schooling entrenched in Alberta Act
1935	Social Credit forms government, remains in power until 1971
1959	Royal Commission on Education in Alberta (the Cameron Commission) recommends private schooling remain unsubsidized
1967	Bill 29 establishes $100-per-student grant for private schools
1970	Per-student grant for private schools increased to $150
1971	Progressive Conservatives form government, hold power until 2015
1972	Per-student grant for private schools increased to $172
1975	School Act allows private schools to move under "umbrella" of public school board, receive full funding
1983	Education minister creates the Committee for Tolerance and Understanding to investigate private school curriculum
1988	School Act that specifically acknowledges the rights of public boards to establish faith-based alternative programs
1998	Provincial Private School Funding Task Force recommends an increase in private school funding from 50 to 60 per cent of basic instructional grant, government acquiesces
2008	Private school funding raised to 70 per cent of basic instructional grant
2020	United Conservative government passes Choice in Education Act

by an examination of the 1950s and especially the 1960s wherein the regime of "faith" is replaced with a regime of "rights" in a transition that looks nearly identical to the one previously examined in the chapter on British Columbia. In fact, it was the exogenous pressures created by the influx of new immigrants in the post–Second World War era, especially those from the Dutch Reformed tradition, that ensured that the rights of parents became the central concern of the debate. This ultimately culminated with the introduction of partial funding for private schools in 1967 to ensure that parents' rights to choose the type of education their children received were, in fact, honoured. Finally, this chapter considers the evolution of the educational system under the lengthy period of Progressive Conservative (PC) rule (1971–2015), wherein an overarching defence of "choice" largely explains key policy decisions made across a variety of educational issues. This is especially so since the mid-1990s when a second set of exogenous pressures, the PC government's ideological commitment to the principles of neoliberalism, including a firm belief in the benefits to be gained by introducing the logic of the market into the education system, emerged. The dominance of the "choice" regime in contemporary Alberta clearly corresponds with the vast network of education options now available to parents in the province, including many educational options rooted in faith.

Historical Foundations: The Constitutional Entrenchment of Faith Education

Much of the initial framework that guided the development of the education system in Alberta was laid prior to the creation of the province in 1905 and was discussed in detail in the preceding chapter on Saskatchewan's educational system. On the land now known as Alberta, various forms of schooling took place well before 1905, initially under the direction of the Hudson's Bay Company, then the Territorial Council of the Northwest Territories. The first schools in the region were private schools operated by Christian missionaries, the majority being Catholic (Hop 1982, 54–8). With the passage of the North-West Territories Act in 1875, the creation of the Territorial Council in 1875, the opening of the first tax-supported school in Edmonton in 1882, and finally the Ordinance Providing for the Organization of Schools in the Northwest Territories in 1884, the basic framework for a public system was installed. Manzer (1994, 56) has labelled this initial public system a "concurrent endowment of confessional systems" model because it allowed for schools to remain affiliated with (and essentially under the control of) either a Protestant or Catholic church, despite the assurance that such schools would receive full public funding. In fact, the 1884 Ordinance created a Board of Education that was independent of the Council and equally staffed with Catholic and Protestant representatives. It further established the right of these groups to form publicly supported schools when they were minorities within a particular community. This approach was quite similar to the initial systems created in both Quebec and Manitoba.

Yet, as early as 1885, the Territorial Council began to weaken the dual confessional model by reducing the power possessed by the religious elements of the Board of Education (Hiemstra 2003). This represented the first in a series of steps taken by the Territorial Council, overwhelmingly supported by the de facto premier of the territory, F.W.G. Haultain, that led to a clear restriction on religious activities in public schools as well as a significantly reduced role for Catholic representatives within the Board of Education, eventually culminating in the adoption of the "minority denominational district" model of public schooling in Alberta encapsulated in the 1892 School Ordinance (Manzer 1994, 55–7). This model, patterned after the Upper Canada (Ontario) approach to public schooling, established a non-sectarian state system that allowed separate schools for Catholics and Protestant minorities and, in the words of Hiemstra, "furthered the creation of a school system based on state control, centralization, and uniformity" (2003, 8; see also Hiemstra 2006, 26–9). Although the 1892 Ordinance and the subsequent 1905 Alberta Act solidified the rights of Catholics to form separate, publicly funded schools throughout Alberta (mirroring developments in Saskatchewan), Hiemstra further argues that the shift from the dual confessional model to the minority denomination district model in the late nineteenth century entailed a significant loss of autonomy for both Catholic parents and the Catholic Church with respect to educational matters (12).

A distinct, although similarly important, historical precedent within the early years of Alberta's education system was the compromise reached with Hutterite communities after they arrived in the province in 1918. An Anabaptist and pacifist Christian farming group of German heritage dedicated to communal-living, most Hutterite communities in Alberta were able to reach an agreement with the province that allowed for the creation of special schools that were funded by the province and followed the basic curriculum but also permitted instruction to proceed in German and included special religion and history classes to be held at the end of each day (Wagner 1998, 192). As Hiemstra has observed, although the public school system essentially outlawed sectarian-based instruction, "in practice it allowed a sectarian-type of minority to segregate within its own public school," a model that was replicated for a tight-knit Dutch Calvinist community in Neerlandia as well (2006, 29). Such schools represented, for Wagner, the first alternative model public school in the province (1998, 192), a model that would re-emerge in both the 1970s and 1990s as Alberta sought to increase both parental choice and competition between schools by supporting a variety of new programs within their public system.

The Partial Funding of Private Schools: Establishing the Right to Choose

Having established the constitutional right to a denominationally based "separate" schooling system in 1905 in parallel with Saskatchewan (though with the important difference that Catholic high schools were immediately funded in Alberta), as well as the precedent of a faith-based public option for a select group of non-Catholic religious minorities, the next significant milestone in the evolution of Alberta's education system was the introduction of partial funding for private schools in 1967. Unlike the evolution of Manitoba's education system, this occurred with little connection to a much quieter (and less successful) push for the creation of a French-language education system controlled by the francophone minority in the province. Indeed, as Behiels (2004) has detailed, despite a determined lobbying effort on the part of various organizations dating back to 1925 that stressed the educational rights of Alberta's francophones, the provincial government only very partially acquiesced over time. In fact, after small concessions were made in the 1960s and 70s that allowed public schools in francophone communities to offer French-language instruction for part of the day, the PC governments of the 1970s and 80s refused to budge further (Behiels 2004, 138–9). Unfortunately for Alberta francophones, the Alberta government's ongoing opposition to a full francophone system would become wrapped up in a much larger constitutional battle with Ottawa in the late 1970s and early 1980s. PC premier Peter Lougheed was especially adamant that the 1982 Charter of Rights (including Section 23, which spelled out the rights to education for francophones) ought to be resisted as an unwelcome intrusion on provincial jurisdiction, further impeding the educational wishes of the francophone community. It took a unanimous Supreme Court of Canada ruling in 1990 (*Mahe v. Alberta*) against the arguments of the Alberta government to finally force the PCs to create a pure francophone system in 1993. In 2018, there are roughly 8,400 students enrolled in the francophone schooling system in Alberta (Alberta Education 2018).

Standing in stark contrast to the experience of the francophone education lobby, the private school lobby in Alberta has experienced a far more receptive political environment. This was certainly not always the case but, beginning in the mid-1960s, a particular contingent of the private school lobby was able to alter the discourse around private education in the province from one essentially hostile to the notion of combining religion and publicly funded education to one in agreement with the notion that a parent ought to have the right to choose the type of education their children receive and to be assisted in this choice by public subsidies. Much like the story that would unfold in British Columbia, this shift in conceptualizing the debate around the public funding of private education from a focus on "faith" to a focus on the "rights of parents" would mark a significant turning point in the history of Alberta's educational structure and continues to underlie a unique approach to education among the Canadian provinces.

This history of private education in the province extends well before 1905. Interestingly, the 1892 Ordinance that Hiemstra identifies as being harmful to Catholic autonomy in educational matters has also been singled out as a key driver in the development of the private school sector in Alberta. As Hop (1982, 55–7) notes, efforts by the Territorial Council to abandon the goal of "Christianization" within the education system and the specific decision to limit explicit Christian instruction to a single thirty-minute period each day did much to revitalize interest in faith-based private schools in the province for non-Catholics. Although limited statistical data exists on private education in Alberta's early years, in 1912–13 there were twenty-one private schools (nearly all associated with a particular Protestant denomination) enrolling over 3500 students (61–2). By 1921 this number dropped to 2,274 as the province closed several schools that were violating the requirement that English was to be used as the primary language of instruction. As the public system continued to move toward a more secular orientation in the 1930s, private school enrolment again increased, and in 1945 2.45 per cent of students were attending private schools (68–74).

In the early 1950s, the Board of the Calvin Central Christian School of Edmonton directly contacted the premier and education minister in search of public funding for private faith-based education (Digout 1969, 43). Although this request was not greeted with much enthusiasm in government, it did represent the first notable effort on the part of specifically Dutch immigrants belonging to the Christian Reformed Church in Alberta to seek such funding. Motivated by a neo-Calvinist philosophy that understood religion and its proper role within the institutions of society in a fundamentally different (and essentially all-encompassing) manner than that of most mainstream Protestants in Alberta, this particular group of citizens would largely become the principal leaders of the movement that sought public funds for private faith-based schools in Alberta (Hiemstra 2005). Strongly opposed to what they saw as the de-religionization of non-Catholic public schools in the province, Dutch immigrants retreated from public schools, leading to large increases in the number of students attending private schools affiliated with the Christian Reformed Church (Cymbol 2009, 10).

That said, the first significant organized lobby group representing private schools in Alberta, the Association of Private Schools and Colleges in Alberta (APSCA), was formed in 1958 without much representation from the Dutch community. This is significant because it helps to explain why the initial brief authored by this group and presented to the 1959 Royal Commission on Education in Alberta (the Cameron Commission) shortly after its creation did not seek public aid for private schools (Digout 1969, 35). The subsequent conclusion by the Cameron Commission that private schools should exist "without cost to the taxpayer" was thus uncontroversial within most of the private school world (Government of Alberta 1959, 257; Bergen 1982, 317). The Social Credit (SC) government shared this perspective. In fact, in 1962 the bulk of the party voted down a resolution brought forward by SC backbench MLA Earl Ansley that requested public funding for private schools. Of SC's fifty-seven MLAs, only six supported the motion. Alberta's education minister Anders Aalborg was forcefully opposed, suggesting that religion was a matter for the home and church, not the school. This was an opinion ostensibly shared by the overtly religious Premier Manning, who routinely dismissed calls from Christian citizens to enforce Christian lessons in the public school curriculum throughout his tenure (Digout 1969, 49–50; von Heyking 2013; Manning 1944, 1948). In 1963 Aalborg reaffirmed the government's position: "No public funding for private schools unless they are ministering to a public need such as assisting [handicapped] children" (Hollaar 2008). Yet, in March of 1966 the Alberta legislature, still dominated by SC MLAs, would pass a resolution by a vote of 34–16 recommending public aid for private schools, leading to a 1967 bill that allowed for a $100 per-student grant implemented for the 1967–8 school year. What explains this shift of opinion in four short years? Fundamentally, it is a story of successful lobbying by policy entrepreneurs who managed to open a policy window in the mid-1960s by shifting the axis of the debate from a focus on faith to a focus on a parent's right to choose – a story that strongly foreshadows the evolution of the debate in British Columbia.

The central policy entrepreneurs in this story are two related groups with strong Dutch Reform roots who launched campaigns for public aid in the early 1960s. The Christian Action Foundation, under the leadership of influential Christian Reformed Reverend Louis Tamminga, initially sought to "explore the direction which political life is taking ... [and develop] a Christian program of action" (The Christian Vanguard 1962, quoted in Digout 1969, 41). Tamminga and fellow group leaders soon narrowed much of their scope, however, and worked closely with the Societies for Christian Education (SCE), a group of parents supporting existing Dutch Reformed Christian day schools in the province, to lobby the government for public financing of private schools. This campaign included meeting individual MLAs and cabinet ministers, authoring articles and briefs addressed to the Cabinet, and gradually working to convince APSCA members to change course and officially seek public funding for private schools. A breakthrough occurred with respect to the last of these activities in 1964 when APSCA, after a couple of years of intense internal debate, passed a motion suggesting that "according to the principles of equity and justice, public funds should be made available to private schools" (Digout 1969, 64–5). A brief expansion of this resolution was quickly drafted and presented to Cabinet. Thus, a united front between those from the Dutch Reformed Christian community and the broader private schools sector represented by APSCA had now formed and would place additional pressure upon Alberta MLAs, ultimately culminating in the passing of a resolution put forth by SC MLA Donald Fleming in March of 1966 that requested immediate public funding for private schools.

In support of the resolution, Fleming stressed the double burden of taxation faced by private school supporters, the fact that Catholic residents already received publicly funded faith-based education, the cost to the public purse should private schools be forced to close for financial reasons, and finally the public system's neglect of "important things, such as the worth and dignity of man, his destiny, and his responsibility to God and his fellow man" before requesting immediate public funding for such schools (Digout 1969, 87). Although successful, support for the resolution was not unanimous. A number of MLAs spoke in opposition, including the new education minister himself, Randolph McKinnon, who passionately defended the public system. Despite this opposition, the government moved forward and, in 1967, passed Bill 29. In 1970, SC would increase this annual grant from $100 to $150 per pupil. Alberta has provided public aid to private schools, at gradually increasing levels, ever since.

Several noteworthy points emerge with respect to understanding the factors behind Alberta's introduction of public funding for private schools in 1967. First, despite being long opposed to the use of public funds for private schools, neither the Alberta Teachers' Association (ATA) nor the Alberta School Trustees' Associations (ASTA), the two most powerful interest groups within the province's education policy community, did much to pressure the government on the issue until just days prior (Bergen 1982, 318) and then *after* Bill 29 had been passed (Digout 1969, 94–7). Second, the decision to offer funding to such private schools was caucus rather than cabinet driven. Given the general assumption that cabinet is the chief policy agenda-setter within the Westminster system, it is surprising that movement on this issue was initially driven by resolutions put forth by government backbenchers in 1962 and 1966. Even more surprising, neither the premier nor many prominent cabinet ministers publicly supported the 1966 resolution (and the education minister was loudly in opposition!) yet it easily captured the required support in the legislature. The caucus-driven nature of this decision speaks to the broader populist conception of democracy inherent in Alberta's unique political culture in that "the people's" representatives managed to overrule the objections of those within the cabinet. Third, the lobbying campaign, led most assertively by leaders from Alberta's Reformed Christian community within both the Christian Action Foundation and the SCE, and later joined by the broader APSCA membership, was clearly a success. The bulk of SC MLAs, including Manning and former education minister Aalborg, were persuaded by this ongoing lobby to change their minds on the issue in a relatively short period of time. Aalborg would later note that, given the potential for private schools to be forced to cease operations without public funding, it was the government's duty to respond because a parent's right to send their children to a public or private school must be protected (Digout 1969, 77–9). An exploration of convention debates, op-ed pieces, and briefs presented to MLAs and Cabinet by the three primary groups who lobbied for public aid was captured well in a 1962 APSCA convention resolution, that "the right to educate their children belongs to the parents, and ... the basic democratic freedom of parents to exercise this right to educate their children or have them educated in harmony with their convictions" must be respected (APSCA 1962, quoted in Digout 1969, 53). In other words, refusing to fund all schools (public and private) across the province was deemed inconsistent with true equality and democracy because it failed to recognize the pluralistic character of society.

That is, the central message espoused by the Alberta-based private school lobby did not utilize pleas related to the defence of the principle of religious liberty nor did they attempt to overtly demonize the public school system's gradual embrace of secularism. No doubt the "de-religionization" of public schools motivated the majority of private school supporters to pull their children from the public system, but the broader message the lobby groups directed at the SC government was one built around the notion of pluralism, the justice inherent in ensuring a multiplicity of approaches to education were supported, and especially the right of parents to choose which approach best suited their children. This message united the private school movement in the province, both religious and secular, and helped convince the vast majority of MLAs that public aid was in fact the right thing to do. These groups successfully changed the focus of the debate from a focus on "faith" to one of "the rights of parents," a strategy and outcome that would play out in nearly identical fashion in British Columbia, leading to the introduction of partial funding for independent schools in that province a decade later.

The Progressive Conservative's Approach to Education: The Entrenchment of Choice

In 1971 Peter Lougheed's Progressive Conservative's toppled the Social Credit government and initiated the longest unbroken reign of any provincial party in Canadian history. It was under consecutive PC governments that support for private schooling in general, and faith-based education in particular, became deeply entrenched in Alberta's educational system. Underlying this outcome was a broad and long-running commitment to promoting choice in schooling, which Wagner (1998, 180–243) labels the "hallmark of the PCs' education policy." Like British Columbia, the broad embrace of "the parent's right to choose" within the education policy system of Alberta in the 1960s made it an easy transition to a regime ultimately built upon the principle of choice in general. Not only would this commitment generate consistent increases in the amount of public funding made available to private schools throughout the PCs' reign, it would also underline the government's eventual support for both alternative schooling within the public sector, including several religious alternatives, the introduction of secular charter schools, as well as the autonomy of religious schools over recent attempts to standardize educational instruction around sexual orientation and protect LGBTQ students from discrimination.

On taking office in 1971, the PCs were immediately greeted by the lobbying efforts of the largest private school organization in the province, formerly APSCA, now renamed the Association of Independent

Schools and Colleges of Alberta (AISCA). AISCA undertook a broad campaign over the next several years reaching out directly to PC MLAs, ensuring ongoing dialogue with the minister of education and department officials, and distributing articles and pamphlets that called attention to the plight of private schools. These efforts were aided by continued action by the SCE that operated as both the largest member of AISCA and as an independent body carrying out additional lobbying where deemed appropriate (Sloan 1980, 72–5, 83–92).

That this lobbying paid off is witnessed most clearly in the PCs' approach to the funding of private schools, which includes consistent and often dramatic increases beginning early in their mandate. In 1972 the annual per-pupil grant was raised from $160 to $172 a year later. In 1974 the funding formula was changed to reflect a portion of the per-pupil grant offered to public schools. Initially, private schools were offered one-third of that provided to public schools (excluding costs for transportation and capital expenditures), although the overall amount would subsequently increase yearly, topping out at 75 per cent in 1982. Such gradual increases were a boon to private school operators, especially to faith-based institutions that tended to draw children from lower income families and were facing ever-increasing financial pressures due to enhanced educational costs (Sloan 1980, 60–2, 65; Bergen 1982, 320–1).

Despite such increases, AISCA continued its pursuit of full funding. Although broadly sympathetic to the plight of private schools (especially the smaller faith-based ones that faced financial hardships), the PC caucus did contain a sizeable segment of MLAs who strongly opposed any public aid flowing to private schools. This opposition was fuelled by both the lobbying efforts of the ATA and the ASTA, who routinely denounced the use of public funds for private schools (Sloan 1980, 67–70), as well as the concerns of certain MLAs that "some religious communities were using the prospect of education as an excuse for following practices that were repugnant" (Interview with David King, 11 August 2014). In response to this divide within caucus in the 1970s, education minister Lou Hyndman proposed a compromise dubbed the "umbrella concept" wherein private schools could enter into agreements with local public school boards, essentially allowing them to become part of the public system with access to full funding, while retaining a certain degree of autonomy to offer lessons grounded in a religious outlook. The potential for this new arrangement was formalized in an amendment to the Alberta School Act in 1975 and represented the early stages of what are now called "Alternative Schools" in Alberta. Although very few agreements were reached between private schools and public boards in the first decade after the umbrella concept was introduced, and a particularly contentious debate unfolded within the Calgary Board of Education resulting in a 1983 decision to prohibit agreements between the board and religious private schools which still stands today (Taylor 2001a), over half of all school boards across the province currently offer a variety of fully funded alternative options, including several faith-based options. Although the Edmonton Public School Board also initially prohibited faith-based private schools from participating in such arrangements, by the mid-1990s it had opened a wide variety of alternative schools, including at least ten faith-based ones, thanks to a very strong proponent of school choice in Emery Dosdall (Dosdall 2001). That these explicitly religious programs exist is largely the result of a section of the 1988 School Act that specifically acknowledges the rights of public boards to establish faith-based alternative programs (Hiemstra 2006, 30–2).

Beginning in 1990, AISCA launched a campaign dubbed "Choices for Children" that emphasized that the public funding of private schools "is a matter of right and also a matter of public interest, rather than just a politically convenient handout" (Interview with Gary Duthler, 19 August 2015). This campaign culminated with the introduction of a private member's bill in 1997 by a PC backbencher calling for an immediate increase of funding for private schools from 50 per cent to 100 per cent. The bill sharply divided the PC caucus between those supportive of funding (including provincial treasurer and prominent evangelical Christian Stockwell Day) and those opposed (including education minister Gary Mar). In an effort to quell caucus infighting over the issue, Premier Klein created the Private School Funding Task Force to investigate the issue of private school funding by way of expert reports and public consultation (Kachur 1999, 111–12). In 1998 a final recommendation was made to government which centred around an increase in funding from 50 to 60 per cent of the basic instructional grant, a decision that "reflects our view that public schools must be the first priority for government funding but also recognizes the public good provided by accredited private schools and the importance of providing choices for parents" (Government of Alberta 1998). Although significant opposition to any increase in funds existed in caucus and the broader PC membership, Klein overruled his education minister and accepted the recommendations of the task force.

The mid-1990s also saw Alberta introduce charter schools into the public system, a development that continues to stand alone among Canadian provincial education systems. Responding to concerns over the state of education in the province generally and a growing sense

that schools were not doing enough to prepare students for the glo-
balizing economy in particular, the government commissioned a study
in 1993. The subsequent report, *Charter Schools: Provisions for Choice in
Public Schools*, suggested that a lack of competition between schools in
the public sector was leading to "the failure of public schools to provide
the level of excellence in education necessary for success in an increasingly competitive society" (Alberta Education 1993, 4). Such reasoning
fit neatly with the Klein government's broader embrace of neoliberal
principles and undergirded a whole host of education reforms, including an increase in funding to private schools, a 12 per cent funding cut
to public schools, and the consolidation of school boards from 141 to
68 (Bosetti and Butterfield 2016; Kachur 1999). But the introduction of
fully funded charter schools was clearly the most revolutionary of the
mid-nineties reforms. The new legislation insisted that charter schools
could not be religiously affiliated nor could they charge tuition or turn
away students unless they were operating at capacity. They were also
required to hire certified teachers and follow the provincial curriculum,
but were autonomous from existing school boards and free to provide
"innovative or enhanced means of delivering education in order to
improve student learning" (Alberta Education 2011, 1). In doing so, the
Alberta government was attempting to break "the monopoly on public
education" in the province. Although the existence of charter schools in
Alberta remains somewhat controversial, in 2019–20, there were 9921
students representing just over 1 per cent of the total student population enrolled in the thirteen existing charter schools (Alberta Education
2020).

In the mid-2000s, AISCA revamped their lobbying efforts to again
have funding rise to account for the growing inflationary pressures
private schools were facing. In 2008 the government of Ed Stelmach
responded with a funding increase from 60 per cent of the basic instructional grant to 70 per cent for private schools willing to adhere to
enhanced accountability measures, a level that remains in place today.
In defending the increase, Stelmach noted the importance of continuing
to ensure education choice for parents ("Provincial Funding for Private
Schools Draws Public Ire," *Calgary Herald*, 31 July 2008).

Undergirding the PCs' general approach to education, at least since
the 1990s, was the desire to introduce market forces into the education system (Harrison and Kachur 1999) – a pattern that would again
be followed in British Columbia under premier Gordon Campbell.
Indeed, responding to a call to defund private religious schools in 2008,
well known PC cabinet minister Dave Hancock spoke directly to this
commitment:

As long as [private schools] are educating their children to Alberta's standards, they are also putting pressure on the public system to be the best that it can be. So I think there's a role for private schools ... I am a strong supporter of the public school system but I'm also a very strong supporter of the concept of choice.

(Legislative Assembly of Alberta 2008, 243)

A long-serving senior Alberta Education official agreed:

Ideologically, there's a belief in Alberta that by providing parental choice you have more engagement, more buy-in, and more empowerment. There's a real ethos in this province ... its certainly clear from this government ... that having choice for parents ... is very powerful and very important. So even at the ministerial level, choice is paramount.

(Interview with K, 17 December 2013)

This commitment is officially encapsulated within the introduction of Alberta Education's handbook on alternative programs, which highlights "the right and responsibility of parents to make decisions that best suit the needs of their children" and emphasizes the notion that, in supporting school choice, "the province strengthens the public school system and promotes the availability of diverse education experiences for Alberta students" (Alberta Education 2010, 1). The United Conservative Party (UCP), which formed government in 2019 and clearly shares the former PC government's ideological commitment to the principles of neoliberalism, extended this support in 2020 by adding the infamous UN's Declaration of Human Rights passage speaking to the "prior right" parents have over the education of their children to the preamble of the provincial Education Act, in addition to encouraging more charter schools and providing homeschooling families more autonomy with the Choice in Education Act ("LaGrange Unveils Changes to Spur More Charter Schools, Unfunded Homeschooling Option," *CBC News*, 28 May 2020).

That said, to understand Alberta's overall commitment to school choice, which stretches back well before Klein's reforms, one must turn to the broader political environment produced by two historical factors unique to the province. The first historical factor is the prevalence in Alberta of a populist political culture suspicious of "elites" and "experts" while favouring the wisdom of "ordinary people" (Banack 2016; Laycock 1990; Stewart and Sayers 2013). Just as the existence of a pre-ideological democratic morality, derived from a belief in the moral and intellectual capacities of the "common people," helps one understand Alberta SC's initial decision to offer partial funding to private schools (both in terms of allowing a caucus-wide vote and the more general acceptance of the private school lobby's arguments regarding parental choice over the dictates of the state), Alberta's populist political culture is a key factor explaining the PCs' long-running endorsement of school choice, especially before the introduction of the neoliberal-inspired reforms of the mid-1990s. Indeed, when asked to identify the reasons behind the PC government's insistence on promoting choice in education in the 1970s, then education minister David King noted the importance of

> A fundamental sense of self-initiated collective activity ... that is deeply embedded in life in Alberta. You can go back to rural electrification in the 1950s and the '60s, or the old telephone co-ops, or the gas co-ops, or the agrarian co-ops, or the United Farmers of Alberta ... There is just a very strong sense in Alberta of both cooperative and self-initiated organization that we're real believers in the commons, and it's not the government that is always the best steward of the commons.
> (Interview with David King, 11 August 2014)

The second historical factor, undeniably related to the first, is the long-running ideological commitment by dominant Alberta parties to "free choice" in general and the benefits of open competition within a free marketplace in particular. As Wesley has demonstrated, successful Alberta politicians have, for more than half a century, consistently preached a "freedom-based narrative" structured around a conservative individualism that emphasizes "personal responsibility, free enterprise, private-sector development, entrepreneurship, a strong work ethic, the evils of socialism, and the protection of individual rights and liberties" (2011, 55–6). More could be said with respect to the origins and development of these factors within Alberta politics (see Banack 2016) but, for education policy in particular, this aspect of the province's political culture has generated a unique and long-running reverence for the right of parents to "choose" the type of schooling their children receive. And this in turn has created significant ongoing opportunities for various faith-based educational institutions in Alberta.

The Autonomy of Faith-Based Schools

Although the funding of private schools has tended to dominate discussions around faith-based schooling in Alberta, the issue of school autonomy has never been far from the debate. Nor has the government of Alberta traditionally declined to weigh in on these sensitive debates. There are many ways in which the issue of autonomy can arise, but the central issues with respect to faith-based schools in Alberta have revolved around the use of accredited teachers and the teaching of religious tenets that challenge widely shared understandings of acceptable social behaviour. The first of these issues rose to the forefront in the early 1970s when a collection of conservative Holdeman Mennonite private schools, for largely religious reasons, refused to employ certified teachers or follow the government-approved curriculum. This was a clear violation of the existing School Act. Although initially reluctant to take legal action against such schools, the attorney general did eventually put one parent, Elmer Wiebe, on trial in 1978 for sending his child to an illegal school (Wagner 1998, 183–6). However, ruling that a prohibition against such schools was a violation of the defendant's right to freedom of religion as protected by the Alberta Bill of Rights, the court found Wiebe not guilty (Bergen 1981, 77–83). Despite calls from media outlets to appeal, Premier Lougheed chose to respect the ruling and created a new category of private schools (Category 4 Schools) that would be permitted to operate without certified teachers but would also be ineligible for public funds. The categorization of private schools has since changed, but there still exists in Alberta a segment of unfunded private schools (Registered Private Schools) that can operate with the approval of the minister of education despite not using certified teachers or following the government-approved curriculum.

As noted above, throughout the 1970s, concerns about the potential that certain faith-based schools "were using the prospect of education as an excuse for following practices that were repugnant" (Interview with David King, 11 August 2014) were voiced by some PC MLAs. Ironically, it was the actions of a public-school teacher, the notorious Jim Keegstra, that reignited this debate in the mid-1980s. In response to the revelations that Keegstra had included explicitly anti-Semitic commentary in his social studies lessons for over a decade, education minister David King created the Committee for Tolerance and Understanding in 1983, which was tasked with recommending ways to ensure Alberta schools were fostering tolerance and respect for human rights and individual dignity.

An initial paper by the commission that focused squarely upon faith-based private schools in the province left little doubt as to the potential danger inherent in such institutions: "private schools, by their very nature, do not adequately meet the spirit and intent of some of the principles [related to tolerance] set out by the Committee" (Ghitter 1984, 15). This line of reasoning was similarly employed by a group called Save

Public Education that led a successful campaign against the inclusion of religious alternative schools within Calgary in the early 1980s (Taylor 2001a, 2001b), and continues to represent the overarching position held by the ATA. In other words, concerns about faith-based private schools and their susceptibility to intolerant messages appearing in their lessons have long existed in the province yet concerns related to protecting the autonomy of faith schools have tended to win out against fears of intolerance. Indeed, the PCs ignored calls from both the Ghitter Report and a separate investigation into private schooling (Woods Gordon Management Consultants 1984) that recommended tighter controls on all private schools in the provinces and the outright abolishment of the unfunded Category 4 Schools.

However, in 1983, King did initiate a legal case against the Western Baptist Academy run by pastor Larry Jones. Although the introduction of Category 4 Private Schools allowed for schools such as Jones's to operate without employing certified teachers or adhering to the provincial curriculum, they were still required to apply for and receive a licence from the minister. A devout evangelical Christian, Jones was convinced that seeking such a licence was tantamount to putting the laws of the state ahead of the laws of God and therefore a sin (Wagner 1999). His arguments were dismissed in court, including an appeal before the Supreme Court of Canada, and Jones would eventually spend ten days in prison. However, upon his release he immediately returned to oversee his unlicensed school. It was becoming clear to newly minted education minister Jim Dinning that further attempts to prosecute Jones would severely damage the generally positive relationship the party had with evangelical Christians in the province (Wagner 1998, 215). Dinning therefore called on Gary Duthler, head of AISCA, in 1988 to assist with brokering a compromise with Jones.

AISCA had already worked closely with the PC government on the writing of the new School Act, which was to be introduced in 1988. One noteworthy aspect of the new act was that it abandoned pre-existing language requiring Category 4 Private Schools to seek permission from the minister in order to operate and instead focused on the conditions schools were to meet in order to possess the right to operate. Although a subtle change, for someone like Jones, who refused to seek permission from the state, it made all the difference in the world. Despite the fact that the School Act had not yet been passed into law, Duthler convinced the government to honour the spirit of the forthcoming Act and allow Jones to operate his school without seeking the permission of the minister, so long as the basic requirements were met, thereby ending the confrontation (Interview with Gary Duthler, 19 August 2015).

A renewed focus on the autonomy of faith-based schools (private, alternative, and separate) more recently emerged in relation to contemporary concerns around instruction on LGBTQ issues and the treatment of LGBTQ students in the province. Interestingly, three recent legislative decisions on this topic suggest a continued influence possessed by the faith-based lobby on the crafting of education policy in contemporary Alberta. The first of these developments was the Alberta PCs' decision in 2009 to enshrine parental rights into the province's human rights legislation despite significant opposition from a myriad of public education lobby groups ("Alberta Education Groups Unite to Oppose Bill 44," *Edmonton Journal*, 6 May 2009). The bill reaffirmed the right of parents to pull their children from any course of study that dealt explicitly with religion or sexuality and added sexual orientation to that list. In doing so, compulsory instruction on sexual orientation was made virtually impossible, an outcome that directly contradicted British Columbia's 2006 decision to place tougher restrictions on the rights of parents to remove children from such lessons.

The second development occurred in the fall of 2012. On the heels of a sustained lobbying effort by religious parents, the education minister announced that the new Education Act would no longer contain a clause stating that all educational programs and materials in Alberta "must honour and respect the *Canadian Charter of Rights and Freedoms* and the *Alberta Human Rights Act*." Instead, the final text would refer to the need to honour and respect "the common values and beliefs of Albertans." For thousands of religious parents, the initial clause represented a potential infringement upon their right to educate their children according to biblical principles, especially those revolving around Christian sexual ethics (Marler 2012). Led largely by the Alberta Home Education Association (AHEA) and aided, in turn, by smaller grassroots parents' organizations and a number of largely unaffiliated religious, private, and Catholic public school supporters, a well-organized campaign was waged targeting MLAs and the minister until the government ultimately altered the offending language and reassured religious parents that their right to teach their children tenants of their faith would be protected. In fact, an explicit recognition that "the parent has the prior right to choose the kind of education provided to the parent's child" was subsequently added to the act.

The third legislative decision encompassed a series of developments related to the introduction of mandatory Gay-Straight Alliance (GSA) clubs in Alberta schools as part of a broader anti-bullying initiative. As interviews completed for this study made clear, legislation mandating such clubs was a source of significant unease for many religious schools and parents who view homosexuality as sinful. Adhering to the demands of the faith-based education lobby, the PCs voted down an opposition motion to make such clubs mandatory in April 2014, citing the importance of choice for school boards ("Move to Mandate Approval of Gay-Straight Alliances in Schools Voted Down in Legislature," *Calgary Herald*, 7 April 2014). In December 2014 a private member's bill was brought forth by an opposition MLA again insisting that such clubs be mandatory, and the PCs again responded negatively, first threatening to vote the bill down then, under increased public pressure, promising to table their own bill which would make such clubs mandatory but also allow faith-based schools to essentially opt out of this provision ("Tories Weaken Stronger Effort from Liberals on Gay-Straight Alliances," *Edmonton Journal*, 26 December 2014). Only after a torrent of critical media coverage, generated largely on the back of public opinion data that suggested most Albertans favoured mandatory GSAs, did the PCs back down and pass legislation that not only made GSAs mandatory across all schools but also rescinded the clause from 2009 that allowed parents to remove their children from instruction on sexual orientation ("Tories Do an About-Face on GSAs; Education Minister Says Students' Stories Helped Reshape Legislation," *Edmonton Journal*, 11 March 2015). In other words, the demands of the faith-based education lobby were eventually denied in this case, although not without significant foot dragging on the part of the PCs.

Like the issue of public funding for private schools, the general deference to the autonomy of faith-based private schools by the Alberta government over the past decades is rooted in their ideological commitment to choice. Asked why the government was willing to adhere to contemporary requests made by their faith-based education group, one senior ministry official replied bluntly:

> The [government] recognizes that ... ultimately choice in educational matters is essential for parents. Parents are the prime educators of all children [and] this minister fiercely believes the family is the central educational unit. This minister recognizes ... that parents should have the opportunity to teach the values they share at home.
>
> (Interview with M, 18 December 2013)

Speaking specifically to the government's response to the campaign launched by religious parents concerned over the wording of parts of the new Education Act, a second senior ministry official noted: "The faith-based community really felt that choice was being eroded ... and it was really tough for this government to say, "Yeah, we believe in choice except here" (Interview with K, 17 December 2013).

When grilled by those who oppose concessions for religious schools on these matters, PC MLAs consistently relied on a two-pronged response that speaks to both populist concerns for parental choice in the face of state enforcement as well as the benefits of marketization generated by school choice. PC MLA Rob Anderson, responding to criticism that the "parental rights" clause in 2009 would breed religious-infused bigotry in schools, chastised the opposition for assuming that

> the state knows better [than parents] what our children should be taught with regard to sexuality and with regard to religion. We need to recognize a parent's role as the primary educator of their children ... We're [defending parental rights] because we want to reassert that the family and not the state is the fundamental unit of a successful society.
> (Legislative Assembly of Alberta 2009, 1468)

PC MLA Thomas Lukaszuk agreed, noting that parental rights would reassure those who worry that their children are learning things contrary to their religious values: "They do not want to give the state the right to have the final decision on what their child learns ... and I think most Albertans would agree with that" (Legislative Assembly of Alberta 2009, 1471).

Defending a 2012 amendment requested by faith-based groups that highlights the role of parents as the primary educator within the Education Act, PC MLA Ted Morton argued that the strong performance of Alberta's education system is directly attributable to it being built atop a foundation of "choice," something which "creates competition between the different systems" thereby strengthening the entire system (Legislative Assembly of Alberta 2012, 545–6). Similarly defending the decision to remove any reference to the Alberta Human Rights Act within the recently passed Education Act, in addition to formally affirming the "role of the family" in educational matters, education minister Jeff Johnson noted: "The *Education Act* is actually the first legislation in Canada to formally recognize the role of parents as a child's first and most important teacher. As a parent, that is something I am very proud of" ("Education Act Passes in Legislature," *CTV News Online*, 20 November 2012).

Conclusion

Viewed comparatively, Alberta's education system is both the most choice-friendly and religion-friendly in Canada. It shares with Ontario and Saskatchewan a commitment to a fully funded Catholic separate system, its levels of public aid to private faith-based schools only slightly trail those of Quebec and British Columbia, and it is the only province in Canada to allow both secular charter schools and faith-based alternative schools to operate within the public system. Moreover, it has arguably led the country in terms of the degree of autonomy granted to its religious schools. The evolution of this system has taken place over one hundred and thirty years and has involved the complex interaction of a number of systematic and province-specific factors. Yet it has also followed a fairly predictable pattern as the education system evolved through the regimes of faith, rights, and finally choice.

Clearly the initial commitment to a Catholic separate system during the "faith" regime was a crucial decision that continues to strongly influence the broader structure of the education system in the province. As a regime of "rights" came to replace that of "faith," thanks in large part to the concentrated actions of a small group of policy entrepreneurs driven by a "neo-Calvinist" religious and philosophical outlook, a policy window opened allowing for the layering of partial funding to private schools in 1967 onto the pre-existing policy of fully funding Catholic schools. Fully grasping this outcome requires one to see how these policy entrepreneurs, having largely arrived in Alberta in the post–Second World War immigration boom, framed the debate over the funding of private schooling as one over parental rights, pluralism, and justice rather than religious liberty. This messaging coincided rather nicely with the broader populist political culture of Alberta, which was already tilted toward the moral and intellectual capacity of the "common person" rather than the "elites," and was thus a rather easy message to accept for most Albertans and their politicians.

Faith-based education lobby groups would continue to win a number of policy victories in Alberta under the consecutive PC governments from 1971–2015. These victories included substantial increases in public money flowing to private schools, the ability to enter the public system under a unique "umbrella" concept, and, more recently, the right to retain an impressive degree of autonomy when faced with broad attempts to standardize educational instruction in Alberta around sexual orientation and the need to protect LGBTQ students from discrimination. As was the case in 1967, these policy victories under the PCs would not have happened without focused and sustained campaigns waged by faith-based and private school lobby groups. Yet, the successes enjoyed by such campaigns cannot be explained solely by the amount of resources such groups have to draw upon in their quest for policy influence. Rather, the broader political opportunity structure available to faith-based groups under the PCs' long reign has been especially conducive to these groups' advances. In particular, they have been aided considerably by the PCs' broader ideological commitment to neoliber-alism in the mid-1990s, a pressure exogenous to the education policy network but nonetheless hugely impactful given the support for school choice inherent in the emerging ideology. And for a broader population that is steeped in a populist and anti-statist political culture, the wide-ranging defence of choice in education consistently employed by con-servative Alberta politicians is generally widely accepted despite the fact the majority of the population is not overly religious. In this way, the story of the evolution of Alberta's education system again strongly mirrors that of British Columbia.

Of course, the Alberta New Democratic Party's (NDP) surprising rise to power in the spring of 2015 dramatically altered the political land-scape of the province in general and the political opportunity structure such faith-based groups faced in particular. Although the NDP govern-ment pledged not to cut funding for private schools in the near term ("No Plans to Change Funding Model for Private, Charter Schools, Says Education Minister," *Calgary Herald*, 25 May 2015), their ideological per-suasion tilts away from the principles of marketization and neoliberal-ism and towards inclusivity for the LGBTQ community, so one would expect the influence of faith-based groups to decline under the new government. In fact, the NDP did engage in a war of words with many in the Catholic separate system over the issue of protective guidelines for transgendered students ("Alberta Education Minister Tells School Boards to Write Transgender Policies," *Edmonton Journal*, 6 November 2015) and threatened to defund private religious schools who refused to implement government mandated policies related to GSA clubs ("Twenty-Eight Private Schools Defying GSA Law Risk Losing Public Funding, Says David Eggen," *Edmonton Journal*, 14 November 2018). However, the United Conservative Party's electoral victory in 2019 seemingly "righted" the Alberta politics ship, and although the levels of public funding received by private schools is unchanged, the UCP did move to protect the autonomy of faith-based schools on certain issues and has passed the aptly named Choice in Education Act in 2020, seem-ingly reconfirming the principles that have long undergirded the prov-ince's approach to education – principles that are expected to remain foundational in the foreseeable future.

Conclusion: Faith, Rights, Choice, and Change

These differences in the place religious and independent schools have found in provincial educational regimes, we argue, are the product of an evolution through historical periods where contention over faith, rights, and choice have defined political debate on this theme. Evolution in the problems faced by policymakers, and in the central issue of debate, led to changes in the institutional support offered to independent and religious schools through both exogenous and endogenous processes. An awareness of these different patterns of change allows for some comparative observations about the process of institutional change. This recognition also allows us to articulate some relationships between the area under discussion, the contentiousness of change, and the manner in which change takes place.

The present-day variation in governance and financial support that initially interested us in this project can be reviewed relatively briefly. In Atlantic Canada, private schools are legal, but no independent or religious school receives government support. Ontario, Saskatchewan, and Alberta all have separate (Roman Catholic) systems which are funded, governed, and staffed in essentially the same way as public schools are in those provinces. Government support for these separate schools is constitutionally protected. Quebec, British Columbia, Manitoba, Saskatchewan, and Alberta all provide partial public support to independent schools on a per-student basis. Although the level of funding varies across these provinces, as does the number of categories, the basic logic is similar: with government funding comes (more or less) adoption of provincial curriculum, teacher training standards, and provincial inspections. Importantly, this means that Ontario, Saskatchewan, and Alberta all treat Catholic schools quite differently than they do those of other faith communities or non-religious independent schools.

Throughout this book, we have seen that there are some commonalities across provinces. Most importantly, from a national and comparative perspective there are successive historical periods where debates about religious and independent schools were defined by disagreements over faith, rights, and choice in most (though not all) provinces and that each period of institutional reform institutionally entrenched the results of these disagreements. A crucial divide, perhaps the critical divide in nineteenth century Canadian politics, was between Protestants and Roman Catholics, leading to the creation of what we have called the faith regime. The religious divide overlapped with that between French and English linguistic groups and, by the turn of the twentieth century, had become solidified in partisan terms as an important part of the division between the Conservative and Liberal parties. It was a very important factor in the institutional paralysis that afflicted the united colony of Canada – paralysis that shoved Confederation towards a federal arrangement that kept education within provincial jurisdiction for the simple reason that there was no solution to the question of faith in education that could be applied across the entire country. Instead, Section 93 of the BNA Act provided protection for existing (officially recognized) separate schools as they existed when the provinces entered the federation. Thus, separate (Catholic) elementary schools in Ontario and separate (Protestant) schools in Quebec City and Montreal received constitutional protection in 1867, as did their equivalents in Saskatchewan and Alberta when those provinces were created in 1905. In the Maritimes, no formal system of separate schools existed even though informal local accommodation to the local majority's religious affiliation was very common until the 1960s. British Columbia, with a small population of Catholics and no existing separate system, enjoyed a similar status when it became a province. Manitoba, on the other hand, saw deeply divisive political disputes between Protestants and Catholics because – once the former were in the majority – they ignored the constitutional protections that had been given to minority religious groups. Finally, when Newfoundland entered the federation in 1949, its terms of union entrenched (after much controversy) the constitutional right to public support for seven denominational systems.

Constitutional entrenchment, however, did not end controversy centred on faith in Canadian education. In all provinces with formalized separate school systems, significant political controversy occurred throughout the twentieth century as political entrepreneurs on both sides of the issue sought to seize opportunities related to the public support that separate schools received. Until around the Second World War, this religious controversy was an important part of politics in all provinces except in overwhelmingly Protestant British Columbia. After the Second World War, there were significant differences in how long the Protestant-Catholic divide defined the politics of education. In Alberta, Saskatchewan, Manitoba, and the Maritimes it seems to have faded fairly quickly. In Quebec, the Church played a dominant role in education until the Quiet Revolution of the 1960s, then was slowly disentangled from education completely over the course of four decades. In Newfoundland and Labrador, the place of religion in schools was constitutionally entrenched as a major issue as there were no schools not run by denominations until a series of exogenous shocks led to the constitutional amendments of 1996.

Beginning in the 1960s, questions of group rights began to layer over disputes about faith and denominational accommodation in some provinces, a period we refer to as the rights regime. With significant variation between provinces, framing the issue of government support for schools outside the public system took a number of forms. In provinces with constitutionally entrenched separate schools, the difference with the previous period was one of emphasis, the use of slightly different arguments to defend the same positions, and the judiciary becoming an even more important venue than before. But, the addition of rights to the mix of arguments also extended the range of groups seeking government support for schools outside the public system. Most politically important of these were French-speaking Canadians in English Canada, but rights claims also gave non-Catholic religious groups and the disabled important ways to argue either for self-governing schools for their own communities or for significant accommodation within the public system. Especially for francophone Canadians in English Canada and the anglophone minority in Quebec, these rights arguments were made in a context where there was a single exogenous shock: the passage of the Charter of Rights and Freedoms in 1982. This had a powerful impact across the country.

But, for religious schools, it is important to note that Section 93 has proven to be one part of the Canadian constitution that can be changed. Both Quebec and Newfoundland went through the process in the mid-1990s to amend the constitution to allow the secularization of their respective school systems. Viewed as an analogy with Manitoba's actions in the 1890s and, perhaps, with the current debate over the use of the notwithstanding clause to protect separate schools in Saskatchewan today, it is clear that the constitutional structure of rights in Canada still allows a determined provincial government to make changes – a reality that runs against our usual portrayal of constitutionally entrenched rights as immutable.

Alternatively, in both Alberta and British Columbia, arguments from the foundation of "rights" emerged not from constitutional interpretations but instead from argumentation drawn from Article 26 of the United Nations Declaration of Human Rights, which identifies both a child's right to an education and especially the parent's right to choose the kind of education given to their children. It was this rights-based strategy that helped sway reluctant governments to support independent schools in Canada's two most western provinces.

The final regime defining question is about the extent and location of choice in education. Beginning in the late 1960s in British Columbia (tightly connected to the "parental rights" argument), but soon emerging as an important theme across the country, what we have classified as policy entrepreneurs argued for choice in education. In this book we have focused on choice between public systems and publicly supported separate or independent schools as the most visible component of this shift. But, it is also true that there have been important movements to increase choice within many large public systems as well. Often, proponents of choice were religious groups who were excluded from the existing separate-public school divide. Importantly, however, they succeeded in those provinces where they focused on choice arguments (BC, Alberta, Saskatchewan, Manitoba) and failed in Ontario, where, although seeking similar outcomes, they tended to frame the debate in terms of religious freedom. In Atlantic Canada, school choice seems not to have been much of an issue outside of Newfoundland and Labrador where there was some discussion of it during the changes of the 1990s. There, however, a relatively homogeneous population, financial constraint, and declining student numbers created a set of practical considerations that prevented change in the direction of greater choice from getting much traction.

Thus, the origins of today's distinctive patterns of school governance lie deep in the origins of the Canadian state but have not been determined or completely bounded by the patterns of the nineteenth century. Instead, periods of political debate produced change in some (though not all) provinces. In some provinces, such as Newfoundland and Labrador and Quebec, changes were more dramatic in character as systems of governance were exogenously shocked. In others, such as Alberta and Saskatchewan, today's pattern of government support for religious and independent schools is the result of consistent incremental change. And some provinces, such as Manitoba, have seen both types of change in play over the last century (see table 8.1).

After 1867, most of the changes to institutional regimes focused on faith were the result of exogenous shocks to a provincial system:

Table 8.1. Patterns of Change in Religious School Regimes in Canada

Province	Regimes	Exogenous Change	Endogenous Change
Ontario	Faith	No	Displacement, Layering
Quebec	Faith, Choice	Yes	Displacement, Layering
PEI	Faith	No	Drift and Conversion
New Brunswick	Faith	No	Drift and Conversion
Nova Scotia	Faith	No	Drift and Conversion
Newfoundland and Labrador	Faith	Yes	No
Manitoba	Faith, Rights, Choice	Yes	Layering
British Columbia	Faith, Rights, Choice	Yes	Layering
Saskatchewan	Faith, Rights, Choice	No	Layering
Alberta	Faith, Rights, Choice	Yes	Layering

mass immigration and federal intervention in Manitoba in the 1890s, the creation of Alberta and Saskatchewan in 1905, the entrenchment of denominational rights into the constitution when Newfoundland entered Confederation in 1949, the demographic and financial crisis that led the government of Newfoundland and Labrador to amend the constitution in 1997, and the massive secularization and constitutional politics that Quebec had gone through before it amended its constitution in 1997. In each of these dramatic moments of change to regimes of the accommodation of faith, the system was shocked from the outside. The resulting politics were contentious. Moments of failed or partial change where the focus was on the question of faith have similar features. Whether due to the sudden decision of a premier (Bill Davis in 1984 in Ontario) or court decisions (the Theodore case in Saskatchewan in 2017), even a shocked set of educational and political institutions has the capacity to resist change. Importantly, almost all political contention over significant, faith-based change where the impetus for change came from outside the political system was very heated.

There have also been elements of endogenous change occurring within the faith frame, of course. The transition from Protestant to secular of what are now public systems is a good example of what Mahoney and Thelen (2010) call conversion, which occurred in every province. The extension of full funding to Catholic high schools in Saskatchewan and the gradual equalization of government support for Catholic elementary schools in Ontario are both examples of policy layering. Some conservative Catholics would argue that separate school systems in Alberta, Saskatchewan, and Ontario have undergone displacement in so far as they emphasize a generic social justice approach more and a specifically Catholic identity less than they once did.

Once constitutionally established, some faith claims were transformed into rights claims almost immediately. In the Manitoba of the 1880s, Ontario in the 1910s, or in 1990s Newfoundland this shift was merely a formal one – all parties concerned were aware that they were really fighting over faith and behaved accordingly. Change occurred following significant political contention and, usually, after exogenous shocks to the existing political system. But rights emerged both as a more central and a more distinctive question in the 1960s as part of a broader social shift and were, at least in the realm of education, driven forward by a change in political strategy by francophone minorities. Rights claims, and the possibility of pursuing judicial as well as political change, gave policy entrepreneurs more gradual and incremental paths to follow. And, often utilizing the openings created by other rights claimants, this is what they did. It is also worth recognizing that rights claims have been a potent weapon for those supporters of an existing religious or independent school regime who seek to stop change which would undercut the existing system. This is most apparent today in the separate school systems in Ontario, Quebec, and Alberta.

Importantly, arguments around choice and movements toward more choice-based systems have been driven significantly more by processes of endogenous change. Even in Quebec – where the necessary constitutional amendment created a clear moment of change – the extension of government support to schools rooted in choice was the product of processes of endogenous layering which gradually led to change. Especially in Manitoba and British Columbia, this was partially the result of deliberate decisions by policy entrepreneurs who knew that they would be more successful if they built broad coalitions on favourable terms. Only in Ontario have these shifts been relatively unsuccessful, partly because opponents of school choice have been successful at maintaining a public focus on faith issues and partly because the existing public and separate systems have been successful at creating mechanisms for parental choice internally.

While politically successful and remarkably flexible, it is also important to note that none of the regimes built on choice are constitutionally entrenched. While constitutional amendments are, of course, a possibility, the difficulty of changing either the constitutional protections for separate schools in the three provinces that still have them or the nation-wide protection of linguistic minorities provides a very powerful judicial defence for those groups, which schooling regimes grounded in choice do not have. To date, choice regimes have been flexible enough that they have been able to accommodate rights claims from the LGBTQ community and the conservative religious identity of many of their schools. But it is hard to see how there will not be continued pressure along these lines.

This book's focus has been the long-term development of a series of distinctive regimes for the regulation and government support of religious schools in Canada's provinces. This distinctiveness has its roots in the founding moments of the provinces, in moments of exogenously driven change, and in more gradual processes of endogenous change within provincial regimes. Though constitutional considerations have been important, the key episodes in each of these evolutions have been political ones, even in relatively recent times. In tracing these long processes of change, we've demonstrated the importance of provincial political considerations in the framing, maintenance, and renewal of one of the most important reflections of diversity by the Canadian state. At least as concerns education, we believe that this long pattern of change is likely to continue as other forms of diversity are layered over top of religion. Highlighting both the differences in provincial regimes that have resulted from more than a century and a half of change and the different types of change therein reveals, we believe, the value in combining a Canadian political development approach that seeks to understand long run change within specific circumstances. By examining these long processes of change and their provincial variation, we hope to have also shown that Canada's incorporation of diversity does not necessarily take place simply at the federal level or through constitutional consideration. Rather, there is an alternative set of governance regimes – in the education sector in our case – where incorporation is the result of decisions made at the provincial level. These decisions played out in distinctive provincial polities and histories and have created subtly different relationships between governments and religious communities in provinces across the country. We've also called attention to the need for a nuanced understanding of what regime change looks like if the long-term evolution of political institutions is to be understood. We do examine moments of dramatic change over a few years in this book. But processes of endogenous change, sometimes over generations, also underpin some of the outcomes we examine. Being attuned to both types of change, in parallel, has allowed us to present such a detailed and nuanced account of "how we got here" in the specific cases we've examined which, through their independent evolutions, have evolved into the Canadian situation that we see today.

In choosing to emphasize provincial comparison and long periods of historical change, we have chosen to operate at a very macro level in understanding the evolution of these policy regimes. This was a reasonable choice, given the existing state of the literature and the evolution of the broad frameworks that we've examined empirically. But, especially in the recent past where polling data is more available and intensive and focused interviewing is possible around key moments of change, there remains much profitable work to be done on, for example, the attitudes of parents towards religious schools (Davidson, Lucas, and McGregor 2020) or the specific roles of different types of actors such as clergy, teachers unions, or school trustees on these questions. By choosing to focus on macro change, we have had to gloss over many episodes that would have been illuminating of public mobilization but not determinative of regime structure.

Of course, while this approach is able to capture the evolution of these regimes and their political dimensions, it does not enable us to comment on the educational or social effects of religious schools. Such questions require a completely different approach to the issue of religion, rights, and choice in schools – one focused on policy outcomes rather than the evolution of governance regimes and grounded in polling and financial data. Such outcome work is outside the scope of this project and, to date, has been relatively sparse in Canada (Davies and Aurini 2011; Bosetti and Gereluk 2016).

In focusing on religion and traditional, formal politics, we have largely left aside questions of race, ethnicity, and Indigeneity. The historical evolution we've documented in this book has been one where white Christian Canadians dominated the policy space to the almost total exclusion of other identities. Only in a few episodes in Ontario and Quebec late in the period under study did intersecting religious or racial diversity become politically salient. At a theoretical level, understanding how these intersecting diversities shape schooling has been highlighted for some time (McDonough, Memon, and Mintz 2013) and there has been some important empirical work done on, for example, Muslim schools (Zine 2008). It is certain that the future evolution of the religious school regimes will be influenced by Canada's increasing diversity. Similarly, as absent as Indigenous education and the reality of residential schools have been from the evolution of this policy area to date, future changes will be affected by the widespread recognition of this terrible legacy that has grown since the Truth and Reconciliation Committee's work in 2015.

Interview Participants

Date	Name	Organization	Title
		ONTARIO	
26 June 2014	Sean Conway	Liberal Party	MPP 1975–2003; Minister of Education 1985–6; 1989–90
10 July 2014	Richard Alway	St. Michael's College	President 1990–2008
19 April 2013	Janet Epp Buckingham	Trinity Western University	Director, Laurentian Leadership Centre
20 October 2014	Bill Davis	PC Party	MPP 1959–85; Education Minister 1962–71; Ontario Premier 1971–85
8 July 2014	Janet Ecker	PC Party	MPP 1995–2003; Minister of Education 1999–2001
17 April 2014	Victoria Hunt	Ontario English Catholic Teachers' Association	Head Government Relations
27 June 2014	Vivian McCaffrey	Elementary Teachers' Federation of Ontario	Head Government Relations
13 April 2013	Mark McGowen	St. Michael's College	History Professor
7 July 2014	Bob Rae	NDP	Leader 1982–95; Ontario Premier 1990–5
18 April 2013	Randall Schnoor	York University	Professor, Centre for Jewish Studies
10 July 2014	Hugh Segal	PC Party	Chief of Staff to Bill Davis, PC Party of Ontario Advisor, Senator
13 April 2013	David Seljack	Wilfrid Laurier University	Religious Studies Professor
13 April 2014	Deani Van Pelt	Redeemer University	Education Professor
7 July 2014	A (Anonymous Source)	Ontario Roman Catholic School Trustees Association	Senior Official

(*Continued*)

(Continued)

Date	Name	Organization	Title
QUEBEC			
27 April 2016	Douglas Farrow	McGill University	Professor of Theology and Christian Thought
27 April 2016	Georges Leroux	Université du Québec à Montréal /Government of Quebec	Section 1.01 Professor Emeritus, Department of Philosophy/Senior Consultant for ERC Program
28 April 2016	Spencer Boudreau	McGill University	Professor of Education (Retired)
28 April 2016	Paul Donovan	Loyola High School, Montreal	Former President
21 June 2016	Fernand Ouellet	Université de Sherbrooke	Associate professor, Centre d'études du religieux contemporain
21 June 2016	B (Anonymous Source)	Coalition pour la liberté en éducation	Senior Official
22 June 2016	Mireille Estivalèzes	Université de Montréal	Associate Professor, Faculty of Educational Sciences
7 December 2016	Jean-Pierre Proulx	*Le Devoir*, Université de Montréal	Journalist, Professor, Chair of 1997 Provincial Task Force Exploring the Role of Religion in Education
7 December 2016	Gary Caldwell	Bishops University	Author, Instructor
8 December 2016	Andre Revert	La Fédération des établissements d'enseignement privés	Senior Official
8 December 2016	C (Anonymous Source)	La Fédération des établissements d'enseignement privés	Senior Official
ATLANTIC CANADA			
23 October 2016	Louise Carbert	Dalhousie University	Political Science Professor
21 October 2016	Don Desserud	University of Prince Edward Island	Political Science Professor
6 December 2016	Gerald Galway	Memorial University	Education Professor
12 December 2016	Roger Grimes	Liberal Party	MHA 1989–2005; Premier 2001–3
9 December 2016	Bryce Hodder	Ministry of Education	Former Curriculum Specialist
9 December 2016	Tom McGrath	Saint Bonaventure's College	President

Date	Name	Organization	Title
7 December 2016	Loyola Sullivan	PC Party	MHA 1992–2006; PC Leader 1996–8
7 December 2016	Philip Warren	Liberal Party	Former Education Professor, Commission Head, Liberal MHA 1989–93; Education Minister 1989–93
8 December 2016	Clyde Wells	PC Party	MHA 1966–71; 1987–96; Premier 1989–96
5 December 2016	Steven Wolinetz	Memorial University	Political Science Professor
8 December 2016	D (Anonymous Source)	Education Ministry, Newfoundland and Labrador	Senior Ministry Official

MANITOBA

Date	Name	Organization	Title
26 August 2015	Lawrence Hamm	Winnipeg Mennonite Elementary and Middle Schools	Superintendent and CEO
20 July 2015	Nick Martin	Winnipeg Free Press	Education Reporter
24 August 2015	John Long	Faculty of Education, University of Manitoba	Professor Emeritus
25 August 2015	Robert Praznick	Archdiocese of Winnipeg	Superintendent, Schools Office
28 July 2015	John Stapleton	University of Manitoba	Former Education Dean and Education Professor
24 August 2015	John Weins	University of Manitoba	Former Education Dean, Professor, Deputy Minister, and School Administrator
25 August 2015	E (Anonymous Source)		Ministry of Education Senior Official
24 August 2015	Sister Susan Wilkeem	St. Mary's Academy	Former Principal
26 August 2015	F (Anonymous Source)	Manitoba School Boards Association	Senior Official

BRITISH COLUMBIA

Date	Name	Organization	Title
22 June 2015	Charles Ungerleider	University of British Columbia/Government of British Columbia	Professor Emeritus, Faculty of Education/ Deputy Minister of Education (1998–2001)
23 June 2015	G (Anonymous Source)	British Columbia Ministry of Education	Senior Official
24 June 2015	Doug Lauson	Federation of Independent School Associations (FISA) in British Columbia	President (2003–17)

(Continued)

(Continued)

Date	Name	Organization	Title
24 June 2015	Ed Noot	Society of Christian Schools in British Columbia	Director
24 June 2015	Phil Hills	Association of Christian Schools International Western Canada	Director
24 June 2015	Peter Froese	Federation of Independent School Associations (FISA) in British Columbia	Former Executive Director (2010–18)
25 June 2015	Jim Carter	Government of British Columbia	Associate Deputy Minister of Education (1977–80)
26 June 205	Kim Franklin	Trinity Western University	Dean of Education
10 August 2015	Fred Herfst	Federation of Independent School Associations (FISA) in British Columbia	Former Executive Director
10 August 2015	Marc Dalton	Government of British Columbia	Member of the Legislative Assembly (2009–17)/ Parliamentary Secretary for Independent Schools
11 August 2015	H (Anonymous Source)	British Columbia Teachers' Federation	Senior Official
13 August 2015	I (Anonymous Source)	Ministry of Education Government of British Columbia	Senior Official
14 August 2015	Rob Fleming	Government of British Columbia	Member of Legislative Assembly (2005–Present) Minister of Education (2017–Present)
14 August 2015	Thomas Fleming	University of Victoria	Professor Emeritus of Educational History
14 August 2015	Alastair Glegg	University of Victoria	Instructor, Faculty of Education
23 September 2015	George Abbott	Government of British Columbia	Member of Legislative Assembly (1996–2013) Minister of Education (2010–12)
SASKATCHEWAN			
22 June 2016	Mark Anderson	Luther College	Principal and Researcher
28 July 2015	Pat Atkinson	NDP	MLA 1986–2011; Education Minister 1993–8
27 July 2015	Lorne Calvert	NDP	MLA 1986–2009; Premier 2001–7

Date	Name	Organization	Title
1 August 2018	Chris Gerrard		Economics Professor, Christian School Principal (1983–90), President of Christian School Association (1988–90), Director Independent Schools Section Ministry of Education (1990–2)
2 April 2018	Richard Holdern	Luther College	Professor and Former College President
17 August 2015	Murray Mandryk	Regina Leader Post	Political Columnist
23 April 2018	John Nilson	NDP	MLA 1995–2016; Cabinet Minister 1995–2006
15 June 2015	Larry Steeves	University of Regina	Education Professor, Former Education Administrator
12 June 2015	Carol Teichrob	NDP	MLA 1991–5; Education Minister 1991–3
23 July 2015	J (Anonymous Source)	Ministry of Education	Senior Official
ALBERTA			
17 December 2013	K (Anonymous Source)	Alberta Education	Senior Bureaucrat
17 December 2013	L (Anonymous Source)	Anonymous Faith-Based Organization active on Education File	Representative of Faith-Based Organization
18 December 2013	M (Anonymous Source)	Alberta Education	Senior Bureaucrat
18 December 2013	Duane Plantinga	Association of Independent Schools and Colleges of Alberta	Director
18 December 2013	Ari Demoor	Association of Independent Schools and Colleges of Alberta	Senior Representative
20 December 2013	Chris Rogers	Alberta Home Education Association	Director
20 December 2013	Ray Strom	Alberta Home Education Association	Senior Representative
21 May 2014	Angela Macleod Irons	Parents for Choice in Education	Director
21 May 2014	N (Anonymous Source)	Anonymous Alberta Parental Rights Group	Senior Representative

(*Continued*)

(Continued)

Date	Name	Organization	Title
13 June 2014 (via email)	Mark Penninga	Association for Reformed Political Action	Senior Representative
2 July 2014	O (Anonymous Source)	Alberta Provincial Government	Alberta Liberal MLA with Responsibilities Related to Education in Alberta
3 July 2014	P (Anonymous Source)	Anonymous Secular Public Education Group	Director of Secular Public Education Interest Group
4 July 2014	Q (Anonymous Source)	Anonymous Catholic School Board	Former Catholic School Teacher and Current Catholic School Board Trustee
17 July 2014	Kris Wells	University of Alberta/ Institute for Sexual Minority Studies and Services	Director, Programs & Services (ISSMS) and Assistant Professor, Department of Educational Policy Studies (U of A)
11 August 2014	David King	Retired. Formerly Alberta Progressive Conservatives and Public School Boards Association of Alberta	Former Alberta Education Minister (1979–86) and Executive Director of Public Education Interest Group (PSBAA) (1990–2010)
21 August 2014	Dennis E. Theobald	Alberta Teachers Association	Associate Executive Secretary
19 August 2015	Gary Duthler	Association of Independent Schools and Colleges of Alberta	Former Executive Director

Works Cited

Alberta Act. 1905. 4-5 Edw. VII, c. 3 (Can.). http://canada.justice.gc.ca/eng
/rp-pr/csj-sjc/constitution/lawreg-loireg/p1t121.html.

Alberta Education. 1993. *Charter Schools: Provision for Choice in Public Schools.*
Edmonton, AB.

– 2010. "Alternatives Program Handbook 2010." https://education.alberta
.ca/media/1626689/alternative_programs_handbook.pdf.

– 2011. *Charter School Handbook.* Edmonton, AB.

– 2013. "Inspiring Education: A Dialogue with Albertans." https://
open.alberta.ca/dataset/45370ce9-3a90-4ff2-8735-cdb760c720f0
/resource/2ee2452c-81d3-414f-892f-060caf40e78e/download/4492270-2010
-inspiring-education-dialogue-albertans-2010-04.pdf.

– 2018. "Student Population Overview." https://www.alberta.ca/student
-population-statistics.aspx?utm_source=redirector.

– 2022. "Student Population Statistics." https://www.alberta.ca/student
-population-statistics.aspx.

Allison, Derek, and Deani Van Pelt. 2012. "Canada." In *Balancing Freedom,
Autonomy, and Accountability in Education,* Vol. 3, edited by Charles Glenn
and Jan De Groof, 79–147. Nijmegen: Wolf.

Anderson, Mark. 2003. "And Justice for Some: The Funding of Historical,
Independent High Schools in Saskatchewan." M.Ed. thesis, University of
Regina, Regina, Saskatchewan.

Association of Private Schools and Colleges in Alberta. 1962. Minutes of the
Fall Convention. 17 November 1962.

Audet, Louis-Philippe. 1964. *Histoire du Conseil de l'instruction publique de la
province de Québec.* Montreal: Editions Lemeac.

Banack, Clark. 2014a. "Conservative Christianity, Anti-Statism and Alberta's
Public Sphere: The Curious Case of Bill 44." In *Religion in the Public Sphere:
Perspectives across the Canadian Provinces,* edited by S. Lefebvre and L.
Beaman, 257–74. Toronto: University of Toronto Press.

– 2014b. "Evangelical Christianity and Political Thought in Alberta." *Journal of Canadian Studies* 48, no. 2 (Spring): 70–99. https://doi.org/10.3138 /jcs.48.2.70.

– 2015. "Understanding the Influence of Faith-Based Organizations on Education Policy in Alberta." *Canadian Journal of Political Science* 48, no. 4 (December): 933–59. https://doi.org/10.1017/s0008423915000797.

– 2016. *God's Province: Evangelical Christianity, Political Thought, and Conservatism in Alberta.* Montreal: McGill-Queen's University Press.

Barman, Jean. 1986. "Transfer, Imposition, or Consensus? The Emergence of Educational Structures in Nineteenth-Century British Columbia." In *Schools in the West: Essays in Canadian Educational History,* edited by Nancy M. Sheehan, J. Donald Wilson, and David C. Jones. Calgary: Destelig Enterprises.

– 1991. "Deprivatizing Private Education: The British Columbia Experience." *Canadian Journal of Education* 16, no. 1: 12–31. https://doi .org/10.2307/1495214.

Baumgartner, Frank, and Bryan D. Jones. 1993. *Agendas and Instability in American Politics.* Chicago: University of Chicago Press.

Beach, Derek, and Rasmus Pedersen. 2013. *Process-Tracing Methods: Foundations and Guidelines.* Ann Arbor: University of Michigan Press.

Bélanger, Claude. 2000. "The Roman Catholic Church and Quebec." Quebec History. Last modified 23 August 2000. http://faculty.marianopolis.edu /c.belanger/quebechistory/readings/church.htm.

Behiels, Michael D. 2004. *Canada's Francophone Minority Communities: Constitutional Renewal and the Winning of School Governance.* Montreal: McGill-Queen's University Press.

Bérard, Robert. 2005. "The Dartmouth Schools Question and the Supreme Court of Nova Scotia." *The Dalhousie Law Journal* 28, no. 1: 199–215.

Bergen, John J. 1981. "Freedom of Education in a Religious Context: The Alberta Holdeman Private School Case." *Mennonite Quarterly Review* 55, no. 1: 75–85.

– 1982. "The Private School Movement in Alberta." *The Alberta Journal of Educational Research* 28, no. 4: 315–36.

– 1990. "The World Wars and Education Among Mennonites in Canada." *Journal of Mennonites in Canada* 8: 156–72.

Bezeau, Lawrence. 1979. "The Public Finance of Private Education in the Province of Quebec." *Canadian Journal of Education* 4, no. 2: 23–42. https://doi.org/10.2307/1494560.

Bosetti, L., and Butterfield, P. 2016. "The Politics of Educational Reform: The Alberta Charter School Experiment 20 Years Later." *Global Education Review* 3, no. 2: 103–9. https://files.eric.ed.gov/fulltext/EJ1098709.pdf.

Bosetti, Lynn, and Dianne Gereluk. 2016. *Understanding School Choice in Canada.* Toronto: University of Toronto Press.

Bouchard, Gérard. 2015. *Interculturalism: A View from Quebec*. Trans. Howard Scott. Toronto: University of Toronto Press.

Boudreau, Spencer. 1999. *Catholic Education: The Quebec Experience*. Calgary: Detselig Enterprises Ltd.

– 2011. "From Confessional to Cultural: Religious Education in the Schools of Quebec." *Religion and Education* 38, no. 3: 212–23. https://doi.org/10.1080/15507394.2011.609104.

Boychuk, Gerald W. 2016. "'Studying Public Policy': Historical Institutionalism and the Comparative Method." *Canadian Journal of Political Science* 49, no. 4: 743–61. https://doi.org/10.1017/s0008423916001220.

Braun, Jacob C. 1991. "A Study of the General Purposes of Independent Historical High Schools in Saskatchewan." Master's thesis, University of Regina, Regina, Saskatchewan.

British Columbia. 1988. *A Legacy for Learners: Report of the Royal Commission on Education*. Vancouver: The Commission.

British Columbia Ministry of Education. 2019a. *BC Schools – Student Enrolment and FTE by Grade*. https://catalogue.data.gov.bc.ca/dataset/bc-schools-student-enrolment-and-fte-by-grade.

– 2019b. *Independent Schools: Enrolment and Funding Data*. https://www2.gov.bc.ca/assets/gov/education/administration/kindergarten-to-grade-12/independent-schools/enrolment_and_funding_data_2014-15_to_2018-19_as_of_feb_11_2020.pdf.

British Columbia Teachers' Federation. 2017. "Priorities for Public Education." August. https://web.archive.org/web/20171212191042/https://bctf.ca/publications/BriefSection.aspx?id=46944.

Brummelen, Harro Van. 1986. "Shifting Perspectives: Early British Columbia Textbooks from 1872 to 1925." In *Schools in the West: Essays in Canadian Educational History*, edited by Nancy M. Sheehan, J. Donald Wilson, and David C. Jones. Calgary: Destelig Enterprises.

– 1996. "Religiously-Based Schooling in British Columbia: An Overview of the Research." *Journal of Canadian Church Historical Society* 38, no. 1: 101–22.

Buckingham, Janet Epp. 2014. *Fighting over God: A Legal and Political History of Religious Freedom in Canada*. Montreal: McGill-Queen's University Press.

Burgess, Donald A. 1992. "Private Education in Quebec." *McGill Journal of Education* 27, no. 1: 85–8.

Buri, George. 2016. *Between Education and Catastrophe: The Battle over Public Schooling in Postwar Manitoba*. Montreal: McGill-Queen's University Press.

Caldwell, Gary. 2000. "Proulx Report and the Role of the State in Quebec Schools." *Inroads: A Journal of Opinion*: 1–8.

Calem, John, and Thomas Fleming. 1988. "Commissioned Papers: Volume 1. Public Support for Non-Public Schooling." In *British Columbia Royal Commission on Education*, 54–7.

Callaghan, Tonya. 2018. *Homophobia in the Hallways: Heterosexism and Transphobia in Canadian Catholic Schools*. Toronto: University of Toronto Press.

Campbell, David E. 2004. "The Civic Implications of Canada's Education System." In *Educating Citizens: International Perspectives on Civic Values and School Choice*, edited by Patrick J. Wolf and Stephen Macedo, 187–213. Washington: Brookings.

Cappon, Paul. 1974. Conflit entre les Néo-Canadiens et les francophones de Montréal. Quebec: Presses de l'Université Laval.

Catholic Schools Section of the Saskatchewan School Trustees Association (SSTA). 1959. "A Brief on Parental Rights in Education." Miller Papers. Archdiocese of Regina Archives.

– 1963. "Catholic High Schools in Saskatchewan." Miller Papers. Archdiocese of Regina Archives.

Christiano, Kevin J. 2007. "Catholicism in Twentieth Century Quebec." In *The Church Confronts Modernity: Catholicism since 1950 in the United States, Ireland, and Quebec*, edited by Leslie Woodcock Tentler. Washington, DC: The Catholic University of America Press.

Chubb, John E., and Terry M. Moe. 1990. Politics, Markets and America's Schools. Washington, DC: Brookings Institute.

– 1998. "Politics, Markets, and the Organization of Schools." *American Political Science Review* 82, no. 4: 1065–87. https://doi.org/10.2307/1961750.

Cook, Ramsay. 1969. "Church, Schools, and Politics in Manitoba, 1903–1912." In *Minorities, Schools, and Politics*, edited by Craig Brown, 19–42. Toronto: University of Toronto Press.

Crunican, Paul. 1974. *Priests and Politicians: Manitoba Schools and the Election of 1896*. Toronto: University of Toronto Press.

Cunningham, Victoria. 2002. *Justice Achieved: The Political Struggle of Independent Schools in British Columbia*. Vancouver: Federation of Independent Schools Association.

Cymbol, Steve. 2009. *Educational Choice for Albertans: History and Implications*. Alberta School Boards Association.

Daniels, Ronald J., and Michael J. Trebilcock. 2005. *Rethinking the Welfare State: The Prospects for Government by Voucher*. New York: Routledge.

Davidson, Adrienne, Jack Lucas, and Michael McGregor. 2020. "Politics and Religion: Identifying the Correlates of Support for Merging the Public and Separate School Systems in Ontario." *Canadian Journal of Education* 43, no. 1: 229–57.

Davies, Scott, and Janice Aurini. 2011. "School Choice in Canada: Who Chooses What and Why." *Canadian Public Policy* 37, no. 4: 459–77. https://doi.org/10.3138/cpp.37.4.459.

De Roo, Joseph. 1963. "An Address Given to the BC State Council, Knights of Columbus," Chilliwack, BC, 26 May 1963. FISA's Archives, Vancouver, British Columbia.

Digout, Stanislaus. 1969. "Public Aid for Private Schools in Alberta: The Making of a Decision." Master's thesis, University of Alberta.

Di Mascio, Anthony. 2012. *The Idea of Popular Schooling in Upper Canada: Print Culture, Public Discourse, and the Demand for Education.* Montreal: McGill-Queen's University Press.

Dion, Leon. 1967. *Le bill 60 et la société Québécoise.* Montreal: HMV.

Dirks, Gordon. 1987. *Review of Private Schooling in Saskatchewan.* Regina: Queen's Printer.

Doern, Russell. 1985. *The Battle over Bilingualism: The Manitoba Language Question 1983–85.* Winnipeg: Cambridge Publishers.

Dosdall, Emery. 2001. "Edmonton's Enterprise." The School Superintendents Association. https://www.aasa.org/SchoolAdministratorArticle .aspx?id=10842.

Downey, L.W. 1986. "The Anatomy of a Policy Decision: B.C.'s Bill 33 – the Independent Schools Support Act." In *Schools in the West: Essays in Canadian Educational History*, edited by N. Sheehan, J. Wilson, and D. Jones, 305–23. Calgary: Detselig.

Eager, Evelyn. 1980. *Saskatchewan Government: Politics and Pragmatism.* Saskatoon: Western Producer Books.

Education Finance Review Commission. 1983. *Enhancing Equity in Manitoba Schools: The Report of the Education Finance Review.* Winnipeg: Queen's Printer.

Eidsness, Brent, Larry Steeves, and W. Rod Dolmage. 2008. "Funding Non-Minority Faith Adherents in Minority Faith Schools." *Education Law Journal* 17, no. 3: 291–346.

Ensing, Gerry. 1980. "Interview with Carol L. Gamey," 4 June 1980. FISA's Archives, Vancouver British Columbia.

Evangelical Fellowship of Canada. 2013. *Falling Short: Manitoba's Bill 18, the Safe and Inclusive Schools Act.* http://files.efc-canada.net/si/Education /Falling%20Short,%20Bill%2018.pdf.

Fagan, Bonaventure. 2004. *Trial: The Loss of Denominational Rights in Newfoundland, a Roman Catholic Story.* St John's: ADDA Press.

– 2012. The Abolition of Denominational Governance in Newfoundland – Unnecessary, Unwarranted. In *Education Reform: From Rhetoric to Reality*, edited by Gerald Galway and David Dibbon, 119–37. London: Althouse Press.

Fallon, Gerald, and Jerald Paquette. 2008. "Devolution, Choices, and Accountability in the Provision of Public Education in British Columbia: A Critical Analysis of the School Amendment Act of 2002 (Bill 34)." *Canadian Journal of Educational Administration and Policy* 75: 1–36.

Farrow, Douglas. 2009. "On the Ethics and Religious Culture Program." Report from Expert Witness, re: Loyola High School et John Zucchi c. Michelle Courchesne, en sa qualité de ministre de l'Éducation, du Loisir et du Sport. Cour supérieure, district de Montréal, No500-17-045278-085.

Fay, Terence J. 2002. *A History of Canadian Catholics*. Montreal: McGill-Queen's University Press.

Federation of Independent Schools Associations. 1967. *Brief Presented to Her Majesty's Council of the Province of British Columbia*. FISA's Archives, Vancouver British Columbia.

– 1976b. *The Independent Alternative*. FISA's Archives, Vancouver British Columbia.

– 1988. *Brief Submitted to The Royal Commission on Education*. FISA's Archives, Vancouver British Columbia.

Fleming, Thomas. 2010. *Schooling in British Columbia, 1849–2005: Voices from the Past*. Mill Bay, BC: Bendall Books.

– 2011. *Worlds Apart: British Columbia Schools, Politics, and Labour Relations before and after 1972*. Mill Bay, BC: Bendall Books.

Forum Research. 2015. "Majority Oppose Funding Catholic Schools." 10 July 2015. http://poll.forumresearch.com/post/314/strongest-among -youngest-wealthy-in-toronto-among-ndp-supporters/.

Friedman, Milton. 1955. "The Role of Government in Education." In *Economics and the Public Interest*, edited by R. Solo, 123–44. New Brunswick, NJ: Rutgers University Press.

– 1962. *Capitalism and Freedom*. Chicago: University of Chicago Press.

Fraser Institute. 2017. "Catholic Schools Popular with Parents across Canada." 17 July 2017. https://www.fraserinstitute.org/blogs/catholic-schools -popular-with-parents-across-canada.

– 2022. "Student Enrolment in Canada, Part 1: Independent School Enrolment on the Rise." February 17. https://www.fraserinstitute.org/blogs/student -enrolment-in-canada-part-1-independent-school-enrolment-on-the-rise.

Froese, Peter. 2010. "Political Action Through Consensus: A Case Study of the Federation of Independent Schools In British Columbia." PhD diss., University of British Columbia.

Fujiwara, Satoko. 2011. "Has Deconfessionalization Been Completed? Some Reflections upon Quebec's Ethics and Religious Culture (ERC) Program." *Religion and Education* 38, no. 3: 278–87. https://doi.org/10.1080/15507394 .2011.609107.

Galway, Gerald. 2014. Educational Governance and Policy in Newfoundland and Labrador. In *First Among Unequals: The Premier, Politics, and Policy in Newfoundland and Labrador*, edited by Alex Marland and Matthew Kerby, 178–94. Montreal: McGill-Queen's University Press.

Galway, Gerald, and David Dibbon. 2012. *Education Reform: From Rhetoric to Reality*. London: Althouse Press.

Garner, John. 1969. *The Franchise and Politics in British North America 1755–1867*. Toronto: University of Toronto Press.

Gaurvreau, Michael. 2011. "From Rechristianization to Contestation: Catholic Values and Quebec Society, 1931–1970." In *Contemporary Quebec: Selected Readings and Commentaries*, edited by Michael D. Behiels and Mathew Hayday, 127–56. Montreal: McGill-Queen's University Press.

Ghitter, R. 1984. *Committee on Tolerance and Understanding Final Report.* Edmonton: Alberta Education.

Gidney, R.D. 1999. *From Hope to Harris: The Reshaping of Ontario's Schools.* Toronto: University of Toronto Press.

Gidney, R.D., and W.P.J. Millar. 2001. "The Christian Recessional in Ontario's Public Schools." In *Religion and Public Life in Canada: Historical and Comparative Perspectives*, edited by Marguerite Van Die, 275–94. Toronto: University of Toronto Press.

Government of Alberta. 1959. *Report of the Royal Commission on Education in Alberta* (Cameron Commission). Edmonton: Queen's Printer.

– 1998. *Setting a New Framework: Report and Recommendations of the Private Schools Funding Task Force.*

Government of Quebec. 1982. *The Quebec School: A Responsible Force in the Community.*

– 1999. *Religion in Public Schools: A New Perspective for Quebec.*

Gwyn, Richard. 1968. *Joey: The Unlikely Revolutionary.* Toronto: McClelland & Stewart.

Hall, Peter A., and Rosemary C. Taylor. 1996. "Political Science and the Three New Institutionalisms." *Political Studies* 44, no. 5: 936–57. https://doi.org/10.1111/j.1467-9248.1996.tb00343.x.

Harrison, Trevor W., and Jerrold L. Kachur, eds. 1999. *Contested Classrooms: Education, Globalization, and Democracy in Alberta.* Edmonton: The University of Alberta Press.

Hayek, Friedrich A. 1960. *The Constitution of Liberty.* Chicago: University of Chicago Press.

Hébert, Raymond. 2004. *Manitoba's French-Language Crisis: A Cautionary Tale?* Montreal: McGill-Queen's University Press.

Hedstrom, Peter, and Petri Ylikoski. 2010. "Causal Mechanisms in the Social Sciences." *Annual Review of Sociology* 36: 49–67.

Henchey, Norman. 1972. "Quebec Education: The Unfinished Revolution." *McGill Journal of Education* 7, no. 2: 95–118.

Heyking, Amy von. 2013. "Aberhart, Manning, and Religion in the Public Schools of Alberta." *Alberta History* (Autumn): 2–11.

Hiemstra, John L. 2003. "Domesticating Catholic Schools (1885–1905): The Assimilation Intent of Alberta's Separate School System." Paper given at Canadian Political Science Association Annual Meetings.

– 2005. "Calvinist Pluriformity Challenges Liberal Assimilation: A Novel Case for Publicly Funding Alberta's Private Schools, 1953–1967." *Journal of Canadian Studies* 39, no. 3: 146–73. https://doi.org/10.3138/jcs.39.3.146.

– 2006. "Faith-Based Alternative School Choice in Alberta: Conservative Revival, Post-Modern Fragmentation, or Principled Pluralism?" *International Journal for Education Law and Policy* 2, no. 1–2: 23–34.

– 2017. "Alberta's Pluriform School System: Beyond the 'Public-Secular' versus 'Private-Religious' divide." *International Journal of Christianity and Education* 21, no. 2: 95–113. https://doi.org/10.1177/2056997116676283.

Hiemstra, John L., and Robert A. Brink. 2006. "The Advent of a Public Pluriformity Model: Faith-Based School Choice in Alberta." *Canadian Journal of Education* 29, no. 4: 1157–90. https://doi.org/10.2307/20054214.

Holdern, Richard. 2013. *The Luther College Story 1913–2013: A Century of Faithfulness in Education.* Regina: Luther College.

Hollaar, Lee. 2008. "AISCA, 50th Anniversary Celebration Keynote." Association of Independent Schools and Colleges of Alberta. https://greywill.files.wordpress.com/2014/09/aisca-2008-talks1.pdf.

Holmes, Mark. 1992. *Educational Policy for the Pluralist Democracy: The Common School, Choice, and Diversity.* Washington: Falmer Press.

– 1998. *The Reformation of Canada's Schools: Breaking the Barriers to Parental Choice.* Montreal: McGill-Queen's University Press.

Hop, Dennis Jay. 1982. "The Development of Private Schools in Alberta." Master's thesis, University of Calgary.

Hoy, Claire. 1985. *Bill Davis: A Biography.* Toronto: Methuen.

– 1992. *Clyde Wells: A Political Biography.* Toronto: Stoddart.

Ibbitson, John. 1997. *Promised Land: Inside the Mike Harris Revolution.* Toronto: Prentice Hall.

Jamieson, John. 1994. "One View of Native Education in the Northwest Territories, Canada." In *The Presented Past*, edited by P.G. Stone and B.L. Molyneaux, 495–510. London: Routledge Press.

Julien, Richard Alben. 1995. "The Legal Recognition of All-French Schools in Saskatchewan: A Long and Often Difficult Odyssey." *Canadian Ethnic Studies* 27, no. 2: 101–44.

Kachur, Jerrold. 1999. "Privatizing Public Choice: The Rise of Charter Schooling in Alberta." In *Contested Classrooms: Education, Globalization, and Democracy in Alberta*, edited by T. Harrison and J. Kachur, 107–22. Edmonton: University of Alberta Press.

Kinahan, Zachary, Stacy Senkbeil, and Matthew Carvell. 2014. "Wedge Issue Politics in Manitoba: Bill 18–The Public Schools Amendment Act (Safe and Inclusive Schools)." *Manitoba Law Journal* 37, no. 2: 177–206.

King, Jane D. 1998. "Education Policy in the Northwest Territories: An Analysis of the Decentralisation Years." Master's thesis, University of

Western Ontario. https://www.nlc-bnc.ca/obj/s4/f2/dsk3/ftp05
/mq30841.pdf.

Kingdon, John. 2003. *Agendas, Alternatives, and Public Policies*. 2nd ed. New
York: Longman.

Klaasen, Peter G. 1970. "A History of Mennonite Education in Canada,
1786–1960." EdD thesis, University of Toronto.

Koning, Edward. 2016. "The Three Institutionalisms and Institutional
Dynamics: Understanding Endogenous and Exogenous Change." *Journal of
Public Policy* 36, no. 4: 639–64. https://doi.org/10.1017/s0143814x15000240.

Langley, Gerald James. 1950. "Saskatchewan's Separate Schools: A Study of
One Pattern of Adjustment to the Problem of Education in a Multi-Religion
Democratic Society." PhD thesis, Columbia University.

Laval Congregation for Catholic Education. 2009. *Circular Letter to the
Presidents of Bishops' Conference on Religious Education in Schools*.
http://www.vatican.va/roman_curia/congregations/ccatheduc
/documents/rc_con_ccatheduc_doc_20090505_circ-insegn-relig_en.html.

Laycock, David. 1990. *Populism and Democratic Thought in the Canadian Prairies,
1910 to 1945*. Toronto: University of Toronto Press.

Legislative Assembly of Alberta. 2008. *Alberta Hansard* (24 April 2008).
Edmonton: Alberta's Government Printing Office.

– 2009. *Alberta Hansard* (9 June 2009, 1468). Edmonton: Alberta Government
Printing Office.

– 2012. *Alberta Hansard* (14 March 2012). Edmonton: Alberta Government
Printing Office.

Leroux, Georges. 2016. *Différence et liberté: Enjeux actuels de l'éducation au
pluralisme*. Montreal: Boreal.

Levin, Henry M. 1998. "Educational Vouchers: Effectiveness, Choice, and
Costs." *Journal of Policy Analysis and Management* 17, no. 3: 373–92.
https://doi.org/10.1002/(sici)1520-6688(199822)17:3%3C373::aid
-pam1%3E3.0.co;2-d.

Lipset, Seymour Martin. 1950. *Agrarian Socialism*. Berkeley: University of
California Press.

Lloyd, Julia, and Laura Bonnett. 2005. "The Arrested Development of Queer
Rights in Alberta." In *The Return of the Trojan Horse: Alberta and the New World
(Dis)Order*, edited by Trevor Harrison, 328–41. Montreal: Black Rose Books.

Lucas, Jack. 2016. *Fields of Authority: Special Purpose Governance in Ontario,
1815–2015*. Toronto: University of Toronto Press.

– 2017. "Urban Governance and the American Political Development
Approach." *Urban Affairs Review* 53, no. 2: 338–61. https://doi.org
/10.1177/1078087415620054.

Lucas, Jack, and Robert Vipond. 2017. "Back to the Future: Historical Political
Science and the Promise of Canadian Political Development." *Canadian*

Journal of Political Science 50, no. 1: 219–41. https://doi.org/10.1017
/s0008423916001207.

Lupul, Manoly. 1974. *The Roman Catholic Church and the North-West School
Question. A Study in Church-State Relations in Western Canada, 1875–1905.*
Toronto: University of Toronto Press.

MacDonald, David B. 2019. *The Sleeping Giant Awakens.* Toronto: University of
Toronto Press.

MacDonald, Heidi. 2000. "The Sisters of St. Martha and Prince Edward Island
Social Institutions, 1916–1982." PhD diss., University of New Brunswick.

MacKinnon, Frank. 1995. *Church Politics and Education in Canada: The PEI
Experience.* Calgary: Detselig.

MacLeod, Angela, and Sazid Hasan. 2017. *Where Our Students are Educated:
Measuring Student Enrolment in Canada.* Fraser Institute. https://www
.fraserinstitute.org/sites/default/files/where-our-students-are-educated
-measuring-student-enrolment-in-canada-2017.pdf.

MacNaughton, Katherine F.C. 1947. *The Theory and Practice of Education in New
Brunswick 1784–1900.* Fredericton: University of New Brunswick.

MacPherson, Paige. 2022. "Student Enrolment in Canada, Part 1: Independent
School Enrolment on the Rise." Fraser Institute. 17 February 2022.
https://www.fraserinstitute.org/blogs/student-enrolment-in-canada
-part-1-independent-school-enrolment-on-the-rise.

Magnuson, Roger. 1980. *A Brief History of Quebec Education.* Montreal: Harvest
House.

– 1993. "A Profile of Private Schools in Quebec." *McGill Journal of Education* 28,
no. 1: 3–12.

Mahoney, James, and Dietrich Rueschemeyer, eds. 2003. *Comparative Historical
Analysis in the Social Sciences.* Cambridge: Cambridge University Press.

Mahoney, James, and Kathleen Thelen, eds. 2010. *Explaining Institutional
Change: Ambiguity, Agency, Power.* Cambridge: Cambridge University Press.

–, eds. 2015. *Advances in Comparative-Historical Analysis.* Cambridge:
Cambridge University Press.

Manitoba. 1959. *Report of the Manitoba Royal Commission on Education.*
Winnipeg: Queen's Printer.

Manning, Ernest. 1944. Letter to Lee, 6 June 1944. Premiers Papers, 69.289,
File 1179. Provincial Archives of Alberta, Edmonton.

– 1948. Letter to Ewers, 6 February 1948. Premiers Papers, 69.289, File 1158.
Provincial Archives of Alberta, Edmonton.

Manzer, Ronald. 1985. *Public Policies and Political Development in Canada.*
Toronto: University of Toronto Press.

– 1994. *Public Schools and Political Ideas: Canadian Educational Policy in Historical
Perspective.* Toronto: University of Toronto Press.

– 2003. *Educational Regimes and Anglo-American Democracy*. Toronto: University of Toronto Press.

Marler, Patty. 2012. "Alberta: Our Work Continues." *Home Matters* (Summer): 20–1.

Martino, Wayne, Lee Airton, Diana Kuhl, and Wendy Cumming-Potvin. 2019. "Mapping Transgender *Policyscapes*: A Policy Analysis of Transgender Inclusivity in the Education System in Ontario." *Journal of Educational Policy* 34, no. 3: 302–30. https://doi.org/10.1080/02680939.2018.1478992.

McCann, Phillip. 1988a. "The Politics of Denominational Education in the Nineteenth Century in Newfoundland." In *The Vexed Question: Denominational Education in a Secular Age*, edited by William A. McKim, 30–60. St. John's: Breakwater.

– 1988b. "Denominational Education in the Twentieth Century in Newfoundland." In *The Vexed Question: Denominational Education in a Secular Age*, edited by William A. McKim, 60–80. St. John's: Breakwater.

McDonough, Graham P., Nadeem A. Memon, and Avi I. Mintz. 2013. *Discipline, Devotion, and Dissent: Jewish, Catholic, and Islamic Schooling in Canada*. Waterloo: Wilfrid Laurier University Press.

McGregor, Heather Elizabeth. 2013. "Situating Nunavut Education with Indigenous Education in Canada." *Canadian Journal of Education* 36, no. 2: 87–118.

McLeod, Keith A. 1968. "Politics, Schools, and the French Language, 1881–1931." In *Politics in Saskatchewan*, edited by Norman Ward and Duff Spafford, 24–151. Don Mills: Longmans.

McNally, Vincent J. 1999. "Challenging the Status Quo: An Examination of the History of Catholic Education in British Columbia." *Historical Studies* 65: 71–91.

Mettler, Suzanne, and Richard M. Valelly. 2016. "Introduction: The Distinctiveness and Necessity of American Political Development." In *The Oxford Handbook of American Political Development*, edited by Richard M. Valelly, Suzanne Metter, and Robert C. Lieberman, 1–27. Oxford: Oxford University Press.

Miller, J.T. 2001. "The State, the Church, and Indian Residential Schools in Canada." In *Religion and Public Life in Canada*, edited by Marguerite Van Die, 109–29. Toronto: University of Toronto Press.

Milner, Henry. 1986. *The Long Road to Reform*. Montreal: McGill-Queen's University Press.

Milot, M., and J.P. Proulx. 1998. Les attentes sociales à l'égard de la religion à l'école publique. Rapport de recherche. Quebec: Ministère de l'Éducation. Task Force on the Place of Religion in Schools in Québec.

Milot, Micheline, and Stéphanie Tremblay. 2017. Religion in the Quebec Public School System. https://web.archive.org/web/20171130185748

/http://www.horizons.gc.ca/en/content/religion-quebec-public
-school-system-change-equality-and-diversity.

Mintrom, Michael, and Phillipa Norman. 2009. "Policy Entrepreneurship
and Policy Change." *Policy Studies Journal* 37, no. 4: 649–67. https://doi
.org/10.1111/j.1541-0072.2009.00329.x.

Morton, W.L. 1969. "Manitoba Schools and Canadian Nationality, 1903–1912."
In *Minorities, Schools, and Politics*, edited by Craig Brown, 10–19. Toronto:
University of Toronto Press.

Mouvement L'École ensemble. 2018. "Opinion sur les subventions aux
écoles privées de la part de l'état." January. https://web.archive.org
/web/20181020165634/http://opineduq.ca/sondage/727.

Mulcahy, M. Nolasco. 1988. "The Philosophical-Theological Foundations
of the Denominational System of Education." In *The Vexed Question:
DenominationalEducation in a Secular Age*, edited by William A. McKim,
11–30. St. John's: Breakwater.

Mulligan, James T. 2006. *Catholic Education: Ensuring a Future*. Ottawa:
Novalis.

Newfoundland. 1968. *Royal Commission on Education and Youth*. St John's:
Queen's Printer.

– 1992. *Our Children, Our Future*. St John's: Queen's Printer.

Newfoundland Teachers' Association (NLTA). 1986. *Exploring New Pathways*.
Memorial University Library Archives LA 418 N4 N49.

Noel, S.J.R. 1971. *Politics in Newfoundland*. Toronto: University of Toronto Press.

Noonan, Brian. 1998. *Saskatchewan Separate Schools*. Muenster: St. Peter's Press.

– 2006. "Saskatchewan Separate Schools." In *A History of Education in
Saskatchewan: Selected Readings*, edited by B. Noonan, D. Hallman, and M.
Scharf, 21–33. Regina: Canadian Plains Research Centre.

Ontario, 1985. *The Report of the Commission on Private Schools in Ontario*.
Toronto: Queen's Printer.

Orren, Karen, and Stephen Skowronek. 2004. *The Search for American Political
Development*. Cambridge: Cambridge University Press.

Ouellet, Fernand. 2000. *L'enseignement culturel des religions: Le débat*.
Sherbrooke: CRP.

Paikin, Steve. 2016. *Bill Davis: Nation Builder, and Not So Bland after All*. Toronto:
Dundurn Press.

Pelt, Michael Van, Ray Pennings, and Deani Van Pelt. 2007. "Faithful and Fruitless
in Ontario: Status Quo in Education Policy." *Policy Options*, November, 25–6.

Penney, Ronald G. 1988. "The Constitutional Status of Denominational
Education in Newfoundland." In *The Vexed Question*, edited by William A.
McKim, 86–101. St. John's: Breakwater.

Pierson, Paul. 2004. *Politics in Time: History, Institutions, and Social Analysis*.
Princeton: Princeton University Press.

Pitsula, James, and Ken Rasmussen. 1990. *Privatizing a Province: The New Right in Saskatchewan*. Vancouver: New Star Books.

Power, Michael. 2005. *Jesuit in the Legislative Gallery: A Life of Father Carl Matthew, S.J.* Welland: Michael Power.

Rasmussen, Derek. 2011. "Forty Years of Struggle and Still No Right to Inuit Education in Nunavut." *Interchange* 42, no. 2: 137–55. https://doi.org/10.1007/s10780-011-9152-5.

Rayside, David. 2008. *Queer Inclusions, Continental Divisions: Public Recognition of Sexual Diversity in Canada and the United States*. Toronto: University of Toronto Press.

Rayside, David, Jerald Sabine, and Paul E.J. Thomas. 2017. *Religion and Canadian Party Politics*. Vancouver: UBC Press.

Read, Anne. 2018. "The Precarious History of Jewish Education in Quebec." *Religion and Education* 45, no. 1: 23–51. https://doi.org/10.1080/15507394.2017.1367595.

Reid, Jennifer. 2015. "Indian Residential Schools: A Governmental Assault on Religious Freedom." *Studies in Religion* 44, no. 4: 441–56. https://doi.org/10.1177/0008429815605774.

Roblin, Duff. 1999. *Speaking for Myself: Politics and Other Pursuits*. Winnipeg: Great Plains Publications.

Rosenberg, M. Michael, and Jack Jedwab. 1992. "Institutional Completeness, Ethnic Organizational Style, and the Role of the State: The Jewish, Italian, and Greek Communities of Montreal." *Canadian Review of Sociology* 29, no. 3: 266–87. https://doi.org/10.1111/j.1755-618x.1992.tb02439.x.

Rowe, Frederick W. 1964. *The Development of Education in Newfoundland*. Toronto: Ryerson Press.

– 1976. *Education and Culture in Newfoundland*. Toronto: McGraw-Hill Ryerson.

Russell, Frances. 2003. *The Canadian Crucible: Manitoba's Role in Canada's Great Divide*. Manitoba: Heartland Associates.

Sable, Martin S. 1999. "Keeping the Faith: The Jewish Response to Compulsory Religious Education in Ontario's Public Schools, 1944–1990." EdD diss., University of Toronto.

Sanders, Elizabeth. 2008. "Historical Institutionalism." In *Oxford Handbook of Political Institutions*, edited by R.A.W. Rhodes, Sarah A. Binder, and Bert A. Rockman, 39–56. New York: Oxford University Press.

Sarrouh, Beesan, T. 2016. "Accommodating Muslim Minorities in Secular Societies: Public Education in England, Scotland, Ontario, and Quebec." PhD diss., Queen's University.

Saskatchewan. 1990. *Report of the Minister's Advisory Board on Independent Schools: Final Report to the Minister of Education*. Regina: Queen's Printer.

– 2018. "Registered Independent Schools Regulations." https://www.saskatchewan.ca/government/education-and-child-care-facility

-administration/services-for-school-administrators/registered
-independent-schools.

– 2022. "Government of Saskatchewan Provides $17.5 Million for the Operation of Independent Schools." https://www.saskatchewan .ca/government/news-and-media/2022/may/11/government-of -saskatchewan-provides-175-million-to-support-the-operation-of -independent-schools-and.

Scharf, Murray. 2006. "An Historical Overview of Education in Saskatchewan." In *A History of Education in Saskatchewan: Selected Readings*, edited by B. Noonan, D. Hallman, and M. Scharf, 3–21. Regina: Canadian Plains Research Centre.

Schryer, Frans J. 1998. *The Netherlandic Presence in Ontario: Pillars, Class, and DutchEthnicity*. Waterloo: Wilfrid Laurier University Press.

Schuck, J.T. 1960. "President's Address Catholic Schools Section Saskatchewan School Trustees Association Convention, Besborough Hotel Saskatoon March 14." Miller Papers.

Sears, Robin. 2007. "How Ontario Got a One-Issue Campaign." *Policy Options*, November, 17–24.

Seljak, David. 1996. "Why the Quiet Revolution Was "Quiet": The Catholic Church's Reaction to the Secularization of Nationalism in Quebec after 1960." *Historical Studies* 62: 109–24.

Sheingate, Adam. 2014. "Institutional Dynamics and American Political Development." *Annual Review of Political Science* 17, no. 1: 461–77. https://doi.org/10.1146/annurev-polisci-040113-161139.

Silver, Arthur. 1997. *The French-Canadian Idea of Confederation, 1864–1900*. 2nd ed. Toronto: University of Toronto Press.

Sissons, C.B. 1959. *Church and State in Canadian Education*. Toronto: University of Toronto Press.

Skowronek, Stephen. 1982. *Building a New American State: The Expansion of National Administrative Capacities, 1877–1920*. Cambridge: Cambridge University Press.

Sloan, L.V. 1980. "A Policy Analysis of Legislation Permitting Public-Private School Agreements for the Provision of Educational Services." PhD diss. University of Alberta.

Smith, Miriam. 2004. "Questioning Heteronormativity: Lesbian and Gay Challenges to Education Practice in British Columbia, Canada." *Social Movement Studies* 3, no. 2: 131–45. https://doi.org/10.1080 /1474283042000266092.

– 2009. "Diversity and Canadian Political Development: Presidential Address to the Canadian Political Science Association." *Canadian Journal of Political Science* 42, no. 4, 831–54. https://doi.org/10.1017/ s0008423909990692.

Smith, William J. 1994. "Linguistic School Boards in Quebec – A Reform Whose Time Has Come: Reference Re Education Act of Quebec (Bill 107)." *McGill Law Journal* 39, no. 4: 200–23.

Stangl, Joseph. 2002. *Life's Challenges: A Man for Others*. Winnipeg: Art Book.

Stapleton, John J., and John C. Long. 1999. "The Manitoba Independent Schools Question, 1957–1996." In *St. Paul's College University of Manitoba: Memories and Histories*, edited by Gerald Friesen and Richard LeBrun, 304–24. Winnipeg: St. Paul's College.

Stewart, David K., and Anthony M. Sayers. 2013. "Albertans' Conservative Beliefs." In *Conservatism in Canada*, edited by J. Farney and D. Rayside, 249–67. Toronto: University of Toronto Press.

Streeck, Wolfgang, and Kathleen Thelen, eds. 2005. *Beyond Continuity: Institutional Change in Advanced Political Economies*. Oxford: Oxford University Press.

Sweet, Lois. 1997. *God in the Classroom: The Controversial Issue of Religion in Canada's Schools.* Toronto: McClelland & Stewart.

Tansey, Oisín. 2007. "Process Tracing and Elite Interviewing: A Case for Non-probability Sampling." *PS: Political Science and Politics* 40, no. 4 (October 2007): 765–72.

Taylor, Alison. 2001a. "'Fellow Travellers' and 'True Believers': A Case Study of Religion and Politics in Alberta Schools." *Journal of Education Policy* 16, no. 1: 15–37. https://doi.org/10.1080/02680930010009804.

– 2001b. *The Politics of Educational Reform in Alberta*. Toronto: University of Toronto Press.

Thiessen, Elmer John. 2001. *In Defence of Religious Schools and Colleges*. Montreal: McGill-Queen's University Press.

Thompson, Debra, and Jennifer Wallner. 2011. "A Focusing Tragedy: Public Policy and the Establishment of Afrocentric Education in Toronto." *Canadian Journal of Political Science* 44, no. 4: 807–28.

Tremblay, Stéphanie. 2012. *École et Religions*. Montreal: Fides.

– 2018. "Escalating Criticism of the Ethics and Religious Culture Program in Quebec: A Cognitive Market Analysis." *Religion and Education* 45, no. 3: 287–307. https://doi.org/10.1080/15507394.2018.1546508.

Vipond, Robert C. 2017. *Making a Global City: How One Toronto School Embraced Diversity*. Toronto: University of Toronto Press.

Wagner, Michael. 1998. "The Progressive Conservative Government and Education Policy in Alberta: Leadership and Continuity." PhD diss., University of Alberta.

– 1999. "Refusing to Be Licensed: Alberta Fundamentalist Christian Schools in the 1980s." *Embrace the Spirit* 1 (Winter): 10–13.

Walker, Franklin. 1955. *Catholic Education and Politics in Upper Canada*. Toronto: Catholic Education Foundation.

– 1986. *Catholic Education and Politics in Ontario: From the Hope Commission to the Promise of Completion (1945–1985).*Toronto: Catholic Education Foundation of Ontario, 1986.

Wallner, Jennifer. 2014. *Learning to School: Federalism and Public Schooling in Canada.* Toronto: University of Toronto Press.

Walton, Gerald. 2006. "British Columbia." *Journal of Gay & Lesbian Issues in Education* 3, no. 4: 97–100. https://doi.org/10.1300/j367v03n04_09.

Warren, Philip. 2012. "The Politics of Educational Change: Reforming Denominational Education." In *Education Reform: From Rhetoric to Reality*, edited by G. Galway and D. Dibbon, 37–71. London: Althouse Press.

Weber, Jerome. n.d. *Report on Separate Schools.* Miller Papers Archdiocese of Regina.

Wesley, Jared. 2011. *Code Politics: Campaigns and Cultures on the Canadian Prairies.* Vancouver: UBC Press.

Westfall, William. 1989. *Two Worlds: The Protestant Culture of 19th Century Ontario.* Toronto: University of Toronto Press.

White, Linda A. 2003. "Liberalism, Group Rights, and the Boundaries of Toleration: The Case of Minority Religious Schools in Ontario." *Canadian Journal of Political Science* 36, no. 5: 975–1003.

Wiseman, Nelson. 1981. "The Pattern of Prairie Politics." *Queen's Quarterly* 88, no. 2: 298–315.

– 2007. *In Search of Canadian Political Culture.* Vancouver: UBC Press.

Woods Gordon Management Consultants. 1984. *A Study of Private Schools in Alberta.* Edmonton: Alberta Education.

Young, David, and Lawrence Bezeau. 2003. "Moving from Denominational to Linguistic Education in Quebec." *Canadian Journal of Educational Administration and Policy* 24, no. 3: 1–17.

Zahariadis, Nikolaos, and Theofanis Exadaktylos. 2016. "Policies That Succeed and the Programs That Fail: Ambiguity, Conflict, and Crisis in Greek Higher Education." *Policy Studies Journal* 44, no. 1: 59–82. https://doi.org/10.1111/psj.12129.

Zine, Yasmine. 2008. *Canadian Islamic Schools.* Toronto: University of Toronto Press.

Zinga, Dawn. 2008. "Ontario's Challenge: Denominational Rights in Public Education." *Canadian Journal of Educational Administration and Policy* 80 (August): 1–44.

Index

Manitoba Association for Equality
in Education (MAEE) (later
the Manitoba Federation of
Independent Schools (MFIS)),
113–19
Manitoba Association of School
Superintendents, 114
Manitoba Association of School
Trustees, 114
Manitoba Catholic School Trustees
Association, 117; "Letter of
Comfort" (1990), 104, 117
Manitoba Court of Appeal, 108
Manitoba Federation of
Independent Schools (MFIS),
115–19
Manitoba Schools Crisis, 26, 38,
103–4, 106–7, 109, 119, 151. *See also*
Franco-Manitobans
Mann, Horace, 124
Manning, Ernest, 168, 174, 176
Manzer, Ronald, 11, 21, 58, 86, 170;
*Educational Regimes and Anglo-
American Democracy*, 9–10; five
political regimes, 10
Mar, Gary, 179
Maritime provinces, 84–7; Acadian
nationalism in, 86; compromise
regarding Catholic and Protestant
schools, 85–6; informal support for
Catholic schools in, 85; legislative
frameworks for government
support of schools in, 84; and
Section 93 of the Constitution Act
(1867), 85, 100–1
Martin, Nick, 200
Martin, William Melville, 153
Matthews, Carl, SJ, 41
McCaffrey, Vivian, 198
McGeer, Patrick, 126, 133, 135, 139
McGowen, Mark, 198
McGuinty, Dalton, 50

McGrath, Tom, 199
McKinnon, Randolph, 175
McNally, Vincent J., 126
Medicare, 156
Meech Lake constitutional
amendment, 99
Memorial University,
Newfoundland, 94
Memorial University College,
Newfoundland, 91
Mennonites, 102, 106–8, 111–12, 118,
121, 128, 153–4, 156, 183
Methodists, 34, 83, 90, 124–5
Métis, 103, 105
Mill, John Stuart, *On Liberty*, 133
Milner, Henry, 64–5
Milot, Micheline, 74
Ministry of Education (Quebec), 20,
24–5, 41, 52–4, 59–66, 69, 75, 79;
Bill 60, 25, 60–2, 74–7
Morton, Ted, 187
Mount Allison University, 87
Mouvement laïque de langue
française, 62–3, 79
Mouvement scolaire confessionnel
(MSC), 64
multiculturalism, 19–20, 72–3, 109
Muslim schools and communities,
16, 78, 197

National Association of Independent
Schools (NAIS) in the United
States, 78
Neerlandia, Alberta, 172
neo-Calvinism, 173, 188
neoliberalism: in Alberta, 28,
30, 168, 170, 180, 182, 189; in
British Columbia, 28; theory and
principles of, 22, 170, 181
New Brunswick, 19, 25, 82, 84–5, 87,
100; Common Schools Act (1871),
84–5. *See also* Maritime provinces